Maggie Wadey is a novelist and screenwriter. Her childhood was spent in England, Egypt, Cyprus and a Sussex boarding school. After a brief time as a model, she read Philosophy at University College London. Maggie is married to actor John Castle and has one daughter and two grandchildren. Among her screenplays for television are adaptations of *Mansfield Park*, *The Buccaneers*, *The Yellow Wallpaper* and the children's novel *Stig of the Dump*. She lives in East London.

By the same author

Sleight of Heart

THE
ENGLISH
DAUGHTER

MAGGIE WADEY

SANDSTONEPRESS
HIGHLAND | SCOTLAND

Published in Great Britain by
Sandstone Press Ltd
Dochcarty Road
Dingwall
Ross-shire
IV15 9UG
Scotland.

www.sandstonepress.com

Editor: Moira Forsyth

The publisher acknowledges support from Creative Scotland
towards publication of this volume.

ISBN: 978-1-910985-13-7
ISBNe: 978-1-910985-14-4

Cover design by Rose Cooper, Seville
Typeset by Iolaire Typesetting, Newtonmore
Printed and bound by CPI Group (UK) Ltd, Croydon, CR0 4YY

To my mother

PROLOGUE

From the beginning, my beginning that is, I had a strong sense of my mother as different. My English family were small, compact and ginger-haired; my mother was dark, taller than average, long-limbed and heavy-boned. She wasn't just different; she was special. She may have told us very little about her life, but I knew her soft white cheeks, her black hair rolled into glossy sausages – one above her brow, one at the nape of her neck – her low voice with its slightly foreign, musical cadence, her strong, careful hands that could suddenly become impatient. Her brown eyes were velvety, her thin brows two perfect arches. Her face expressed emotion very subtly, sometimes to the point of invisibility. A better indicator of her mood was her movements, the set of her shoulders, the exact position of her hands. As a child – and I was her only child – I learned to read these signs very accurately, not to understand her, but to predict her behaviour.

I knew my mother had come from Ireland alone on a ferry-boat that bucked and reared on the October night sea. All the passengers were sick as dogs. Grown men (but Irish and therefore more susceptible) called on the Holy Mother of God before vomiting into the wind. My mother travelled with only a hatbox (though it contained no hats), having left home in a hurry after poisoning her mother's geese. I felt I'd been born imprinted with this mental image: my mother standing in a twilit field – a very green field, for I knew Ireland was called the Emerald Isle, as green as the stone in my mother's engagement ring – surrounded by a litter of geese as dead as pillows and scalded with my mother's tears. She was crying because she was afraid of her own mother who was a tall woman, pale-faced and, being from long ago, wore a black shawl, a crucifix, and laced boots. 'She was a hard woman,' my own mother said. 'Father was a sweetheart, but she was hard.' And when she said that I was sad for her velvety eyes, for her lost homeland and the sky darkening over the battlefield of soft white bodies.

Agnes Teresa Kavanagh was born on July 16th, 1915. Or maybe not. In the drawer where my father kept our papers – birth certificates, marriage certificates, medical records and such – there was no birth certificate for my mother. Once, perhaps when applying for her first passport, she had written to Dublin for a copy of her birth certificate only to be told it was unavailable due to a fire which had burned down the Custom House during the War of Independence in 1921. To my father and me this was an unlikely story which only confirmed the reputation of the Irish for quaint ineptitude. Another date kept cropping up, July 18th, 1911, but this was apparently the birthday of another child, an infant who had died and after whom my mother had been named. 'When I was a child,' she told us, 'birthdays didn't matter.' In other words, my mother was evasive about her age, and this inclined us to suspect that she was older than she'd have us believe.

I was born into a world of women. My infancy was spent in the company of my mother, my paternal grandmother and my aunt, my English aunt. We lived at the top of a tower which was part of Collyer's Boys' Grammar School in Horsham, Sussex, where my widowed grandmother was cook. I always understood that this represented some kind of fall from grace, that I wasn't to look on myself as the grandchild of a school cook any more than she ever considered herself to *be* a school cook, even though she finally held the post for over twenty years.

My grandmother was plump and petite. With her white hair and powdered face, she was sweet and light as a meringue dipped in icing sugar. I liked every so often to pat her cheeks and then to lick the powder off my fingers, murmuring exaggeratedly, 'Mmm, delicious!' My aunt was the same shape as her mother, small and round, with ginger hair and freckles. She had an easy way with practical affairs. She would lie on the lawn hour after hour reading instead of tidying up, and she stopped the holes in the soles of her shoes with pieces of cardboard cut-out of Player's cigarette packets. 'This is stitchwort,' she used to say as we went along the tangled path to the chicken run. 'Here's Jack-go-to-bed-at-noon. And milkmaid.'

The chicken run opened on one side into an elderly orchard, grey with lichen. Dodging under the barbed-wire fence one day, I sliced my cheek open and narrowly missed spearing my right eye. There was a certain amount of friction between my mother and my aunt on these matters. My aunt believed not so much in scars, but in risk. My mother was indifferent to risk but wanted me unblemished. I was her creation, perfect, and the rituals of everyday life, my washing, dressing and feeding were, as she perceived them, not unlike holy rituals. We were mother and child, age-old icons, timeless, impersonal almost. My sweet-ration was given away – presumably to children whose teeth didn't matter. A lot was expected of me. I had to be worthy of my privileges, such as the red coat bought at great expense and tailored in the same style as the coats of the little Royal Princess Margaret, in whose honour I was named. I was pleased with the coat and even more pleased with my three-year-old self in it. But it made the schoolboys yell 'Tally-ho!' and gallop up and down the playground spluttering with beastly laughter.

No wonder my aunt sometimes felt sorry for me. It was a relief to accompany her along the muddy path to the chicken run, fighting my way through the brambles in her wake, close up against her generous rump, watching her sturdy white legs thrust into short black gumboots flash left-right, left-right. 'This is catmint,' she would say, bruising a leaf between finger and thumb. 'Speedwell.' And with a laugh, 'Here's pissenlit. Don't chew that or you'll wet the bed.'

At night my mother put on a trench coat and walked the streets, firewatching. She had a torch and a whistle to summon the help of men with water-hoses. But I pictured her swallowing the fire. I saw her throw back her head and open her mouth wide to swallow the flames – which was why fire sometimes came back out of her mouth, fire, and spittle, and angry words. At night the streets were dark and empty but my mother wasn't afraid, not even when searchlights picked out heavy-bellied aeroplanes in the sky and distant guns began to fire. There were no men in our lives. Sometimes I heard the insubstantial voices of male announcers on the radio and I had a teddy bear made, so I'd been told, from the fleecy lining of my long-dead paternal grandfather's raincoat.

But, on the highly polished sideboard in my grand-mother's sitting room, between the tin of macaroons and the empty sherry decanter, stood the photograph of a beatifically good-looking young man. I was told this was my father and that he was away fighting in the war. I very much enjoyed being given his photo to look at. Nana would buff the glass with her sleeve and, stooping, put it reverently into my hands. She reserved a special smile for this ritual, similar, I thought, to the smile with which I looked at my teatime egg before bashing it on the head and eating it. The young man wore a soldier's uniform and looked at me benignly and, because I was his daughter, his eyes followed me all round the room when I moved. Looking at him, being looked at by him, was quickly unsatisfying. Much later on I realised the photograph had been heavily touched up, a process that romanticised and stereotyped his face.

One memory poignant above all others, from the time before everything changed: I see my mother and me, hand in hand, mounting slowly up the rim of a hill, going towards but never reaching the horizon, accompanied by the shrill song of skylarks. The curve of the horizon divides the world into two parts, one green, one blue, except for one small bright cloud floating in the sky. And on closer inspection the grass is dotted copiously with flowers: buttercups, daisies, clover and, closer still, with filigree spiders and tiny beetles. On this occasion I'm four. We have the whole late summer afternoon to ourselves. I've set out proudly to teach my mother the names of the flowers but she seems a bit absent-minded. I give up. But I don't mind. On the contrary. In my mother's world things don't need naming and I should like our walk to go on forever through a field of nameless flowers.

Then one day the guns stopped, and the sirens, and the nights spent sheltering under the table in the school kitchen. People sang in the streets and the church bells rang even though it was a weekday. My father was coming home. The war, it seemed, was over. England had won! Peace came like a fever. A man, his face lit up like a lunatic, spat at my mother outside the big post office. The gob landed at her feet. 'No thanks to you, bloody Irish!'

7

he said. My mother's hand tightened on mine. 'Take no notice,' she said, and because her head was high I felt she addressed the remark not to me but to the world at large. That the shame reflected more on the man than on her. The world at large was suddenly engaged in a passionate search for extra sugar, extra butter, extra eggs. Infected by the adult excitement, I began to dash about, too, pumping my elbows and puffing up my cheeks. I fell and grazed my knee and at teatime I got hiccoughs. I must have done something else, too, because my mother sent me in from the garden. I met my aunt at the foot of the stairs and gasped out:

'Mummy said "GET indoors"!'

'Well,' said Dorothy dryly. 'You'd better get.'

That evening I was sent early to bed, where I bit my teddy bear's fat bristly legs and cried myself to sleep.

Life as I knew and loved it was over. I drove the three women slowly out of their minds with questions: What will he be like? Where will he sleep? Where will he put his clothes? Which chair will be his? One moment I favoured the yellow, winged chair by the fire; next the old horsehair armchair with crooked wheeled feet like eagles' talons. I spent a lot of time rearranging the cushions and dragging the leather pouffe from the sitting room into the kitchen for my father to put his feet up on. I'd noticed in my Little Grey Rabbit books that Hare had his slippers put by the fire to warm, but here there were no slippers. I went on relentlessly hammering away at the same questions, whining that there was no place where a daddy could fit in, until my grandmother turned on me.

'This is his home, too, you know. Your daddy was here long before *you* were even thought of.'

The day of my father's return arrived. My mother had a new dress for the occasion and new, uncomfortable shoes

8

that gave her a new, loose-kneed walk. But her hair was still the same: divided at the back and pulled forward to sit on either side of her head just below her ears in two fat shiny black sausages. Every so often she cuffed them gently with the heel of her hand, checking that they were in place. I liked to stick my fingers inside the sausages, but today it wasn't allowed, and I felt the tension in her neck, like a bow strung taut for the arrow. Earlier, my mother and aunt had carried my bed out of the bedroom – the room I'd shared with my mother every day of my three-and-a-half-year-long life – and put it into a poky little boxroom next to the sitting room where Nana slept on the sofa. I was told this was because my father was going to sleep in here, in the big bed with my mother, something I wasn't allowed to do unless I was ill. Now, turning to the mirror, my mother plastered her upper lip with lipstick then pressed both lips together, leaving a precise, unnatural-looking print on the lower one. She smiled tremulously at herself and took a deep, shuddering breath. Her pretty new dress had oblong buttons like little biscuits, and a narrow belt with an oblong biscuit buckle. My mouth was dry with anxiety. I pressed my hand hard between my legs for reassurance that some things at least wouldn't change.

'Don't touch yourself down there!' cried my mother, rounding on me to slap my hand away. 'Nice little girls don't do that!'

My hair was yanked out of its paper-curlers and sprang up like corkscrews all over my head. Was I to be ridiculous as well as not nice? I kept my eyes fixed on the buttons on my mother's dress. I considered biting them, but didn't. Then, as we went along the corridor, we heard the women's voices in the kitchen and the radio playing: 'You are my sunshine'.

My mother halted, her eyes fixed on me but absent-mindedly, as if attending to something I couldn't hear. I looked back up at her, holding my breath, and we became outsiders together, shadows in the dim corridor that for that moment lead nowhere, both of us insubstantial as ghosts. Then in the headmaster's study on the floor below, the clock softly chimed three times and my mother, stooping awkwardly, clutched me to her breast. I glutted myself on her love and her remorse – if remorse it was – before breaking free and running ahead of her into the marzipan-scented kitchen to show off my dress. I stood in the doorway swinging a leg and humming: 'You are my shunshine, my only shunshine...'

A booming sound rose from the distant hall. I froze. The door into the schoolyard had been opened and then banged shut, the way I was told off for doing. You had to keep hold of it right up to the moment the latch clicked. You had to be careful, that was all. I ran to the top of the stairs and looked down, four flights to the bottom. For a long moment I saw nothing, though I could hear quick footsteps. Then, rising up out of the dark into the sunlight on the first landing came the top of a man's reddish-fair head. He took the stairs in twos the way Dorothy sometimes did and I saw his hand on the banister and the dark cuff of his suit. I fled back into the kitchen where I buried my face in my mother's lap, overwhelmed by an emotion I still have no words for.

Moments later, I was safe down amongst the legs and the soft stuff of the women's skirts as his mother, his sister, his wife went on tiptoe to kiss, to touch, to pat my father until he became himself again under their doubting fingers, familiar, their own in spite of the evidence of their eyes. For he'd changed. They laughed, questioned, exclaimed, their voices coming in short breathy gasps. From under their flapping elbows I studied his face. Whatever had gone wrong with it? The photo of the romantic young soldier was bland and smooth as a pebble. This man was thinner, older, with a fierce suntan and a ginger moustache, and when I broke away and repeatedly hurled myself at the yellow armchair his eyes didn't follow me the way they did in the photo. He gave me an uncomfortable squeeze. His hair and clothes smelt of dust, metal and oil, the smell of faraway unknown places, the unfamiliar smell of man. Then he embraced my mother and something terrible happened. She turned to jelly. Her smile went lopsided, her proud head drooped, her body sagged. His kiss left a 'burn' on her white cheek, which he proudly kissed again.

The night my father came home from the war I slept apart from my mother for the first time in my life. In the little boxroom where my bed had been made up I found a bag of sweets hidden under my pillow. Apparently, even my teeth didn't matter any more.

Now, my father lives alone, and every day in his pretty suburban garden he feeds the foxes. He comes home late at night with chicken carcasses, lamb bones, leftover mush and gravy like some kind of eccentric recycler of waste from the kitchens of friends and relatives. Which prompts my father – a retired civil engineer – to quote the old joke: 'It may be sewage to you but to me it's bread-and-butter.' He trots in from the car and unloads in the kitchen, rustling plastic bags as he sorts what will be used immediately from what will be frozen in the coffin-sized freezer in the garage. Outside in the dark the foxes, a mother and three cubs, are prepared to wait as long as it takes. My father reports their imagined remarks: 'What's this?' they say to one another. 'Late again? What does the silly old boy think he's up to?'

As well they might ask. Aged ninety, my father is rarely at home, independent, fit, and maintaining a style of life that might tax a man twenty years younger. When the foxes step out of the bushes on to the lawn a security light on the wall comes on like a flash-photo, freezing them in its white glare like ghosts. The foxes squabble over their food. The cubs snarl and snap at one another and the mother always yields. My father puts the flat of his hands together and rolls his eyes. 'Poor mothers! 'Twas ever thus.' Having eaten, they dig holes in the lawn and roll in the flower beds. One of the cubs always craps in his own feeding bowl. 'That doesn't make sense, my son,' my father says indignantly.

How odd, almost outlandish their presence seems, these feral, stinking foxes in my father's garden. The nearest open space is maybe a quarter of a mile away, alongside the motorway, a long narrow stretch of scrub and grass beside a stream, where blackbirds sing sweet as pie in the stinking May trees, where my mother used to walk my infant daughter amongst the daisies. As my father cleans away the fox crap he shakes his head and mutters:

'Davey-boy, you must be going soft in the head.'

He claims heartily to dislike the wretched creatures with their filthy habits and their nocturnal shrieks and snickering, none of which had appeared to bother my normally fastidious mother. It was she who had begun the habit of feeding them, and my father tells me the only reason he continues to do so is out of deference to my dead mother's memory.

There's a whole lot of other things he does for the same reason. So many things he learned from her over the years: how to iron and fold linen, the correct way to lay a table for dinner, how to remove red wine stains from the carpet, the exact way to julienne carrots, to cut bread

12

as thin as tissue paper and to butter it without having it crumble to pieces. My mother was no slacker. She had a tireless insistence on getting things right, and a quick sensitivity to what counted as 'right' – a characteristically feminine trait, perhaps. Now, if my father fails to dust behind the chair, or forgets to draw the blind to stop the carpet fading, he hears my mother's voice chastising him. He knows that raw and cooked meats must be kept separately in the fridge, that vinegar and newspaper is better to clean windows with than hot water and a shammy. As he goes about the household chores, he reminds himself of these things and bows to my dead mother's rule of law.

The house is as it was when she left it, and most of it was as she had wished, comfortable and pretty, with a small collection of silver and Venetian glass on display – though my father's taste prevailed in the embossed green wallpaper for the dining room. My mother's armchair is still 'hers'. Her Marks and Sparks slippers are still where she kept them, placed neatly side by side at the top of the stairs. My father has shown no desire to get rid of her things but I have, of course, looked through her clothes and jewellery, giving away a few pieces to relations, and taking some to the Sue Ryder charity shop on New Malden High Street, where the personal effects of the dead are somehow rendered as harmless, as anonymous, as clothes on the factory rail. Some, I have kept for myself: a mohair shawl, my mother's engagement ring (so-called, though my father didn't in fact buy it for her until they had already been married for sixteen years) and two or three silk shirts which had been gifts from me. I genuinely like these things, but also want to possess a little bit of her. For weeks after her death I slept in the mohair shawl. I have kept a string of cultured pearls which I loved as a child. I remember knowing that 'cultured' meant they were in some way disappointing or inferior, in spite of which they were precious and beautiful. My mother and I certainly thought so.

I was allowed to wear them once. I was on holiday from boarding school, visiting my parents in Malaya where, as members of the local British community, we were guests at a party in the sultan's palace in Johore Bahru. I was fifteen and this was my first adult party. Even with the pearls gleaming at my throat I was excruciatingly shy and appalled at the prospect of being asked by a stranger to dance – an art I'd only very imperfectly mastered. I was intimidated by the European women's indecently bare backs and arms, by the womanly white nakedness of their skin, and by the grace of the Malay sarongs. My self-consciousness expressed itself in a naïve faux pas. I refused to dance with our host's son, the Tunku, accepting instead the invitation of a handsome young Indian doctor. Against the formal backdrop of the palace, the touch of the doctor's dark hand on mine became the perfect emblem of feral eroticism.

Tunku Mahmud was graciously tolerant of my childish rudeness – as were my parents, who might have been expected to be mortified and extremely cross. My parents' tolerance was, in fact, characteristic of them: I was never forced to eat food I disliked, nor pushed to shine at school. In consequence, I ate adventurously and enjoyed examinations. As an adult I never danced with men I didn't fancy.

In the 1970s, when foxes first visited my parents' garden, they were still a novelty in towns. My mother could scarcely believe her eyes. It was a bright early morning in spring and the pretty young vixen seemed proud to display her adorable cubs, playing with them on the lawn, then falling asleep in the sun. Later, the vixen

14

became skeletal, the cubs infested with mange, and my mother's pleasure in them turned to a fretful sort of pity. She bought expensive antibiotics from the vet to dose their feed with. It was impossible for her to believe that the vixen's blood-curdling scream was lust, not pain. On summer nights, when the foxes loped out from under the shrubs, my mother would reach over to her reading lamp, turn it off and sit in the darkness, watching. Now, sometimes I sit in her place, faintly bored by the ritual which still pleases – or irritates – my father, who has never quite got over his astonishment at the animals' proximity, their boldness, and their greed. Silently, I wonder what it was the foxes had meant to her. Infinitely adaptable creatures, native to woods and mountainsides, yet making successful new lives for themselves not just in suburban gardens, but in inner cities, too. As adaptable as man, but less changeable.

I know my father sensed something disproportionate in my mother's pity for them. It had the same note of violence as her extreme hatred of war, her almost child-like recoil from the brutality of so much of life. Which is not to say she was sentimental. Her solution to repeated famine in Africa was not charity. 'Why don't these people stop having children if they can't feed them?' she would ask, with something like fury in her voice.

My mother was the eighth of nine children. It seems unlikely that her parents, Irish Catholics who married in 1899, would have stopped having children because they couldn't afford to feed them, much as they might have wanted to. Poverty would not have prevented my mother's birth, though she might have died of it. Did my mother's fury faced with the intractable problem come from personal experience? I didn't know the answer to that question, nor to many others I might have asked, and my mother volunteered only the minimum of information about her background. Her many brothers and sisters were a shadowy chorus I met only at funerals. And since my mother did not allow me to attend funerals until I was in my teens, I grew up knowing only her youngest, favourite sister, Nancy, the ninth and last of the Kavanagh children. 'Nancy and I were like that,' my mother used to say, holding up two tightly crossed fingers.

The Kavanagh funerals were always in North-West London: in Hanwell, Southall, Edgware, depressing places reached by a long tedious car journey in which, in my adolescence, I took a kind of masochistic pleasure. Our route took us through Willesden and Hendon on to the North Circular, and I threw myself deep into the angst of the post-war urban sprawl, in my mind composing poetic metaphors for the loneliness and ugliness of the place. This was the late 1950s. I had begun to read Sartre and Camus. I had come across the concepts of 'existentialism' and 'alienation' and in my egotistical immaturity, wrapped in moody silence on the back seat of our car, I was at the perfect age – sixteen – to understand them. The tabula rasa of existentialism especially spoke to me with its dizzying freedom of self-invention. I owned a precious 45 rpm record of Juliette Gréco singing 'Sous les ciel de Paris'. Here was a woman who embodied both sexual and intellectual freedom, whose Parisian nonchalance and black eye make-up I took as my model.

Our destination was the Catholic church of St Michael and All Angels in Hanwell. Built in the 1930s to resemble an ark, it was, to my critical and would-be sophisticated eye, a shrine to embarrassingly bad taste. Here both the lengthy funeral service and the mourners were full-blown Irish in a way my mother was not. My mother's voice still betrayed her origins – something in the cadence, in

16

the way she pronounced 'th' and the short 'o' in donkey – but my aunts and uncles all spoke with unashamedly ripe brogues. I met them in damp cemeteries in north London in winter, standing under umbrellas with a steady drip from the trees behind us. They were watchful, white-skinned, garrulous. I felt the claim of their flesh but they remained foreign, unknowable. Like shadows in the underworld they seemed stranded there – for I could imagine them nowhere else – a chorus in black, murmuring together at the graveside or inside the dark interior of a north London pub. They sent a bolt of excitement through me, not of recognition, but of otherness.

Ever since I could remember, I'd been uncomfortably aware of a whiff of anti-Irish feeling. I'd picked up on the fact that the Irish were seen as comic, or stupid, or untrustworthy. Sometimes a romantic gloss was added, where it did no harm: in the way, for instance, my father referred to Nancy as a 'colleen', or in the way that even English eyes filled with sentimental tears when they sang 'Danny Boy'. But my English family wasn't above exchanging 'Irish' jokes in my mother's presence: 'Did you hear the one about the Irishman who fell down a mineshaft and his friend called out to him: "Paddy, did you break anything?" And Paddy called back: "No! there's nothing down here."' My mother would sit with a very faint, fixed smile on her face, eyes downcast, not unlike a woman enduring male jokes about her own sex, little acts of cruelty licensed in some way by the intimacy between the two parties: man and woman, English and Irish. Sometimes my English family only exchanged glances, or kept a significant silence. Later, during the Troubles in the 1970s, the anti-Irish jokes turned sour, the silences deeper. At such times my unspoken loyalty, passionate and totally uninformed – unthought, almost – was to my mother.

Still, whenever I actually met up with them, when my Irish relations looked searchingly into my face, I resisted their familiarity. In the crowded pub after the graveside ceremonies I was made uneasy by the sense that they knew things about me I didn't know, deep, clannish, sticky things they were too polite to mention. Where my English relations, in their outspoken Sussex way, would have teased and challenged, I was aware of my Irish family thinking a good deal more than was said. My Uncle Dan had a devilish smile and broad, pale hands. A strong erotic charge crackled around him and he, more than the others, with his sly smile and his pale hand on my shoulder, suggested that I was in some way a fake. Of course I was a fake: I was in my late teens, hot with the desire to escape everything in the background I knew about and not at all keen, as I might have been, to embrace the other side, the side about which I knew nothing, but *nothing* at all.

It was always my mother who wanted to leave the funeral breakfast first. As the noise levels rose she embraced her sisters with diffident graciousness, murmuring something about the long drive home. My father and I were relieved to be freed to follow her out of the smoke-choked pub where the mythical companions of her childhood stayed on, their black suits gently steaming in the heat, to finish their ham sandwiches and their whiskey. She was always silent on the way home, her face turned away from us, eyes glazed. She was full to the brim with otherness. Amongst my parents' possessions from Egypt, Cyprus, Malaya, there were scattered items inherited from my father's mother – a gilded rose-vase, a silver inkstand, a dark oak coffin-stool – but nothing from Ireland. During my childhood I took this for granted. Only when I was adult did my mother wistfully express her regret that the lovely copper pots and brass lamps she remembered from home had 'vanished', and that nothing had come down to her. Not a chair she might have sat in as a child. No books, no jewellery, no knick-knacks. Not even a photograph. I grew up without touching a single thing my Irish grandparents had ever touched, without a single photograph of them, or of their home, or of my mother as a child or as a very young woman. That is to say, no photos from her life before she met my father.

But then, in 1996, after the death of one of her sisters, my mother finally received her inheritance. It's a photograph, a single black-and-white photograph – taken in the late 1920s to judge by what the women are wearing – of the Kavanagh home. I have the photograph in front of me now. On the reverse I've written, 'The house on Knigh Hill, Tipperary, approx. 1928.' It is a pretty, stone house with a slate roof and trailers of some kind, roses, perhaps, or wisteria, rambling over the walls. There are six windows in what can be seen of the front of the house – not quite all of it is contained within the frame of the snapshot – the front door stands open and there's an archway, part stone, part trellis, leading into a walled front garden. It looks substantial, comfortable, and charming. Behind the house is a stand of trees, thinly leaved, as if winter is approaching. A smudge rises at an angle above the chimney, possibly windblown smoke. In front, a dog lies on the gravel path, his tongue out, looking keenly towards two women and a small boy who stands stiffly by the garden wall. The boy, who is perhaps five or six – too young to be one of my mother's brothers – has bare forearms, his hands are clasped in front of him, his face averted. The older woman, my grandmother, is in profile, arms crossed on her chest, her features indiscernible. Beside her stands a strong-looking young woman who faces directly into the camera but is made unidentifiable by her twenties bob and twenties 'uniform' of white knee socks and low-slung waist.

My mother had no recollection of when the photograph was taken or why. Incredibly, it was only now, when she was in her eighties and I had this photograph in my hand – and to be honest when certain things were happening in my own life – that I began to ask her to tell me more. For the first time since I'd left home more than thirty years ago, we began to have a regular period of time each week together, alone. On Monday evenings my father was out playing bridge. My mother used to partner him, but latterly the game had become too competitive for her and she no longer enjoyed it. My father had found a new partner, a young married woman with small children, keen to keep her brain and her killer instincts sharp. So, on bridge evenings, it became my habit to keep my mother company.

After supper we went into the sitting room. My mother sank into the armchair with the kind of exhaustion which suggested she was unable to resist the over-upholstered chair's gravitational force, that at any moment the cushions would swallow her, leaving only a sigh. As if acknowledging this fancy, she gave me a lopsided grin. She kicked off her slippers then leaned her head back, mouth ajar, hands dangling over the arms of her chair. Silence and darkness lapped all around the house. We were adrift. My mother's eyes seemed curiously large, almost black, as if the pupils were dilated. The light went on outside. My mother flicked off her reading lamp and parted the blinds so that we could watch the little drama of the foxes on the lawn, the struggle amongst the cubs to be top dog. After a moment she remarked dreamily, 'My father used to feed the foxes. He'd put out chicken bones for them, and sometimes he blocked their holes so the dogs couldn't get at them.'

I didn't think that could be right. Foxes' holes are blocked to prevent them going to ground, to keep them out in the open for the hunt. But I said nothing. If I didn't contradict her, maybe she'd continue talking. She was silent. Then I saw a faint inward smile fleet over her face. Was she finally going to tell me more?

PART ONE
CHILDHOOD

1

My grandfather, John Kavanagh, was born in Borriso-kane, north Tipperary, some time in the second half of the nineteenth century. My mother doesn't remember the date of his birth, or rather, she never knew it, only that he was his parents' firstborn and, as such, was destined to live out his life in the cottage where he was born. My mother, who adored her grandmother, described her home as 'a darling little thatched cottage', standing on its own land where 'Grammy', as she was known, kept goats and grew vegetables: potatoes, of course, and, in spite of the goats, leeks and cabbages too.

Behind the little thatched cottage was my great-grandmother's bog, a precious resource from which my grandfather would have been able to harvest enough peat to keep himself – and his children, God willing – warm for the rest of his life. Here on this rather flat, upland area the furze comes into such abundant blossom it sets the land ablaze, a forest of burning bushes shrill with birds, droning with bees. In marshy places cotton grass puts up its little white flags and pale pink bog-flowers flare like stars.

One late afternoon in May, 1887, my grandfather, John, goes walking up here alone. He knows and loves every inch of this place. But today he's filled to the brim with a woman, with her face, her voice, with the question in her eyes, and with her name which he murmurs to himself from time to time. Today – in spite of the fact that some indefinable quality in Kate Buckley tells him she will be forever beyond his reach – he has asked her to meet him, there where the gorse gives way to ancient heather, where remoteness provides a sense of privacy under the vast sky. And he expects to have to wait. Of course he has to wait. Even so, he's almost given up when at last he sees her figure approach, straight, unhurried, unmistakable. He doesn't move to meet her until he can read the look in her eyes. An hour later, having touched no more than her strong, dry hand, John turns back to the cottage where he will have to face – and face up to – his mother. He has decided to reject what she's always assured him will be his and his alone: the cottage, the land, the bog, a place forever at her side. He shrinks from delivering such a blow, but knows he must. Kate has said, 'Yes. Yes, I will.' John's mother, as he'd known she would be, is deeply distressed. As he speaks, she occupies herself with folding the washing, smoothing each article of clothing with the flat of her small hand. She frets that, by rejecting what he has in hope of more, John will end up with nothing. She frets at the idea of losing the son she had expected to be her companion until her death. Of course in principle she wants her son to marry. In practice it's a different matter. This young woman whom John had feared was 'too good' for him will, of course, not be good enough in the eyes of his mother. Never mind that Kate Buckley – daughter of the coachman to the Bishop of Killaloe – is generally considered 'a natural born lady'. It's also widely known she will come to the man she marries with nothing. Five months later, that man is John Kavanagh.

This is the story of my grandparents' courtship as their children were told it. I don't quite understand what was at stake – why John couldn't live at home with his wife, for instance. Perhaps it was inconceivable that Kate and his mother should live together under the same roof. And though I understand that my grandfather might want to go his own way, to make his own life, it surprises me he's prepared to do so at the cost of abandoning his mother and his inheritance. By the time of their first child's birth, the young couple were facing into a century of massive upheavals. But my mother, in telling me the story of her upbringing, didn't mention – except very glancingly – the great events that formed the turbulent backdrop to her childhood. Like most ordinary people her life was formed by, yet innocent of, the epic flow of history.

When my mother was ten months old she was set down for safety inside an old rubber tyre. As she sat kicking her fat little legs, turning her own chubby hands under her amazed gaze, all around her the haymaking proceeded. The rhythmical sweeping of scythes came closer and closer until at last, to the older children's mock-surprise, she was revealed like a baby found under a thorn tree. But for an endless-seeming time before that the baby had been marooned in a world of her own, the others out of sight and out of mind beyond the grass, their voices faint and far-off, just herself inside the circle of tyre in a circle of yellow grass under a circle of sky. Beetles shimmied up the stalks, from time to time a ladybird landed with a little rattle, and filigree spiders ran over the infant's hot, damp head. The field lay aslant the south-western side of the hill, a wide green lap of bounty at the very centre of the world. The baby considered her toes and smiled.

The rubber tyre surprised me. 'What sort of tyre?' I asked. 'A car tyre?' My mother laughed. 'No, no! There were no cars, or lorries.' A pause. 'Some of the old farm vehicles,

27

they had rubber tyres, great big things.' She gave a little shrug. 'I don't think I really remember sitting in the thing,' she said. 'But I was told. And then, when Nancy came along, I had to mind her in it while the others worked.'

Agnes Teresa, the eighth of nine children, was born when the oldest was only eleven years old. Three boys and five girls, with a sixth girl already in the making – a fact known only to the mother. The whole family took part in the hay-harvesting. To Agnes, aged one, this was a blur of meaningless activity, but by the time she was four she would understand every aspect of the harvest and she knew it was about to begin again when, some twilit night in early summer, a little old man turned in off the road to sit on the Kavanagh doorstep. Scholar O'Connor – Schol, as he was known – was regular as the swallows. It was time: his bones told him the dry spell would continue. It took him an eternity to ease off his decomposing boots, groaning and cursing, and releasing an awesome stink.

Once hot sweet tea and tobacco had done their work, Schol – who could never remember where he'd had his last meal – opened his mouth and out came yard upon yard of the old ballads, ballads that told the fate of the Sons of Usnach, of Conchobar and the beautiful Deirdre, of the four children of Lir who were turned into swans and whose only consolation was that their voices were so sweet there was no music on earth to equal them. To say that Schol had once upon a time committed these poems to memory does the case no justice: the man was made of them, the stuff of them had formed his muscles as much as his mind, he walked and worked to their rhythm. The older children could have cried for boredom. But upstairs in bed Agnes felt a fleeting touch of swan's wing brush

28

her cheek. She knew that tomorrow the haymaking would begin.

At noon, Kate Buckley and two of her daughters would go up to the house to make tea and cut squares of bread. Agnes wasn't big enough yet to help her mother carry the bucket of tea back out to the workers. She could see how it would be – with her so small beside her mother, they'd be all at sixes and sevens and the precious tea would end up spilt. But this was the task she longed for, to put her small hand close to her mother's large one there on the handle where it had been wound with string so as not to cut into their fingers. Instead, she had to take the bread, crammed into her apron pocket, and as they returned to the field her stomach growled with hunger. She ran in circles round her mother and Bridie, like a dog. After some minutes, her mother said mildly, without looking at her, 'Whatever that child's got, I'd like to bottle it.'

By the time Agnes is seven she understands how everything on the farm lives and dies. She hasn't been taught to wring a chicken's neck yet, but she dislikes the noisy, stupid creatures and watches as her mother goes about it: catch it, hold it between your knees, a quick sharp twist – 'like twisting a firelighter' – and the neck snaps. Nothing to it. The pigs, who'd given her so much fun when they were sharp-eyed little piglets who screamed when they were tickled, grow fat and spiteful, and are taken for slaughter at the Slatterys'. The Slatterys live on the other side of the hill, out of sight, but not out of earshot. The Kavanagh calves are pulled by whoever happens to be around at the time. Agnes quite enjoys this scary, bloody business that turns like a miracle into milky peace. The job they all hate, painting the sheep with a vile sticky stuff to get rid of parasites – taking special care with the area under the sheep's' clinkered tails where the maggots hang in white clusters – is taken strictly in turn by everyone over the age of eight.

In a large white farmhouse at the bottom of the hill beside Knigh crossroads live the Clearys. They are famous for advertising their surplus hay for sale in the local newspaper. Their name is the first thing Agnes remembers ever seeing in print: CLEARY, on a page beside a picture of ladies' underwear. And when she's a little older she puts Rody Cleary down as the most dashing man she could ever imagine, a strong farmer with a watch on a silver chain.

Sometimes, the figure of a child in a white smock appears over the brow of the hill. This is Annie O'Brien, the carpenter's daughter, come to collect eggs or milk to tide the family over. Annie's father is a famously good carpenter, the son of a carpenter who was himself the son of a carpenter; nevertheless he is frequently in the business of waiting, empty-handed, on his money. Agnes likes nothing better than to see Annie receive the Kavanaghs' bounty. She especially likes to see Annie's eyes go longingly to the baking board, and then to observe the girl's gratitude when Mrs Kavanagh gives her a piece of cake. She wishes Annie would ask for butter. Having helped her mother make it, Agnes knows there's plenty of it, but butter is a luxury the O'Briens can live without and it doesn't do to owe more than you have to. Agnes thinks of the pork salting in a tub of brine in the outhouse and hopes that when winter comes Mr O'Brien will still be in the business of 'waiting, empty-handed' for his money so she can impress Annie with the gift of a slice of luscious shiny fat. Meanwhile, she stands at her mother's side to watch as Annie goes carefully away, treading as if the jug she carries contains liquid gold. Her figure in the patched white smock dwindles away through the yellow field accompanied by butterflies. The mother explains that butterflies are attracted to the colour white but Mary Rose, her oldest child, says white isn't a colour at all. Her mother doesn't reply.

Once long ago before Agnes was born, Mary Rose had done a terrible thing. She'd picked her little brother Patrick up by one arm and one leg and swung him round, laughing, and she'd broken his leg against the hearthstone. At first, no one realised the gravity of what had happened. But when the following morning Patrick's leg was blown up like a purple balloon the parents panicked. Dan was sent racing down to the Clearys' and Rody Cleary brought the tram cart up with his wife on it for womanly support. They loaded the boy on to it and got him down the hill to the surgery at the blacksmith's where, two hours later – after one of the Slattery boys had raced into Nenagh on his bicycle looking for him – the doctor arrived. Ever since, Patrick had worn a leg iron, and Mary Rose was the one who had done it. Patrick, her first son, was the mother's favourite, both before and after the accident. But even that word 'favourite' doesn't do justice to the power of her feelings. Sometimes, it's as if Patrick is her only child and the others are foundlings. Even as a boy, Patrick didn't complain about his leg and it makes no difference to his appetite for hard work.

Near the Slatterys, in a dark little cottage, lives old Mrs Foley, who has 'the evil eye', and Agnes has an idea where she keeps it: in the breast pocket of the man's jacket she wears. The jacket is pockmarked with burns from the pipe Mrs Foley – known as Mud Foley – makes a habit of putting away whilst it's still smouldering. She doesn't put her pipe away to mutter 'Goodmorning' or, which is more usual, 'The Devil take you,' but only to say her confession to Father O'Brien of whom she has a high opinion, always saying of him, 'There's a man who can tell the difference.' Mary Rose claims that, on the morning she broke Patrick's leg, she'd seen Mud Foley standing at the edge of Knigh Wood looking towards the house.

Agnes is very small when she's given charge of the newest – and the last, another fact known only to the mother – addition to the family, baby Nancy. Nancy has taken Agnes's place inside the rubber tyre. Sitting at the centre of the cornfield late one August afternoon, Nancy takes it into her head to crawl out and explore the larger world. Her ambition takes her away from the sunlit field and away from the silent harvesters working all around her in a haze of golden dust. When Agnes looks up from her gleaning – a task she's been employed in for the first time – Nancy is gone. The little girl turns her back on the awful absence and scratches feverishly at the corn-stubble. She looks over her shoulder. No Nancy. She thinks of Mud Foley. She thinks of the little people. The fear is so extreme it hurts and she lets out a wail piercing enough to bring the adults running. The baby can't be found. Nancy, a placid fat little nine-month-old, has never been known to move before. Has she been bundled up by mistake inside one of the stooks? Is she lying scythed in half under the mown corn? The mother thinks of sibling jealousy, and rabid dogs. She thinks, too, of the paid strangers who've come to help, drawn out of the surrounding unpeopled countryside as if by magic at the clatter of the mowing machine. Her eyes run over them, counting. Were there only five, or should it be six? She shields her eyes with one hand and looks towards the wood. It's nearly an hour before one of the labourers finds the baby tumbled happily into a ditch, her fist full of the cow dung she's been cramming experimentally into her mouth. The mother darts forward and slaps her baby daughter, then she slaps Agnes, and everything goes back to normal.

Except that, in Agnes's mind, the aura of danger always hung over Nancy. Nancy herself didn't seem to know the meaning of the word.

Agnes is cautious, sensitive, quick to learn and, like her mother, surprisingly quick-tempered. 'Surprisingly' because both mother and daughter move in an aura of calm and reserve, both give the impression – a true one – of delicacy. Disliking her own temper, the mother is determined to stamp it out in the child. Agnes suffers much bitter recrimination and punishment for her lapses – which only strengthens both her reserve and her temper. The most usual punishment is for her to be sent upstairs alone and without her tea.

The bedroom window looks directly down on to the slate roof of the outhouse where her father and brother Pat store their tools. The door to the shed stands open and from inside Agnes is aware of the little click of stones and hisses of impatience that tell her Cathleen and Nancy are playing fives without her. If she presses her face to the glass and squints to one side she can see into the yard. There are coals on the lid of the bread-oven but her mother isn't there, only the poultry pecking and tiptoeing about. Mrs Kavanagh keeps duck, geese and chicken – no turkey because she believes them troublesome to rear in the Irish climate – and, as pets, guinea fowl. When Agnes is let free she means to offload her temper in chasing those idiotic guinea fowl, sending them scattering, shrieking and dropping their glossy feathers in their own dirt.

A movement takes Agnes's eyes. Turning the other

33

way, she sees her mother drop to her knees between the flower beds with newspaper spread out around her. She is using a trowel to lift the corms of her begonias and the even more precious gladioli. Later she will store them in shallow boxes made for her by Pat. Now Nancy comes spinning out of the shed and hurls herself at the swing, kicking off with one foot, sending up a cloud of dust that settles on the flowers. A bolt of agony goes through the child at the bedroom window. She can't stand it a minute longer. She'll go down to her mother, touch her skirt, try to provoke a smile and then beg to be let out. Please, Mammy, please, please. But no tears. Agnes is too proud for that. Besides, tears disgust her mother.

But when Agnes runs into the garden, her mother is gone. She is standing away just outside the wall on the hillside as a flock of thrushes sweep down around her in what looks like an ecstatic greeting. Safely arrived through the clouds from – according to Mary Rose – Russia, they settle, sighing, on the moss-soft turf, the red on their sides showing like wounds. Mrs Kavanagh loves all birds, but songbirds especially, and nothing would distract her from this rare moment of forgetfulness. Knowing this, the girl turns away, her impulse to demand forgiveness and affection gone. Besides, isn't she out anyway? She dances away to join Nancy on the swing.

My mother and I sat in silence a moment with that picture in our minds. My picture must have been similar to hers but, of course, no matter how hard I listened, it couldn't be identical. Would she even have recognised it? Just then, as she spoke about her mother, there was unusual emotion in her voice. Sometimes as we talked I managed to coax an extra detail out of her, as when I asked, 'Did Schol recite those poems in Gaelic?' to which she retorted, 'No one spoke Gaelic!' And though my mother was only telling me all this because I'd asked her, still I had the impression she was enjoying it. Which made me wonder what needs of her own were being satisfied? She wasn't idly turning over familiar memories. She hadn't spent time with her brothers and sisters saying, 'Remember when...?' Even with Nancy, I didn't think there'd been much talk about the old times. Did some of the pleasure, I wondered, come from telling me her own version with no one there to contradict her?

One winter day, when Agnes is seven years old she is sent on an errand alone for the first time. She is to walk over the hill to Carney to visit her newly married sister who is mysteriously unwell. She has a dozen eggs, a pound of butter, and a twist of paper containing parsnip seeds. Agnes herself had shaped the butter into four pats, two square, two round, and, with the letter 'A' cut into a wedge of potato, she had printed her initial on top. Her desire to please was so intense the procedure had caused her great anxiety and exhausted her mother's patience. But finally, with the butter wrapped in dock leaves to keep it fresh, and the twelve eggs all properly uniform in size and different in colour, the girl is satisfied.

As she goes beyond sight of home, Agnes chides herself for being a little nervous at being sent off alone like this. Doesn't she know everyone along the way, and doesn't everyone know her? She tells herself she is Agnes Teresa Kavanagh from Knigh, Kate Buckley's daughter. Kate Buckley's eyes are famously beautiful, not blue – as you might expect – but dark, dark brown and, in so far as she has any awareness of her own appearance, Agnes knows she has her mother's eyes because she's been told so.

A small dun-coloured bird flits across the path, then

back again with a twig in its beak. Cold as it is, the birds are beginning to make their nests, which is how Agnes knows it must be St Bridgid's Day. She crouches for a moment by the hedge to watch. The bird pauses to look at her, bright-eyed, its head on one side. Neither of them moves. In this moment of intense watching, the child is at one and the same moment a narrow dart of consciousness and the vast circle of her entire known world, the pulse of her own being indistinguishable from the great pulse of life. She looks into the eye of the world, and the world looks back. Then the bird flits away, Agnes shifts the basket on to her other arm, and walks on.

Once past the clump of blackberry bushes on the left, Agnes is walking where she's never before walked alone. A little thrill of excitement goes down her spine. But with the sun up, she doesn't think of the headless coachman who is said to drive along the lane at midnight, down to Knigh Cross and away along the road to Nenagh. The lane, known as Blind Lane, skirts the wood, a green wood of ash and oak and elm, at present still and leafless. The wood is her brother Pat's responsibility, so maybe that's why there are no wolves and no bogeymen hiding in its dark interior, only foxes, and local children thieving kindling and wild strawberries when Pat isn't looking – and why should he look? Isn't there enough for everyone? She passes several deserted cottages, little more than a tumble of stones and brambles. Suddenly the vista opens up clear to the distant horizon, and ahead of her the white lane falls like a dry river in silent curves towards her grandmother's cottage, the place her father had said 'No' to, where his mother and his two sisters still live side by side without touching, like apples stored in a box.

On top of the hill is a circle of ancient stones. Agnes knows this is a fairy ring. So far, she's neither seen the

little people nor found any trace of them, only sheep droppings and flowers in the grass. But knowing this is a fairy
fort, she approaches with respect, solemnly and quietly,
perching her bum on one of the stones and placing her feet
neatly side by side, pointing in the direction from which
she's come. From up here she can look down on the grey
roof of her own house. To one side, on the side the sun
comes up, is the small pastel-blue splash of Lough Eorna.
Agnes knows that Lough Eorna was once a huge field of
barley that was flooded by God's wrath, and she knows
that two young girls drowned there when the ice gave
way beneath them. On the other side, the side where the
sun sets, is Lough Derg, as vast, as blue, as mysterious as
a lake in a saga. Agnes knows that St Patrick himself had
walked there and blessed the Nenagh river. Because of his
blessing, swans still come down in their tens, sometimes
hundreds, until the mouth of the river has the appearance
of being heaped with snow. The swans dip their beaks
to drink like pilgrims at a shrine. Between Knigh Hill
and the lough stands Lisduff House, a house so large the
Kavanagh children imagine it a palace. To the south, in
the direction in which the child's feet are pointing, is a
circle of blue hills, among them a mountain my mother
knows by name: Silvermine Mountains. Agnes knows no
more about it than its name, but she's heard that rocks
have veins and she imagines deep cuts being made into
them, and rivers of silver gushing out to coat knives and
forks and spoons with, to make rings and necklaces to fit
on women like chains.

The Silvermine Mountains were beyond the Kavanaghs'
reach. Even the loch, only a couple of miles distant, seemed
far off. In his entire life John Kavanagh – eight of whose
children would grow up to emigrate to England – never

moved beyond a radius of about fourteen miles, with Knigh Hill standing almost exactly at the centre of that circle. The little girl sitting up there on the fairy fort believed this to be the most beautiful place in the world. A place St Patrick had blessed. She knew she never wanted to leave.

2

Since 1878 Mrs Griffin had stood guard over the girls' entrance to the school in Puckaun. An increasingly stout figure buttoned tighter and tighter into black bombazine – a dress rumoured to have belonged to her grandmother – Mrs Griffin had begun teaching as a girl of sixteen. By the time my mother was one of her pupils she was in her late fifties and had long ago acquired a reputation as a dragon. Indeed, as Agnes knew, 'dragon' was what her name meant. Not only that, but Mrs Griffin had been born and raised on Silvermine Mountain, so it was a good deal easier to imagine her a little dragon, scuttling about on iron claws, than to think she had ever been a human child. Mrs Griffin had no children of own, only a dead baby born when she was a young married woman and rumoured by the children to be carried always inside her black bag, along with her dog-eared prayer book and a box of clove-scented lozenges. But Agnes didn't think that any of this this excused Mrs Griffin's dragon-like habits in the classroom. The child took with her to school an unusually lively sense of fairness that had been nurtured at home where, in spite of the mother's passion for her first son, there was never any sense that girls were inferior to boys and the last three children were, as it happened, all girls: Cathleen, Agnes and Nancy. These three made their own tight little circle inside the larger world of the school.

My mother hadn't recalled Mrs Griffin for over sixty

years. Even to find her name come back so readily surprised her. She thought the Puckaun National school was 'quite old' and that it had fifty or so pupils. The oldest boy at Puckaun school was fourteen, almost an adult in the eyes of my mother, who began her schooling at the age of four. She disliked the boys at school. She couldn't say why. It wasn't as if she wasn't used to boys – having three older brothers at home – she just didn't like them. One had a fancy to her and when school was out he chased her around, which she hated but endured in silence, as if it was something to be ashamed of, beating him off furiously but ineffectually with her schoolbag. No one ever came to her rescue except Nancy – who was half the boy's size – which only added to his fun. Agnes and Nancy. Nancy and Agnes.

Happily for my mother, inside the school the sexual divide went deeper than the religious one: boys and girls were taught under the same roof, but separately. They had separate entrances leading into separate classrooms, separate playgrounds and separate lavatories. Catholic girls sat with Protestant girls – though in my mother's day there were no Protestant girls – and Catholic boys with Protestant boys; at Puckaun just two, sons of the rector of the local Church of Ireland. The Reverend Brittain Lougheed was a young man with a parish of sixty or so souls, the majority of them gentry. Canon O'Meara, on the other hand, ministered to close on six hundred and was known for his many acts of kindness. But he was an old man, wrapped in a great old-fashioned frieze coat, wearing his wide-brimmed hat set at an angle on his white head. On weekday afternoons these two men liked to walk up and down Kelly's Lane discussing the great issues of life and death. Outside the church gate stood a few thin trees. In summer, the men strolled in their shade, like Frenchmen in a village square. In winter they trod the leaves underfoot.

Naturally, being of different religious dispositions, they came at most things from a different angle and sometimes, especially in the case of the younger man, they generated more heat than light. When this happened the reverend's gentle, hard-working boys were embarrassed by the sound of their father's light, rather high voice, clearly audible inside the schoolroom. They blushed and hung their heads, and the classroom fell silent, gleefully anticipating the Reverend Lougheed's predictable explosion: 'Surely to God, man, you can see my point of view!' and Canon O'Meara's calm response, always the same: 'Indeed I can. But to see both points of view, my dear friend, *that* is the great thing.'

Many of Canon O'Meara's parishioners repeated his sayings like mantras: 'To see both points of view…to mind your own business…to take your time, that is the great thing.' These sentiments could be heard spoken with the greatest sincerity by the greatest bigot in the land and no one would argue with him.

'True! True enough!' came the Reverend's rueful reply, upon which the men would turn and walk back the other way, their black skirts trailing the dust, their voices fading.

Beyond the schoolhouse and the church stood the barracks of the Royal Irish Constabulary, housing four armed policemen, and on the other side of the road was Kennedy's public house. The walls of the church had been erected around a little old thatched chapel, now vanished, that had stood on that site for generations. Agnes knew this story and sometimes during the sombre eternity of the Mass she liked to imagine the chapel, standing before the altar, a chapel inside a church and inside the chapel… Father O'Meara had told the children that the stone used

41

to build the church was famous for 'weeping', and for a long time my mother believed this was a miracle that marked Puckaun Church out as special.

But though Father O'Meara was frequently referred to as 'a walking saint' he wasn't the man to bother with church walls, weeping or otherwise, and in my mother's time the church was badly in need of renovation, both to its fabric and to some of its customs. In the front portion of the nave stood twenty private pews. Several had been made by Annie O'Brien's father, who complained bitterly that the pious kept him in the business of waiting to be paid a devil of a lot longer than your average sinner.

Mrs Griffin owned a private pew, so did the Royal Irish Constabulary. And the local publicans. The well-to-do, naturally, had their private pews, too. Exclusivity was jealously guarded. The majority of the congregation was left to stand in the unfurnished rear portion of the church. As a little girl attending a packed 'mission' – to which everyone was expected to contribute 'in coin or kind' – my mother noticed that not one of the privileged invited any of those standing, or kneeling on the cold stone floor, to share their comfort, not old people who groaned as they knelt, nor the exhausted mothers. And then it would be read out who had given what and if you gave too little you were reprimanded and if you gave more than you could afford you were looked down on for vanity or idiocy. Even in the house of God social distinctions mattered. Wealth, and its necessary complement, poverty, mattered. The Kavanagh family always gave an appropriate and unremarkable shilling.

The door of Kennedy's pub, like that of the church, always stood wide open to those seeking comfort. From its gloomy interior came a low masculine babble like stones turning over on the bed of a stream. The place was much frequented immediately after Mass, or in some cases immediately before it. This was especially true of those men needing to blunt their shame before stepping into the dark confessional – or of course to celebrate afterwards by setting themselves well on the road back to committing the same sins for which they'd just asked forgiveness. To the children who passed by – or in some cases hung about outside waiting for the head of the family to re-emerge – the pub, with its little windows darkened by curtains, had an air of shame and secrecy not unlike the confessional itself: a place of licence from which red-faced men stumbled out happier than they had gone in. Women did not go into pubs.

Nancy runs ahead of her sisters along the Mass path. It's her first day to school and she is carrying a few sticks of kindling. Agnes and Cathleen both carry a penny in their pockets but kindling is less likely to be lost and just as acceptable to the school as a penny. Agnes keeps her eyes fixed on her younger sister, but her head is full of a poem. She's been learning it all summer, painstakingly and out loud, so that the entire Kavanagh family has got it by heart. It's driven them half mad.

Today Mrs Griffin will ask Agnes to stand up to recite the poem in front of the entire class. But Agnes is confident. The words sing in her head as if they're remembering themselves. The path runs for a couple of miles through both Kavanagh and Slattery fields before it comes out on to the road a hundred yards or so from the village. Here, hidden from view under a thorn bush, the girls sit down and take off their boots. Nancy needs help, just as she needs help to get them on, because her boots are buttoned, which is even more difficult than laces. The girls then roll down their garters and black stockings, stuff them inside the boots and hide them in the hedge. Having staked their claim to be one with the poorest of the poor they scamper on barefoot, impervious to the rough surface of the road.

The walls of the classroom are covered in maps so old they look like stains in the plaster. Agnes has searched them for Puckaun but so far she hasn't even been able to find Ireland, perhaps because she's looking for green but, as she later comes to understand, it's coloured pink, like England. On a shelf behind the teacher's desk is a row of shabby books covering subjects such as history, geography, bookkeeping, a little Euclid, and some poetry.

From the other room the girls hear the regular tap of the master's cane on his desk as the boys launch into their multiplication tables, low and quiet at first, but increasingly loud and shrill as they work their way up into the tens until the master's voice roars at them to 'Shut up! Be quiet! Start again! Behave yourselves!' And off they go again, chugging along through the twos and threes and then, like a steam train, gradually building up speed until they career out of control and come off the rails.

Physical punishment is regular as mathematical tables in the boys' class and its administration is clearly audible to the girls. On rare occasions a boy's reaction is audible, too, and if he has a sister she hangs her head, sharing both the pain and the shame. Mrs Griffin does sometimes whack one of the girls with the blackboard rubber but usually she needs nothing more than her tongue, the look in her eye. Her breath. Agnes annoys her. The child's watchful habits, perhaps, her unsmiling face and immaculate apron, the way she has of setting out her slate and chalk. It's not clear yet whether Agnes is clever or merely keen, but keen she certainly is, and the slow fading of the look of anticipation with which she always arrives is like a criticism. Mrs Griffin has her favourites, of course, one of them a tall girl who's learned the value of a smile and a

well-chosen lie. Agnes doesn't even wonder at Mrs Griffin
not seeing through this girl, not seeing that the smile is
stuck on her face too long to be sincere, or that the lies are
always self-serving. Agnes knows perfectly well that Mrs
Griffin sees and doesn't care. Indeed, that Mrs Griffin is
tacitly approving of lies and insincerity as the best tools
for improvement in life, and that that is the real lesson her
girls are expected to learn.

The school lavatory is a place to avoid, but today Agnes
has no choice. The wooden seat, worn to a satiny sheen,
has a hole in it over a stinking zinc box. Birds wearing
hobnailed boots land and clatter over the corrugated roof.
Agnes has a horror of being spied on in here. She kicks her
heels against the box as spasms of pain knot and release
her guts. The idea of succeeding in pleasing Mrs Griffin
has a peculiarly sour taste to it. The prospect of failure
tastes even worse.

Mrs Griffin's look follows her as she returns to her
place. Over her bombazine shoulder Agnes fixes her eyes
on the spine of the large poetry book but as she does so,
even the poet's name – until now branded on her memory
– slips from her head like a sliver of wet soap. When told
to stand up to recite, every word she's learned goes clean
out of her head. She turns stiff as a board, her mouth
tight shut. The sight of the dragon's lopsided imitation of
a smile, and her bright blue eyes like bullets, turns Agnes
to stone, and neither threatening nor coaxing nor even
Cathleen's wail:'She knows it! She knows it better than
her own name!'

Nothing can wring the poem out of her.

Agnes's punishment, the usual one, is to be made to
stand out in front of the class, an example of a fool who
hasn't taken the trouble to do her homework. 'Unless she
cares to prove otherwise?' hisses Mrs Griffin. The child

shakes her head and is fascinated by the flush of vexation that washes up over the teacher's face. Word by word the poem returns, but the lesson Agnes has learned today has less to do with poetry than with silence. Not only is silence always within her power, it IS power.

School officially ends at three o'clock but in practice there's still half an hour of catechism, which means that in winter they go home in the dark. Setting off early, the lucky little Protestants hear the others inside sweetly chanting: 'Our intellect is darkened, our will is weakened, we are subject to suffering and death.' But the very last thing of this and every other day is the hymn.

There's no piano so the monitor, a plump young woman with a squint, plays the whistle. Agnes thinks it must be because of the whistle they have a rather narrow repertoire. Very narrow. To be exact, a repertoire of four hymns and one song, but much anyone cares. They'd happily sing the last lesson written up on the board. With fluttery little motions of her hand, like a woman tapping a cake to see if it's done, Miss O'Leary readies the girls and then, delicately, eyebrows slightly raised, she lifts the whistle to her lips. If you can't sing you're supposed to beat time with your hands and if you can't do even that, then you listen. It's soon obvious that listening is all Nancy can do, but she does it so well, lifting her face a little, opening her blue eyes wide and parting her lips as if expecting a sweet to drop into her mouth. A couple of the others don't find even listening that easy and Miss O'Leary – all too aware of Mrs Griffin at her back – gets agitated.

'If you've no voice, then isn't it still and quiet you must be.' Sometimes the pleading tone has effect. Some kind of fellow feeling works on the girls who have neither voices nor any sense of rhythm. They resign themselves to still-ness and silence and Miss O'Leary's face is like sunshine after rain. 'Will you take it away now, girls!'

And they do. For the singers, this is an experience of pure joy: the prospect of imminent freedom, the sensation of their own voices spurting strongly out of their throats, the beauty of the melody and its mysterious relationship with the beauty of the words, all these elements fuse together in an echo of Agnes's mystic moment on the way to her grandmother's. But that was solitary, this is communal. Every girl is gathered in.

At intervals during the afternoon the girls have noticed unusual noises coming from the boys' room: crackling, sudden piercing whistles, a curious babble of what sounds like voices but scarcely human and certainly unintelligible. Now Mr MacDonald suddenly puts his head round the door and with the kind of grin on his face that turns every muscle in Mrs Griffin's body rigid, he invites the girls into his classroom. There is a stunned silence. But when Mr MacDonald throws the door wide open and stands aside, the girls crowd forward to be confronted by a circle of raised bottoms.

Every last one of the boys, including Tom and Dan Kavanagh, are doubled over like little Mohammedans at prayer in front of a construction of metal and wires and knobs. This doesn't strike the girls as particularly amusing but definitely odd, and elicits some titters. In a compelling male basso Mr MacDonald demands silence, strides over to the construction and with a flourish turns one of the knobs. There's a good deal of spluttering and crackling and then, from a great distance, like a voice trickling through an electric storm, comes the unforgettable, incomprehensible announcement – made in a rip-roaring accent the children have never heard before – that 'we have made radio contact with the US Red Star Line SS Zeeland bound east...!'

47

Agnes is paralysed by a thrill of violation.

'It's the USA!' yells Mr MacDonald. Then he stands stock-still and with shining eyes he whispers, 'Boys and girls, it's the US of A.'

The moment school ends, the children's feet hit the road outside. As the Kavanagh girls race past Kennedy's, Nancy bumps into a pair of familiar, muddy trousers: Schol O'Connor, the man who is 'made of poetry' and labours in their father's fields. He drops on to one knee, grasps Nancy's ribcage in both hands and peers into her ruddy face.

'So, you're after getting yourself an education at last, is it?' His eyes are bright with mischief. 'Tell me the dates of the kings of Ireland and where the cuckoo builds her nest?'

'There's no kings of Ireland!' says Cathleen scornfully. 'And cuckoos don't have nests.'

Schol laughs ruefully and goes through the curtain into the darkened bar where a policeman with a gun on his belt is buying ten Woodbines and a packet of Peg's Legs.

Returning to the spot where they'd earlier hidden their boots the girls find them gone. A quick search of the surrounding area reveals precisely nothing and this nothing has the power of an unexpected blow to the head. The absence of the boots is like infinity, ungraspably vast, awesome, dizzying in the consequences that stack up behind the one massive, relentlessly awful consequence: their mother's anger. They can't go home without the boots. It occurs to them not to go home at all. To stay out on the hillside all night and offer up their suffering to propitiate their mother's awful fury. They will be cold, hungry. Lost. Surely they can earn her pity?

Cathleen sits down on a tussock and refuses to budge. So Agnes goes on alone, lugging their sister – Nancy has suddenly lost the use of her legs – over the difficult bits and through the whitethorn with which the ditches are planted. Nancy doesn't complain. And maybe because she always feels protected by Agnes, she just can't seem to grasp the inevitability of maternal anger. Her good-tempered moon-face is scarlet, her legs scratched with brambles, her eyelids drooping with exhaustion. Her bare, mud-caked feet are the first thing the mother notices.

With the worst of the storm over, their father – in an unusual gesture – briefly puts a hand on each child's head and suggests mildly that he'll go back with them to make a proper search. Who knows but the girls mistook where they hid their boots? They may still be there, or lying just some little way off having been the playthings of foxes. As they go back down the path they can hear the sound of Cathleen humming where she sits on the tussock, hugging her knees. A thorough search of the ditch and the field yields nothing. Then, passing under an ancient crab tree at the edge of the wood, John Kavanagh's head collides with something. Three pairs of boots dangle by their laces from a branch, out of sight amongst clusters of sour little green apples. Without proof, accusations can't be made, but the culprit is identified with passionate certainty by all three girls as little Mick Foley, one of Mud Foley's boys. From this day on Mick is known, to his professed incomprehension, as 'Boots' Foley.

When the father and his girls get back to the house Mrs Kavanagh has gone out to the outhouse, where she's making up a wreath for a wedding. She works standing at a long, slate counter, and the outhouse is cold. As she moves about, she coughs, a hollow sound the children have become so familiar with they scarcely hear it. Before stepping on to the clean kitchen floor, John Kavanagh takes off his boots and puts them down beside the step.

The girls do the same with the boots they've carried home in their hands. They put them, as always, neatly side by side and Agnes goes down on one knee to do what the others don't bother to do: that is, to pull the laces loose and very exactly even in length, and to yank the tongue of the boot out to facilitate getting her foot into it in the morning – or maybe it's her way of sticking her tongue out at her mother. Who knows, even Agnes doesn't know, but that's the way it has to be. Then the girls grip the doorjamb with one hand and with the other they brush the dirt from the soles of their feet. Agnes drives one of her mother's guinea fowl out, finding relief in an outburst of scolding and rushing about. The day's baking stands on a wooden board on the dresser. It goes without saying they can't touch it. The sisters perch on the edge of the settle, their stomachs growling. Then, at a nod from their father, they dash outside to find the donkey.

As the girls haul the water barrel up on to the donkey's back, they hear his low voice, and hers, the mother's, answering. The children listen gratefully a moment, but as they set off down the hill they don't say anything themselves. It could have been worse. They could have been sent to bed hungry. The coolness of the path descending under the trees is like an augury of the well they are going to. On the way down, with an empty water barrel, the donkey can take the weight of one of the girls and this evening it's Agnes's turn. She presses her face into the dear beast's neck, and grips his grey flanks needily between her legs. She breathes in his donkey smell and pats his broad, hard cheeks that remind her of the cheeks of the bellows they keep by the hearth. She runs his ears through her hands, testing the slightly greasy texture of his fur on her palm. Then, having assured herself that everything is as it should be, she lies limp, allowing the donkey's warmth to seep into her, lolling in time with the smooth, quick scurry of his hooves.

There are ferns growing around the mouth of the well. Cathleen fixes the rope to their bucket and drops it down. It smacks the water, rolls on to its side and slowly at first, then in a great rush, it fills. Cathleen leans out over the side until she can see her own outline shuddering on the bright coin of water.

'Arse!' she shouts. 'Arse, arse, arse,' replies the well with the weary tone of someone humouring an old joke.

'ARSE!' screams Nancy, shrill enough to wake the well up.

They count the echoes.

'That's seven arses,' says Agnes gravely.

It takes all three of them to haul the full bucket up and, careful not to get soaked, to hoist it high enough to tip the water into the barrel. Eight buckets in all. They lean on the wall to get their breath back. Nancy faces down into the dark damp hole.

'Where do all the arses go?' she asks, and not entirely unaware of her own whimsicality.

Cathleen gives her a punch.

'They lie down there waiting for the next time you come by and then they'll all blow off together in one enormous great fart till you faint dead on the ground.'

'POOH!' they scream, pinching their noses.

'Holy Mary SAVE ME!' they shriek, reeling, and fainting dead away on the puddled grass.

The donkey turns his eyes to look at them over his shoulder. By the time they're halfway back up the path, pushing the loaded donkey ahead of them, they don't have the energy to laugh any more.

From deep inside the wood, Patrick, who has meanwhile been told the story of the boots, sees their small figures

51

toiling up the hill, the sun on Cathleen's fair head. Patrick is cutting scallops to sell for thatching. The wood is his territory and, since his fourteenth birthday, his responsibility. He knows every tree here, oaks, elm, beech and ash as well as the hazel. He would know them blindfold by the feel of their bark. He clears them, removing some of the dead trees and branches, leaving some to nature. He treats the wounds inflicted by storm or wildlife. His leg is tiring him. It feels twice the weight it was when he got out of bed in the morning. He's used to it, of course, and won't say anything when he goes home, avoiding his mother's pitying eyes as best he can. He touches his fingers to the roll of baccy in his pocket.

The evening meal is over. The family is down on its knees for the saying of the rosary. They're in a semicircle, more or less facing, without really seeing, the Sacred Heart with its little red oil lamp. Mary Rose, symbolically, kneels somewhat apart, her neat brown head bowed. She's the oldest child, the plainest, the quietest, the most inclined to do her parents' bidding. Next to their mother, shifting about on their knees like pilgrims on Mt. Croagh Patrick, wincing, giggling, tugging at the hems of their dresses, are the two middle girls. Like the youngest three, Bridie and Josie form a separate unit, paired as opposites, complementing one another so exactly it's like a little joke on nature's part. Josie is the beauty of the family, so fair and blue-eyed that Bridie's had to make do with being strong and handsome. And secretive. Bridie never gives anything away, not even the time of day. Agnes, late and in a dither one morning, asked had she got the parting down the back of her head straight? Bridie said God only knew if it was straight or crooked and why did she want to know anyway? It may be her pairing with Bridie that has brought out an independent, not to say stubborn streak in Josie. Josie has never asked an opinion of anyone, let alone permission, and now, aged twelve and pretty as spring, she's growing up to be a cause of anxiety to the parents who no more worry about Bridie than the iron by the fire.

As to the younger boys, it would be perverse of the parents to worry about the elder, Tom, who is hard-working and loved by everyone. And Dan, at the exact middle of the family, is the one who somehow always slips their minds – the child who can get away with murder because his mother and father are mostly looking the other way. Just now, kneeling almost hidden behind the upright back of the settle, Dan experiments with sticking his thumb up his nose then wiping it on the settle to make the others laugh. But the only one who notices is Agnes. She closes her eyes in disgust and searches her teeth for pips, for a trace of strawberries.

Earlier that evening, as the girls came up from the well, Pat had come limping out of the woods. Cupped in his black hat were wild strawberries. As he trickled an equal portion into each of their aprons, the girls smelt cigarettes on his fingers. The woods were already darkening behind him and Pat's fifteen-year-old face had something sly, ancient, derisive about it, unwilling to acknowledge his own act of kindness.

Now, kneeling beside his parents, the only one of the children to have a sugan chair, his position is as symbolic as that of Mary Rose – who is apart, and has no chair. Naturally, the three youngest girls don't have chairs either so they face the settle, a position Agnes dislikes because the settle is where visitors plant their bums and she fastidiously refuses to put her face anywhere near it. Sometimes she sinks down with her forehead almost touching the ground, an image of exaggerated and unconvincing piety.

Usually, avoiding the stomach-churning sight of the Sacred Heart, she looks off to one side at the dresser, or towards the door, whilst her father's voice, accompanied by the little clicking sounds of eleven sets of rosary beads, intones the prayer.

'Hail Mary, full of grace, blessed art thou amongst women and blessed is the fruit of thy womb, Jesus.'

Obediently, the children give their bored replies: 'Holy Mary, Mother of God, pray for us sinners...'

On shelves just inside the door is a display of glass. In summer, when sunshine falls in at the open door, it sparkles like the best crystal and Agnes promises herself that when she's grown up she'll be like her mother and make a collection of crystal. Her eyes go to a shelf on the dresser where there's a double pack of cards and a box containing a game of Lotto. Sometimes after prayers the three youngest are allowed to stay up a little, long enough for just one game. The illustrations on the cards are scenes from the Bible and this is one of Agnes's most intense pleasures: examining every last detail of these tiny pictures which are printed with only three colours, green, blue and yellow. Here is the Good Shepherd, and here the widow giving her mite. Here is Moses descending from the mountain with the Ten Commandments. Here is Jonah curled safe inside the belly of an enormous, friendly looking fish. And here is Agnes's favourite: the flight into Egypt. Mary's cloak, which shelters the sleeping baby, is the deep blue of an evening sky. The noble grey donkey carries them tirelessly, his little feet scurrying over the sand.

When the three little girls go up to bed, the sound of their parents' voices continues downstairs, just a few words, batting quietly back and forth between them while the mother sews. The children can also hear the

54

creak of the trees behind the house, and the squeak of their mother's lamp as she runs it up on its chain then sits for just a few moments – you might be able to count to fifty before hearing her feet on the stairs – hands folded, doing nothing before she goes to bed. Tom lies on the settle reading a Zane Gray western, of which he has quite a collection. Dan mooches up and down outside the open front door, kicking the gravel until his father, without taking the pipe from his mouth, growls, 'Will you stop that!' Dan has had his moment of attention. After everyone else has gone up, Pat – with the independence of his fifteen years – steps outside, rolls a cigarette and, with eyes as large and deep as the donkey's, he watches the stars turn.

Just as everything has gone quiet and still, as the last of the girls is dropping off to sleep, the rattle of a carriage starts up in the distance. It is the headless coachman, driving full pelt up and over the hill, past the house and away along the road to Nenagh, leaving the Kavanaghs safe and sleeping, deep in the ocean of night. On occasion a dark figure might then be seen leaving the house. John Kavanagh is going out to secure the foxes' holes.

A good Irish Catholic, my grandfather owned neither a gun nor a Bible. But he and each of the children had his or her own confirmation prayer book, bound with a hard creamy-coloured front of mock ivory with a cross embossed on it. I saw the one belonging to my Aunt Josie on her bedside table, after a lifetime of use bulging with little holy images, broken-backed, with her name and the date September 1915 written in a rather bold, scrawling hand – her mother's, I supposed (or perhaps, as in my own prayer book, her father's) – on the marbled flyleaf. Aunt Nancy went to the grave with hers, for all she had

55

married an Englishman, but my mother did not keep hers. She kept nothing from Ireland.

Just once, in the summer of 1938, my father went to Ireland to meet my grandparents. A reliable but uninformative witness, he remembers them as 'nice, decent people'. When pressed, my father (who can recite mile upon mile of Kipling and Gilbert and Sullivan) could add only that they were both tall and dark. John Kavanagh would take a coal from the fire with his bare fingers and hold the live part to the baccy in his pipe to get it going. My mother remembers him looking through the local paper, shaking it out, then smoothing it flat with the careful gesture of a man smoothing the flank of a nervous horse. He played cribbage with his 'cronies' – my mother's word – and both he and his mother smoked clay pipes. He never in his life visited a doctor and he had no toothbrush: all his life he kept his own teeth, which he cleaned with little twigs cut from oak wood. It was his custom to get up at first light in order to walk the horse in the dew.

Now my grandparents lie in an unmarked grave, under a white hawthorn tree in a little graveyard in a field that has run wild. Thirty years ago, I travelled to Tipperary with my husband and nine-year-old daughter. We found the house on Knigh Hill, derelict, used only to store farm machinery in. I don't believe it occurred to me to try finding either the Slatterys or the Clearys, names my mother had mentioned with affection. It was all too long ago, too far away. In a field of blowing grass beside the ruin of an old chapel we discovered the graveyard. But it scarcely registered on me that these ancient ghosts, this romantic fragment, was all that was left of the flesh-and-blood parents who had loved and raised my mother. The tide of my own life was strong and it was carrying me in the opposite direction. We were on our way to Donegal on holiday. Donegal, the best part of two hundred miles away from Puckaun, meant nothing more to me than a beautiful, rocky coastline. The weather was perfect. The beach, made up of exquisite shells the size of pinheads, was divine. We might as well have been in the Mediterranean – which, the following summer, we were.

3

Recently, the sounds from Kennedys' bar had changed: the voices were harder, more like flint striking stone than pebbles turning companionably over in water. Although the children had been told that the war in England was over – my mother was referring here to the First World War, of course – there were soldiers and police everywhere, English soldiers and still more English policemen. My mother offered no explanation for this except to say that for some time there'd been a notice up in Kennedys' window informing honest young men that the Royal Irish Constabulary had need of them. But either there were no honest young men in Puckaun, or they'd not taken a fancy to life in barracks.

So it was these Englishmen who'd come instead, though why they'd want to was a mystery, especially when they had to put together some kind of mismatched uniform for themselves. There were bottle-green trousers enough to go round – unless you examined them closely they looked black – but the men had had to top them with any old khaki jackets they could find. When these men were around there was an explosive atmosphere. They winked and joked with the children but Agnes took a violent dislike to them. When they laughed in her face and flicked her pigtails over her shoulder, she thought their hearts must be as sour as their breath. Nancy fell for the jokes and the sweets, but Agnes hated them. Behind their backs she heard them referred to as 'scum', even by the people who, having no choice in the matter, took their money.

The children never see any of these men away from the village or the road, but sometimes as they go home along the path beside the woods they find themselves looking over their shoulders. If they catch one another at it they give each other mocking shoves, then explode with laughter and race up the hill. Home is all the sweeter.

One day, a man of a different sort walks over the hill and along the lane that's white with dust so deep the fellow seems to be an inch or two off the ground, walking on cloud. A thickset man with grey eyes. On either side of him the thorn trees are in bloom, like clotted cream, and high above him larks are singing. When he reaches the house his boots and his black hat are dredged white. Seeing the mother throw him that look of hers, a frown that draws a fine mesh of lines like a net over her face, the man – who had been about to set foot over the door-step – flushes and stoops awkwardly to pull off his boots. As he does so, his bowler hat falls off his head and rolls across the kitchen floor to take its place at the fireside. A suitor has come courting Mary Rose. He and Mary Rose are allowed to go walking, formal as a couple on a promenade.

Mary Rose is twenty. She works as a junior in the office at the Ballyartella Woollen Mills where she's allowed to handle the money, and when she comes home her fingers smell of coppers. The three youngest sisters are in awe of this smart young woman with money in her pocket and first call on the hot water. There's a hook behind the office door which is specially hers to hang her coat on in the mornings.

At Christmas, when she'd been working at the Mills for

close on five years, Mary Rose was given a bolt of green cloth. What more does she want? For all Mick Gavin is a local farmer, with twenty-five acres of land near Borriso-kane, he's never before shown his face at the Kavanaghs' so far as the little girls know – and they know most things.

Still, here they are, together, she leaning on his arm, her neat dark head bowed, her companion holding his hat flat against his chest like a man marching in a funeral, the breeze tumbling his greying curls. That submissive look on their sister's face and the masterful cut of Gavin's shoulders produces an odd, contradictory state of emotion in the girls: irritation mixed with excitement, mockery with awe. A stranger has come courting their sister. This fact, this atmosphere as strong as liquor, affects them all, the way the approach of bad weather affects cattle, making them restless, excitable, nervy.

Blood-curdling screams are what Agnes would in retrospect associate most with the preparations for Mary Rose's wedding. Once or twice a year, Pat takes a pig down to the Slatterys' to be slaughtered. Of course the pig, known to the children by name and nature, always screams. It's only fitting that not a morsel of him, not a strip of skin or a cup of blood, is wasted. Soon his living flesh is transformed into pink slabs of meat, into washed tripe and black pudding. His trotters are split open, breadcrumbed and fried, a treat of such mouth-watering delicacy that even the girls are reduced to silence while the brothers quarrel over who is to get a share of the meatier, hind feet. The leftovers are taken and boiled down for gelatin and Mrs Kavanagh will use every last little scrap of flesh to make brawn. For the wedding breakfast a mountainous joint of bacon is salted, boiled with a bucketful of herbs and onions, and set aside to cool in its coat of glistening fat.

Although John Kavanagh will go from house to house inviting those closest to the family – and many who are not – to his daughter's wedding, this is widely thought of as an unnecessary formality. In fact, some of the invited will feel insulted, taking it as a sign that their presence at Mary Rose's wedding wasn't taken for granted. It's a fine line the parents have to tread. The mother judges she must provide for fifty. But then, to avoid the shame of guests standing at a bare table, provisions rise adequate for eighty: as well as the bacon she decides there must be rabbit stew with dumplings, and four boiled chickens. Which is how Agnes gets her first, long-awaited chance to wring a chicken's neck.

She has already chosen her victim: the white Rosecomb with pink eyes, a great one for self-important clucking when, as Pat puts it, 'She's done no more than lay a fart, which I can do very well for myself.' Having observed her mother's technique well, Agnes dispatches the bird quickly and efficiently. Gutting it is another matter, but the mother isn't going to allow her little assassin the thrill of a kill without having to deal with the smelly aftermath. The neck, heart and liver are put aside to be used in the pot. The white feathers are added to the bag of feathers, mostly black and red, that Mrs Kavanagh is collecting to stuff a cushion with. The head, the feet, the entrails are fed to the remaining pigs.

A long table has been set up on the gravel outside the front door. The cloth lifts in the breeze and petals from a jug of roses scatter over the food. The wedding cake stands out of sight on a cold slab in the outhouse, its snowy perfection protected under muslin, chastely awaiting its moment with the knife. The kitchen settle has been turned to face the open door and the elderly sit either here – where they complain of not being able

61

to see or hear anything, but no one takes a blind bit of notice – or on the wooden chairs and boxes that have been placed outside for them in the shade. Every familiar thing is out of place and strange. It's a hot day and the men, having walked up from the church faster than usual, stand panting and mopping their faces, waiting for the beer barrel to be tapped and the drinking to begin. Their women gather awestruck before the table where Mrs Kavanagh has done exactly what she said she would do and laid out enough food to feed a small army. The sun reflects off the white cloth, off the glass, off the knives and forks to dazzle the women into the closest thing to silence they are ever likely to achieve: a low sibilant murmur, like a crowd at prayer. Considering the splendour of the wedding breakfast, there is the same thought in every head: the Kavanaghs have five more daughters to marry.

Behind them a cart is crawling laboriously up the hill. It's crawling because of the nature of its load, both heavy and precious: a piano. A small, black, upright piano. Having had their attention drawn to it by the creaking of the cart's wheels, the guests move away from the table and go to the wall where they jostle one another for a better look. The lid of the piano is open; the keys are yellow, like teeth in an old mouth, and the brass-plating on the foot pedals has been worn away.

Mick Gavin, looking unexpectedly handsome and expansive, has been moving amongst the guests with a lordly air. His double-breasted jacket, buttoned for propriety, only gives away its not being brand new by being too tight across the belly and showing a shine on the right elbow. He has given his arm to one woman after another to escort her to the table, and if he hasn't remembered or perhaps never knew the woman's name, he makes up the shortfall with a throwaway 'Darlin', the easiest fellow in the world. He overloads plates in the most generous manner imaginable. His grizzled curls shine. Now he crosses to the wall and shouts in recognition of the bowler-hatted man with the cart.

It turns out the piano is a wedding gift from the groom to the bride's family. Weren't there five girls left to enjoy a chance to tinkle the ivories? The five said girls look askance at one another. Could the man be serious? The gift is of course thought excessive – foolishly, embarrassingly excessive – but there seems to be more against it than that. A flush spreads up Mrs Kavavangh's neck.

'That piano's got Lisduff written all over it,' someone observes under his breath. Agnes is aware that Lisduff House has recently been vandalised, and there is laughter as someone else claims to know who it was had smashed the chandelier: 'With a sheep hook!' But when Agnes edges over to get a look at the piano she can find only three words written on it. In flowery brass letters across the inside of the lid it says Broadwood and Sons.

When their bellies are satisfied the guests turn their attention to finer things. Those in the know tell of how people from miles around walk up the lane on a summer evening to see Mrs Kavanagh's garden, to smell the flowers – 'Sure, you can come up in December and she'll have a bunch of flowers, those are her flowers you'll be seeing in the church' – and they are proprietorially familiar with them, getting the names wrong and exaggerating the work involved. They squint in through the open front door at the immaculate floor, the jars of red apple jelly on the dresser and the brass lamp glinting on its chain above the mother's chair – and Mrs Kavanagh herself, now isn't she a fine sight today?

More than any of the guests, it's Agnes who's fascinated by her mother's public manner – 'queenly' she thinks of it.

How straight her mother's back is, how clean and white her strong hands which she'd spent an age scrubbing that morning – how impressive her garden, her table, her handsome and well-dressed children – the jelly made from their own apples, the rabbits from their own woods, the slab of pink ham from their own pig – the roll call of plenty makes Agnes dizzy. Most thrilling of all, the belief that thrums through her all that glorious day, is her certain knowledge that this, one day, is what her mother will do for her.

The fiddlers, the two Lynch brothers, with a middle-aged woman from Terryglass who plays the melodeon, have set themselves up with their backs to the blossoming flower beds. Now the woman taps one booted foot and, with a nod to the fiddlers, she begins to squeeze the melodeon on her lap with the grim-faced determination of someone reviving a corpse. The sound galvanises Mud Foley who until now has divided her attention between smoking and eating. Either way, her mouth was full and she had kept an unusual silence. Now she taps her pipe out, puts it in her pocket and asks Father Fogarty, is he dancing? The young priest undertakes this office without flinching and the pair go at it with such enthusiasm they set the others off. Soon a dozen or so couples are batting off one another, apologising, laughing and having a fine old time showing off their paces. Pat nods to Tom and the nod means, 'Remember, if old Mud Foley catches fire it's our job to put her out.'

But Pat has already taken a little too much interest in the beer, and Tom is consumed in a fire of his own making as he takes his girl by the waist and, for the first time, feels the soft dough of her hip under his hand. The musicians, to give their pumping elbows more room, have stepped back into the flowers, but even Mrs Kavanagh doesn't seem to mind. She turns to smile as her husband comes up beside her. Agnes holds her breath: she sees that her parents are about to join in. She sees her father take the mother's hand, sees the mother hang back a moment, then step into him until they are touching from breast to knee – then they move together for all the world as if they've done this before, many times, in some other, secret life that Agnes knows nothing about. She's never seen them so close, never seen them touch except in the act of working together. Shyly, her heart pounding, she looks away.

Agnes moves quietly amongst the boisterous guests, treading as softly as one of her mother's guinea fowl, practising graciousness. She sees the last of the pig fat – Brian, the pig was called – disappear into the maw of an old woman with eyes like soot marks. The men begin to load the cart with furniture, including a couple of the upright chairs the guests have been parking their backsides on, and the contents of Mary Rose's 'bottom drawer', and her clothes – Agnes recognises a dress made from the bolt of creamy-white cloth which was Mary Rose's 'leaving present' from Ballyartella Mills and to which Agnes had contributed, in an act of generosity so painful it had almost killed her, six mother-of-pearl buttons she'd spent her twopence on in Blake's.

The loading of the cart turns into a shambles due to the alcohol the men have consumed. The groom himself has remained impressively sober. He staggers only very slightly as he hands Mary Rose up on to the seat, and she's disappointed in him only in that by now he's given up on his appearance and undone the buttons of his jacket so his belly can be seen hanging like a bag of flour over his belt. Now, with Mary Rose's aunt, John Kavanagh's sister, as 'companion', the happy couple climb up amongst their belongings. Mary Rose's long white skirts, laced with muck, trail, in danger of catching in the wheel. One of the male guests, to the cheers of the others, throws himself after the cart and embraces the voluminous skirts like a man catching a steer. Having got his arms full, he throws them on to Mary Rose's lap where they lie, a white bundle, for all the world like a newborn baby.

As one of the fiddlers strikes up a lament, the cart goes away along the track over the hill. The youngest girls rush after it, waving and shrieking. That's the last memory Agnes will keep of her sister's wedding day: Mary Rose sitting up straight and proud, with her husband's arm around her waist and her sunlit head shining like thistledown.

At the beginning of this narrative I described my mother's story as hanging by the fragile thread of one woman's voice. True, but at the same time it wasn't strictly a monologue. My mother wasn't speaking into a neutral recording machine. We were classically placed, two women alone by the fireside at night, the older spinning out her stories of the past, the younger weaving them together as best she could. And I should remind myself that it was my English aunt Dorothy who was the storyteller, not my mother. Ironically, that side of my nature isn't part of my Irish but of my English heritage. My mother would never have turned a real incident into a 'story', a little drama told for laughs or shock value. Which isn't to say I didn't occasionally get the feeling, not just that my mother was telling me what she thought I wanted, but that I was only hearing what I wanted to hear.

The boots, for instance. Of course I love that, the story of the three little girls hiding their boots on the way to school.

But aren't barefoot Irish children just the kind of thing I'd read about elsewhere? And surely they, unlike the Kavanaghs, went barefoot because they couldn't *afford* shoes?

'Oh we had boots,' my mother said. 'But we wanted to be like the others.'

So then I was bound to ask, 'Wouldn't the foxes have found the boots?' I remembered how foxes had taken my shoes from my doorstep in London. And then, 'What if it poured with rain while they were in school?'

'We hung them upside down,' my mother told me. She laughed. 'The only one who ever forgot, of course, was Nancy.'

'So Nancy would arrive home with squelching boots? Did she get scolded?'

My mother shrugged.

'She most likely got a clip round the ear.' Her head fell back against the chair. 'And if I'd ever done the same I'd have got two.' Without looking at me she held up one hand, the first two fingers tightly crossed. 'But Nancy and I were like that.'

Like recognizing the sound of a 'true' note I recognised the truth of what I was hearing. I have an old-fashioned resistance to relativity in matters of truth. If I believed my mother was telling me the truth, then I believed there was a correlation between her words and what she was describing. Which isn't to say she didn't make use of the censor's scissors. I could see it amused her to watch me hoarding all these little details. At the same time it disturbed her. She didn't quite trust me. As we went on, that was what I became increasingly aware of: gaps, silences, a growing sense I'm not being told everything. She talked, for instance, of walking out as a girl of sixteen with a young man called Jim Cooney who wore a black beret – but she claimed to have no idea of its significance.

'A black beret?' my husband exclaimed when I told him. 'Then he was a member of the IRA.'

Perhaps my mother was scarcely aware of leaving things out – if she was – perhaps gaps and silences are all the true work of memory, or rather, forgetting. On these Monday evenings, she and I are quite alone but, in speaking to me, is there still a level of discretion at work – good manners, even? I am English. My father is English. Does it seem impolite to mention the hatred and the violence that lies between the English and the Irish? As Elizabeth Bowen has it, 'large areas are left unexplored by both sides, for reasons of bad conscience, good manners and convenient amnesia.' Ah, yes. 'Convenient amnesia.' When my mother mentions the black beret, for instance, or when she describes the best way to wring a chicken's neck, there's that faint mocking look, a quick sly glance to see what I make of it, a quick changing of the subject. She was telling and not telling in the same breath.

I had some larger, brighter copies made of the photograph of the house on Knigh Hill. One evening I asked her about the little boy. Who was he? For a moment she seemed unsure, then she told me the child was Sean Gavin, Mary Rose's little boy. So, is the young woman Mary Rose, I asked? My mother became rather vague – no, she thought not. Bridie maybe. Then she said, 'Sean lived with us for a while. We girls hated it. He got into everything.' Surprised, I asked, 'Did he live with you for long?' There was a pause. 'Oh, a while,' my mother said. 'Then he went over to England.' Of course. Sean's mother was 'Manchester Mary'. I'd learned the story of Mary Rose bit by bit over the years. When I was small I knew she was called Manchester Mary but I'd no idea why. Later, I learned she'd gone to England where she ran a boarding house in Manchester. I hadn't pictured a son at all, but here he was, a little cuckoo in the Kavanagh girls' nest. Was he there until things were set up for him to join his parents, I wondered? My curiosity was aroused but, sensing an uncomfortable area, I asked no more. My questions could wait until another of our Monday evenings together, evenings that seemed to stretch endlessly ahead of us.

PART TWO
THE AGE OF REASON

1

*'One starts out light as a feather, then everything gets
difficult.'*
– Henry Green, *Concluding*

My parents had very different natures. He was fixed, she
was spontaneous. She, who disliked planning, lived with
a man one of whose favourite maxims was, 'Time spent
in reconnaissance is seldom time wasted.' An intelligent
man, my father could sometimes be misled by an idea of
how things *ought* to be into expecting them to be that way
in reality – and being seriously put out when they weren't.
A mistake my mother never made. As a younger man my
father was habitually not just punctual but a little early for
engagements. She would insist that if you were asked for
seven o'clock you shouldn't arrive at seven, nor even ten
past. No, you wouldn't be welcome before seven fifteen.
To which my father's reply was, 'If I'm asked for seven
then I take it that's when I'm expected.' My mother never
believed the weather forecast (always part of my father's
reconnaissance) nor anything else she read in newspapers.
She attributed selfish or corrupt motives to everyone in
authority – long before it became fashionable to do so –
and whereas my father has certainly never suffered fools
gladly, my mother was less easily fooled. The only thing
that occasionally wrong-footed her was her own scepticism. My father certainly thought so. He was angered when

she whispered after the cremation of his much-loved uncle, 'I bet they give you any old body's ashes – I bet they just shovel up a few pounds of the stuff and write a name on it.'

My mother saw through things. Yet when she tried to express her ideas, when she stood up to my father – knowing in her bones sometimes that she was right – the ineffectiveness of her arguments made her grind her teeth in fury. My mother loathed, feared and was mortified by the IRA with whom she felt *she*, as an Irish woman in England, was unjustly identified. This didn't always prevent her from racing hotfoot to the defensive position from which she argued, 'Why is it, when the IRA throw bombs they're murderers, but when the English go to war and drop bombs that kill thousands of innocent civilians, then it's patriotism and principle? The IRA are patriots, and no matter how mistaken they are, they have principles. What's the difference?' Of the war that had taken her young husband away from her for five years, she once said provocatively, 'You young men only went off to fight because you had to.'

And he, with little snorts of derision, answered, 'Well, m'dear, if you would have *preferred* to live in Hitler's Nazi Empire…'

Those snorts of derision maddened her. They maddened me. I'd like to think this put me firmly in my mother's camp, that no matter how much her obtuseness in argument irritated me, I was on her side, her passionate, untamed, recalcitrant Irish side. But my feelings in the matter were never quite so straightforward.

By the time of my fourth birthday I was already devoted to my father. Once recovered from the shock of his return, and from my agonised sense of exclusion, I trotted at his heels asking questions I had quickly realised only he could answer: What makes snow? Where does the sound on the radio come from? Before long he began making me things. As he made them, he whistled. He made a little cart out of an old fruit box. He gave it four cotton-reel wheels and a string to pull it by. Then he made me a stool. This was for me to stand on so I could reach the electric light switch myself. I had been given power over light and darkness. Intuitively I recognised it for what it was: not magic, but science. I saw my father held the key to the real world where everything had a name and where every name could be learned. I was not only devoted to my father, I identified with him. I was going to be like him and certainly not like my mother who walked loose-kneed and dreamy-eyed in a big, circular skirt, who couldn't even name the wild flowers I snatched up in my fist.

Looking back, I wonder if she ever felt – as I began to flex my adolescent intellectual muscles – as if my father and I were ganging up on her. My mother never quite lost her capacity to become unpredictably, awe-inspiringly hectic with rage and, though my father never, ever criticised her to me when push came to shove, we did everything we could – we used sarcasm, logic, WORDS – to repress her female force and fury, the power of the old regime under which I was born. We made out that her insights weren't insight but emotional bias, that her temper was a disgrace in the face of our own sweet reason, that her intuitions were inferior to our logic.

At one level, we were right. She changed her mind at the last minute and if you dared ask her why, she couldn't say. She had a thoroughly reprehensible gift for spontaneity. She might refuse to go to a funeral – though she'd already bought a hat – and sometimes even dropped out of weddings at the last minute. Worse, dropped out of

Christmas. As to her temper and her irrationality, they of course were put down to her being Irish as much as to her being a woman. I don't mean that either of these points were ever made explicitly; they didn't need to be.

It was only as I turned from neuter into woman, I saw the misogyny in my father's scorn. Perhaps I'd instinctively recognised it earlier, but I'd been able to hide from myself the appalling fact that *I* was potentially its object as much as my mother. It became a matter of survival never to be scoffed at for my feminine – or 'female' as my father would say – lack of logic. I remember sometimes feeling a shiver of panic, as if I'd set out on the wrong road. But there was no going back. I'd made the decision long before I could construct an argument: never to be like my mother, never to vanish into that maelstrom of female blood and emotion. From my father's shoulders I could see further. Up there the air was drier, cooler, clearer. And the rules made sense, didn't they? They were fair, consistent, reliable. That was the point: I could rely on him.

Once I'd reached my teens, my father and I loved to 'argue'. It was my mother who called it arguing. My father and I thought we were having a bracing discussion. I would scarcely have sat down at table before we'd be engaged in sparring, throwing down our thoughts on life after death, on drowning unwanted kittens, or new facts on the possibility of space travel. Though my mother sat dreamy-eyed at the foot of the table she rarely joined in. Intellectual discussion made her uneasy. In her eyes, we were like poor Monsieur Laurent who threw himself confidently off the Eiffel Tower wearing a pair of brown-paper wings and moments later crashed to his death on the Champ de Mars. So, though she professed routine admiration for our confident theorizing, her smile was qualified by a certain shrewd scepticism that got on our nerves. In my mother's company we were more dogmatic than when talking alone together.

But I didn't need my father's help: as a child I could infuriate my mother all on my own, though I often didn't quite understand why. Of course I knew stamping my foot at her was wrong. But I couldn't see why she had to pour scorn on my misery at having my hair lopped off: 'Who do you think is going to notice YOU!' she snapped as I sobbed on the bus home. When roused, she was quite capable of giving me a clip around the head. I remember once being chased around the house with the broom. But I was only ever beaten once, and that was by my father. This was for repeated and blatant disobedience, the kind of thing my mother would have ignored as childish attention-seeking – unless, of course, she'd lost her temper.

My father's law couldn't be applied in anger – nor could it be waived in sentimental change of heart. My usual punishment was to be sent to bed early without supper. Although my mother had sent me to bed countless times, because I could never be sure what would provoke her into it, it didn't have much effect on my behaviour. Left to her own devices, she nearly always relented anyway, and sneaked up the stairs with an apple or a bowl of bread and milk. Then I was kissed before I went to sleep, one quick, shy kiss that stood in for the words she could never say.

By the time I was twenty I was already married and things had gone awry between my mother and me. I had been left feeling guilty – so, perhaps, had she – and as a young married woman I was seeking to be invulnerable to her, to be perfect. To demonstrate loud and clear that I had made the right choices in my life. If ever I did let down my guard sufficiently to approach my mother with a problem – moving sideways, needing her support but trying to make out things weren't as bad as they were – her eyes went vacant and she'd shred the tissue that was always in her hands, not listening to a word, head cocked, picking up on what I didn't say, what I knew she didn't want to hear: 'I've wasted my time working on something that's come to nothing, I don't know what I should do next, I'm worried about money.' My attempts at manipulation were always resisted. Like a woman finding a ladder in a stocking, she held my offerings up to the light and found them wanting. But of course I didn't find trust any easier than she did. I used a wide variety of techniques to keep people at arm's length, including a kind of wit and a very credible insouciance. Pride. Silence.

When I became the mother of a baby daughter I was still at university, studying for an MA in Philosophy. Like my father, I believed the world was an intelligible place and I was setting out to understand it. The person who enabled me to do this, by taking care of my daughter twice a week, was, of course, my mother. In spite of the fact that she did *not* share my belief in the world as intelligible. On Monday and Thursday mornings she arrived – sometimes even a little early, since I had an appointment to keep in a world she could scarcely imagine, of lecture halls and fully grown adults sitting around arguing about the nature of Time – bringing with her flowers, home-cooked food and new dishcloths. Sometimes when I got back with my thesis on Kant under my arm I'd find her on her knees cleaning the kitchen floor. I was an only child, a '60s feminist who didn't identify with her mother (not so uncommon) and took all this rather for granted. I only hope I didn't show it too much.

Once, fitting my daughter back like a piece of Lego on to her hip, she asked irritably what it was all about. I launched cheerfully into a description of the joys of epistemology, the virtues of logical positivism versus existentialism. Of why it matters to *know* that we know. And how much more difficult that is than it seems because of the intrinsic uncertainty of reality, which some philosophers believe is no more than a bundle of sensations. I told her the story of Bishop Berkeley walking with Samuel Johnson, the Bishop asserting that nothing is real outside our perception of things, that, in effect, the physical world is all inside our heads, and Johnson vehemently responding that when he stubs his toe on a stone he knows it's real because it HURTS, this being – as the Bishop should know – the moral role of reality: not to bend to our wishes but to be *difficult* and *painful*… In telling this, I concluded by kicking out and sending my daughter's fallen drinking cup flying across the floor.

My mother's eyes glazed over. She fell into that mood in which, for some perverse reason, I loved her most – no doubt I'd taken a leaf from that ancient book of the patriarchs and was feeling benignly superior. What I had adopted as simple and irresistibly persuasive arguments for the life of the intellect left her cold. While I droned on, my mother smiled that faint, dreamy smile of hers, like the smile of a woman riding a richly caparisoned camel whose big soft feet know the desert, and whose hump is so richly stocked with nourishment she doesn't even have to bother herself with watering him.

I have foxes of my own here in the city. I don't feed them but, like my mother, I'm fond of them. All those things people most dislike about them – their smell, their screaming on the street like murdered children – this juxtaposition of the wild with the domestic has always given me a pleasurable thrill. A sandy-coloured young dog fox used to curl up to sleep in the ivy on our garden fence, like a bird in a nest, like a verse by Ogden Nash. But recently the smell of their urine has begun to sicken me. It's too constant, too strong, hanging like fumes in our front porch and needing to be explained away when people call. I try to get rid of it with bucket after bucket of hot soapy water, to little effect. Then, a couple of mornings ago there was fox shit on the doorstep: two little dollops of it, and the soft cement round the base of the step was all dug up and scattered over the path. This ignites a flare of disgust in me.

But speaking to my father later on the phone I don't mention any of this. I don't admit my new dislike of the foxes for fear it will encourage him to stop feeding his own feral visitors, the ones that freeze in his security light like flash-photos, like ghosts. I don't want to release him from his nightly ritual, performed in memory of my mother. The idea brings me close to tears.

My mother's death was sudden. Although she was eighty-four years old – possibly older – she'd not been ill, only exhausted, which at that age wasn't so remarkable though it may already have been a symptom of the heart disease that would kill her. Her exact age was still a mystery because of the missing birth certificate and no doubt she was oversensitive about her age because my father was younger. Increasingly, she longed for quiet and stillness, for both of which she had a special gift. She may have given David the occasional shove earlier in their marriage to get him going places, but in later years – when he became habitually restless – she tried to insist he stay still at least some of the time. 'Don't keep jumping up!'

she would cry out in exasperation as he darted off for the nth time to ferret out a paper-cutting or to find his latest cup. In that enforced stillness, his love of music, opera especially, flourished.

Often, when my mother took herself off to bed early, my father sat downstairs wearing headphones and listening to Verdi: *Rigoletto* and *Otello*. He especially liked small, sweet, blonde heroines (his mother, Ella's, type, not the tall, dark type he had married) and the not-so-small, sweet, blonde singers who sing them. The glorious Frederica von Stade singing Desdemona's death scene – I should say, her murder scene – was a favourite, with its heartbreaking aria in which the girl reflects on being forsaken by her lover: 'The sad girl wept, O Willow, Willow, Willow! singing in the lonely land, the willow will be my funeral garland.' Sometimes, with a sheepish smile, he'd say, 'I'm just a sucker for the ladies.'

Where it mattered to her, my mother made a brave effort to keep up. She was an adventurous cook, keen to try out all the latest fads in ingredients and styles. Like the little girl making butter pats and stamping them with her initial 'A', it was still her pleasure and her pride to do things well. 'I've a reputation to keep up,' she used to say with a grin. There was her other reputation, too, as a snazzy dresser, and right to the end, my father appreciated it. 'Look at her!' he used to say. 'Doesn't she look lovely?'

The day she was taken ill they'd had a young woman from Australia, a distant relation they'd not met before, to lunch – or 'luncheon' as my mother sometimes preferred to call it. A superb lunch of chicken with lemon grass, and French apple tart. The small Ercol dining table was laid immaculately in my mother's characteristically pretty way with starched napkins, tiny bowls of flowers, and silver. Michelle, remarking gently that her Auntie Agnes looked tired, left them around four o'clock. My father said he would do the washing-up but my mother replied, 'No, we'll do it together as always.' Having done so, she took herself off upstairs to rest. When my father went to see how she was he found her in bed, but unable to get comfortable. Not in pain, but uncomfortable. Tea, more pillows, no pillows, warm milk. Nothing seemed to help. They passed a restless night.

In the morning my father got up to make tea and Agnes followed him downstairs, saying she might be more comfortable in the armchair. She asked my father to go to the chemist, tell the pharmacist her chest hurt, ask him to prescribe some medicine. This was a Sunday morning. My father at last found a chemist that was open. He described my mother's symptoms, and the pharmacist said he couldn't possibly prescribe anything, that a doctor should be called. This was done. The hours ticked by. Finally, at four thirty in the afternoon, a doctor examined my mother and diagnosed a heart attack. He told her she should be taken into hospital immediately.

My mother mistrusted doctors and had a horror of hospitals. She seemed unable to believe she had had a heart attack. The doctor said, well, he couldn't force her into hospital, but she must at least see her own doctor the following morning. Meanwhile she *must not* climb the stairs. 'Your husband can make you up a bed on the floor down here,' he instructed. My father returned to the chemist with the doctor's prescription. When he got home, my mother had taken herself back upstairs to bed.

That night my father dozed in the bedroom chair and my mother continued in great discomfort. She also continued to say, no, she would not go into hospital. It wasn't until six o'clock on Monday morning my father finally called for the ambulance, and the first thing they said at Kingston Hospital was, 'A pity she didn't come to us earlier.'

The medicines that would have been given immediately after the heart attack to disperse the clot were no longer considered appropriate. She wasn't in pain any more but very, very weak. On the phone to me, my father stressed that she was so very exhausted and must have rest, sleep. He thought it best if I didn't visit until the following day. She was in good hands. Let her sleep.

For an hour or two I was an obedient daughter. In a distraction of anxiety I even prepared to go out to dinner that night. But after speaking to a dear friend who urged me to '*Go*, visit, in these circumstances *always* visit,' I drove like a madwoman the five miles or so to Kingston Hospital.

I found my mother drugged and serene, propped up on pillows in a single room in intensive care. The hospital gown had slipped off one shoulder – her white skin with a violet tinge at her throat, the white curve and blue veins of her breast partially revealed. She smelt of L'Air du Temps, my last earthly impression of her warm and alive. I sat beside her, holding her hand as she smiled and talked, the words all garbled: 'Something lovely,' she said. 'Gladness your coming tomorrow.'

It was only for two or three minutes but the moment I left her, as I stepped out into the corridor, I could see she was already drifting asleep again, with that look of surprise, euphoria almost, on her face. She was in good hands. Let her sleep.

On Tuesday morning she rallied. My father and daughter visited briefly. She was sitting up in bed joking and demanding her favourite nail varnish. By three o'clock that afternoon she was dead.

'I'm so very sorry,' said the soft-voiced Chinese nurse

who was with her as she died. 'I'm so very sorry.'

My mother's heart and lungs had failed in a dramatic and final double act.

It had happened whilst she was having a catheter inserted. We were told that everything possible had been done to resuscitate her. She'd died so quickly, she would scarcely have been aware of anything. That's what we were told but we hadn't been there. We'd only just arrived – and been asked politely to wait a few moments – with flowers and talcum powder and, as ordered, her favourite nail varnish.

My father's face screwed up in shock and incredulity. Thrown into this too fast to disown it, he twisted sideways as if looking for some safe place, but there was no safe place to be had. We'd been ambushed. Robbed. I wept instantly, uncontrollably, as if a layer of my skin had been stripped away. When my arms went round my father he felt very frail. Someone brought us tea – a dark blue teapot and thick china cups. Sugar. Then, too soon, we were allowed in to see her.

There was no difficulty now in believing her dead: her head was thrown back, her mouth open, her face and neck streaked with dark violet, violet pools surrounded her eyes, deep violet-coloured streaks like claw-marks scoured her cheeks and neck, as if some wild animal had been interrupted in the act of devouring her and this was where its maw had torn at her pale flesh. The upper half of her face was untouched: austere, beautiful, white, the same – yet totally metamorphosed by death. What had been tender, tremulous, surprised, was rigid and vandalised. A bolt of terror went through me. Horror, grief, and pure animal terror.

Two days later, my father and I returned to the hospital to collect her belongings. In the car, in the overheated hospital corridor, in the lift, he chattered constantly.

'So many things to be done,' he kept saying, 'but I'm getting there. Telephone calls, letters, people to notify.' Then, 'Third floor, turn right into the corridor, second office on the left,' he muttered anxiously under his breath, for the third or fourth time. 'I phoned the Department for Work and Pensions this morning to cancel your mother's old-age pension and spoke to a very pleasant female. She was grateful I was notifying them so promptly. She said some people take weeks and months. I've written to the Council to ask for my rating status to be reassessed. And then there's your mother's bank card, Bentalls card, her chequebook – I've destroyed those, of course. Should I cancel her passport? I don't know. So many things to be done.'

We weren't coming to the hospital to see anyone who had cared for my mother, neither a nurse nor a doctor – and we never did do so, though I assume we could have done if we had asked. We could at least have asked Why? and How? We could even have questioned the treatment she had received, if only to put our minds at rest. The person we had come to see was a middle-aged woman in a windowless office who, with a professionally sweet, tired smile, recited a list of what we must do. She gave us directions to the register office. Then she handed us a small weekend case belonging to my mother, and a plastic bag which had her nightie, slippers and sponge bag in it. With a deferential nod, my father thanked her. Carrying my mother's things we walked away down a pleasant road lined with safe, pretty houses to the register office on the corner of the main road. This was where, years earlier, my youthful wedding had taken place. At the top of the steps by the door is a sign: No confetti please.

The registrar of births and deaths turned the greenish screen of his computer towards us.

'The deceased's maiden name was Kavanagh, Agnes Teresa,' he told us in the flat voice of a man patenting some dubious industrial device. 'Correct me if I'm wrong.'

He went on to hazard a guess that Agnes Teresa's official date of birth was 'unknown', and to state the stark fact that she was 'female'. As to her place of birth, 'the Irish Republic' was sufficient, he suggested, since Nenagh was tricky to spell.

On the computer screen my father and I read the cause of her death and this, in a sense was new to us, the official account of how that shocking metamorphosis had taken place:

1: (a) *Cardiac and Respiratory failure [stroke]*
   (b) *Pulmonary Embolism [clot],*
   (c) *Myocardial Infarction [heart muscle/tissue death], and*
2: *Ischaemic Heart Disease.*

We watched in silence as these incomprehensible words came up on the screen – the registrar did not attempt to pronounce them. On to my father's face came that twisted, wrinkled-up look again, as if he was sucking on a lemon. The registrar printed out a copy of my mother's death certificate and handed it to my father, her widower of forty-eight hours, who thanked him.

Now at last we began to talk about her, my father and I. We talked a great deal, offering memory after memory, mostly instigated by me, by my obsessive need to talk about her. Neither of us tidied her things away. But my father didn't mind.

86

'Why should I mind?' he asked. 'I have nothing but good memories.'

Privately, my husband admitted to finding this 'odd'. Surely, once someone had died it was intolerable to be constantly reminded of them. But in this instance I was on my father's side. In fact, my husband's point of view made me unreasonably, unfairly angry.

'It isn't a question of being *reminded*!' I cried. 'It's a question of not being able to forget.' Adding, unpleasantly and with a note of hysteria, that I hated the habit my husband had of scratching over the names of the dead in his address book. It brought to mind vile phrases like 'rub out', 'waste' and 'snuff'. Criminal words. Nazi words. It wasn't just that I couldn't forget my mother, I didn't *want* to.

My body was like lead. Faint nausea was accompanied by a constant desire to eat, long hours of insomnia were interspersed with hours of heavy sleep and brief bursts of weeping. Dealing with shock and grief took all my energy. But one night when my husband took me in his arms, my fury surfaced. Fury that my father had expressed no grief, that he had failed to act soon enough, failed to assert himself, to make demands, to insist – against no matter *what* resistance on her part – that she needed immediate medical attention. To me, her grieving daughter, this epitomised a certain masculine inertia which finds it easier to do nothing rather than to act. It was something my mother must on occasion have needed all her strength to break through.

In the weeks after her death one image played itself over and over in my mind: Agnes, aged about eleven and wearing a dark blue pinafore dress, is coming towards me with that dancing step she sometimes parodied in her old age, her head on one side, her dark eyes melting with some secret amusement, mischievous and charming. I've no source for this image – no old photographs, of course, no verbal description, even, of her as a girl to draw on – yet in my mind's eye, there she is, like something vividly remembered, an eleven-year-old girl dancing closer, brimming with half-flirtatious amusement, teasing, giving nothing away.

A month later, my father invited his sister Dorothy and her family to come up from Sussex for dinner, his first invitation since the funeral. Dorothy, like my mother, is an excellent cook, and has indeed cooked professionally for many years. The occasion involved hours of pleasurably nerve-wracking preparation for my father, promoted from kitchen skivvy to chef. When my mother was alive he used to prepare the vegetables, whip the cream, do the washing-up. For this evening he wrote himself the most precise instructions, scattered about on little bits of paper in the kitchen and dining room. He was eerily successful in reproducing what my mother would have done. There was a moment's uncertainty before it was decided I should take my mother's chair at the head of the table – a place I never accepted again.

Everyone was in a skittish, almost ribald mood. There was a lot of sparring between my cousins and their spouses. Outside the uncurtained window, spring was in the dark blue air. My father, anxious in case silence fell – about as likely with his family as being struck by lightning – had the scene set to entertain us after dinner with a display from the foxes. Dorothy, meanwhile, was remembering the first new dress she bought after the war, having saved up two years' worth of clothing coupons.

'Blue velvet collar and cuffs,' she told us, 'with French pleats and a nipped-in waist.'

Proudly, she'd put it on to show May – I'm never quite sure who May is, only that I associate her name with slowness, unreliability, and loneliness. Anyway, May it was who looked Dorothy's dress over a moment, then said in her slow Sussex way, 'It's a bit tight across the dairies, Doffie.'

My aunt Dorothy, once plump and red-haired, was by now rather charmingly fat. Sitting on the dining chair she filled it from side to side, her plump white legs crossed neatly at the ankles. Both her skin and her hair were like demerara icing: dry, crisp and ginger. Her mind was still rapier-sharp, her small brown eyes, quick as mice, missed nothing and her memory was fabulously encyclopedic. Now she patted her mouth with a napkin appliquéd with pale pink flowers, one of six I remember my mother buying in Singapore.

'Delicious,' said Dorothy, nodding at her brother. 'Clever boy.'

Everyone agreed. It was also agreed that David had had a good, strict teacher – 'the sort who doesn't allow you to lick the spoon.' Always that tone of irony when my mother was mentioned: her over-fastidiousness, her demanding ways and, of course, her *Irishness*. 'You know the one about the Irishman who plans to fly a rocket to the sun? "But Paddy," his friend says, "the sun will burn you up." "Don't worry," says Paddy, "I've thought of that. We'll go at night."' Ho-ho, the Irish! An endless source of humour.

Dorothy licked the last of the cream from her lips and told me, 'Agnes used to iron even the ribbons on your vest!'

Vests which, my cousins reminded me, *they* had to 'inherit'.

'So?' I said. 'At least you didn't inherit rubbish. Ribbons indeed!'

Even my little boy-cousin John – metamorphosed into a soft-hearted fireman with a big pale face and arms the

89

size of my thighs – he, too, had to wear my cast-off vests, ribbons or no. But in my cousins' case, the vests weren't ironed. Dorothy's method of ironing, slapdash and creative like everything else she did, was to fold damp clothes, stick them under a cushion and sit on them. All through my childhood there were times when what I most passionately wanted was to lose myself in my aunt's empire of chaos where the washing piled up in the bath and a mob of shrieking children clambered over the furniture *with their shoes on.*

Over the pudding my father told a joke I'd not heard before, one he certainly wouldn't have told if my mother had been there. It involved a string of boys arriving late for school and, on being asked where they've been, replying 'Up Sandy Lane, sir.' The last boy to appear *was* Sandy Lane. I remembered my cousins telling me how, when they were children, they loved to get my father to tell his slightly blue jokes – but always out of Auntie Aggie's hearing.

Does that mean Agnes was a prude? She called herself that sometimes, but in a slightly surprised tone of voice, as if quoting someone else. Yet she wasn't above laughing at rude noises and she was a flirt, in the mischievous, light-hearted way of a very young, inexperienced girl. A way that's maybe particular to her generation. But she didn't like dirty jokes and she didn't like sex on television or film. Whilst my father was away during the war, my mother was famously icy towards the sex-starved Canadian soldiers billeted in town. When she firewatched she walked alone. She was by nature chaste, pure, uncompromising. Sometimes these qualities amounted to hardness.

Driving home that evening, on the car radio I heard a jazz version of Purcell's famous aria, 'Dido's Lament', the first classical aria I fell in love with, and I remember

Dido's dying words: 'When I am laid in earth, Remember me, remember me…' In my mind's eye I saw my mother's eyes, her pale forehead, her hands – quite large hands, with clear nail varnish and a platinum wedding ring – her way of smoothing her skirt and, recently, a new, jaunty way of walking with an exaggerated swing of her shoulders that was both girlish and at the same time an old woman's mocking comment on her own age and frailty.

Grief thinned into depression. My work dried up. The simplest decisions were beyond me. Increasingly I spent my time walking, turning her image this way and that. I made notes. I jotted things down, my own memories, and hers.

With my daughter, my husband and I chose March 17th, Saint Patrick's Day, to scatter her ashes. During the ten days or so after my father collected them from the crematorium he kept them in their canister beside his armchair in the sitting room. At teatime they watched Countdown on the television together. The landscape at Shere was still wintery but awash with pale sunlight, the earth seamed with golden celandines. The canister, made of sturdy green plastic, was astonishingly heavy. My father took it out of the car and tucked it under his arm. As we went through the kissing gate into the meadow my mother whispered in my ear, 'I bet they give you any old body's ashes.' We chose a spot under a beech tree. My father opened the canister and we scattered half of the ashes, several pounds – maybe as much as five – of coarse white ashes down amongst the roots of the tree. Then a moment of helplessness paralysed us. My daughter, with characteristic pluck, took the initiative. This is the stretch of the river where she and my mother used to paddle together searching for crayfish. Now she waded out into the water, upended the canister and poured the rest of her grandmother's ashes into the stream. She did this slowly, with a controlled air of ceremony. Some of the ashes moved away downriver like smoke, the rest – the heavy granules – fell in a steady stream to lie on the bed, a silvery pool that glimmered palely through the water, like a featureless face upturned to the trees and sky above.

In 1994 my parents went on a brief tour of Ireland. I joined them at Shannon. My mother made the usual remarks about the loveliness of the landscape and the charm of the people. But of course, it was all a good deal more complicated than that and most of the time we were in Ireland it was difficult to tell what my mother was thinking and feeling. It must often have been difficult for her to know herself. What she did know she wouldn't have wanted to offer up to us, her husband and daughter, who must have seemed disconcertingly alien here. She would surely have needed a long, slow time, possibly on her own, to re-establish a relationship with her birthplace, even to recognise it.

She chose not to go back to Knigh – neither to her old home nor to the graveyard at Knigh Cross. We did visit Puckaun and we went into the church. I suspect my mother was often fearful that the places she was returning to would be dirty, mean and poor. Or that she would be brought down by emotion. But the Ireland she'd come back to was a very different place from the Ireland she'd left in the thirties, different not just in reality but *in the way it was perceived*. The tourist industry was thriving and a generation of successful Americans, Australians and even English – anyone who boasted that fabled creature, an 'Irish grandmother' – was keen to buy a second home back in the old country. Ireland wasn't a joke any more. It had become fashionable.

As we rubbed up against the more obvious signs of Ireland's trendy new status, my mother's confusion was at times tangible. For sixty years her memories had been private, precious as a handful of coins kept in your pocket for the comfort of turning them over occasionally, hearing them jingle, knowing they're there, yours, safe and secret. Now the coins had been yanked from her hand, buffed up and made into common currency.

At Gurtalougha House in Tipperary there was an exquisite air of privilege and exclusion. The enclosed garden was open on one side only, on to the water of Lough Derg, a pale-blue shifting silk screen that gave the illusion of being within touching distance of my parents' window. It so happened that the owners of the hotel were friends of my brother- and sister-in-law, and I'd made this booking supposing it would be a happy experience for my mother to be back, within a ten-minute drive of her old home, staying in style. I made sure my parents had the best room, with a balcony overlooking the lough, a room that was all green shadows and shifting light like a tree house.

As we were shown into the room, my mother – wonderingly fingering the fine material of the curtains – suffered a dizzy fit. Without a sound, she fell and banged her forehead on the radiator. It seemed to happen very slowly, as if the solid floor were far, far away. She lay on the rug in a foetal position. I soaked a flannel in cold water and held it to her forehead until she stirred. She was unharmed, but very shaken. We sat her in the soft movement of air by the open window and she turned her face away from us towards the lough.

On the ferry back home to England, as we came into Holyhead, I asked my mother if she'd been excited all those years ago when she left Ireland.

'Of course I wasn't excited,' she said, her voice unexpectedly snappy. 'Why should I be excited?'

'You were starting a new life,' I suggested.

'I was terrified. I got on the train and sat alone in the compartment with just one man and we didn't speak a word to one another all the way.'

I tried to picture this.

'A compartment without a corridor?'

'No. It had a corridor.'

The ferry slid between the turrets that marked the harbour and the quay appeared, grey and damp. Crumpling a tissue in her fingers my mother added, 'My feelings about leaving Ireland were mixed.' She shot me a look. 'You know what mixed feelings are, don't you?'

2

About ten years before my mother died, I entered an unhappy time in my life. All the usual reasons: work, a difficult period in my marriage, the loss of youth. I was in my late forties, full of self-doubt and dissatisfaction. My two inheritances, the feminine and the masculine, the Irish and the English, were at war. I'd come to feel it was my own desire to assimilate into the masculine, the rational and the English – as much as my mother's reserve – that had kept half my inheritance from me. I went through a period of incandescent rage with everything masculine before arriving at a new sense of solidarity with everything feminine. I gave up struggling to be always rational. Drawing closer to my mother was all part of a slow process. Not long after, the Monday nights spent with my mother began. The old rift between us was neither resolved nor exactly forgotten, but it was out of sight. Here I was, 'at my mother's knee' looking for clues not just to her but, of course, to myself.

As it happened, this was a difficult time for my mother, too. The difference in my parents' age and sociability was part of it – at the time I'm describing, my mother was in her late seventies. My father not only *was* younger but, as time passed, he seemed to lose a year for every year she gained. His new bridge partnership had turned out very successfully and, now that he was retired, he would have liked to play more often than just one evening a week.

My mother may have felt she was holding him back. Or maybe not. Superficially, however, nothing much had changed. My father still made a fuss of her, and Agnes Teresa Kavanagh still had something queenly, patrician, even, in her manner. My father still liked to tell the old joke: 'I will be master in my own house! I WON'T get out from under the table!' And it still made my mother laugh.

But certain physical gestures of hers had become more noticeable – her shoulder blades were drawn high and tight, her fingers forever moving as if rolling tiny pellets against the pads of her thumb – and for some years, a skin condition, rosacea, spoiled the lovely skin of her cheeks. Eventually she found a cream that cured it, but her skin never quite regained its old flawless perfection. For some time I was both very aware of my mother's unhappiness, and too bound up in my own to give hers much attention. My own problems, though not discussed, must have been an added burden to her.

Still, my mother often gave the impression of having got more out of life than she'd expected. She had, for instance, a low opinion of her own intelligence. Once, when we were talking about her school days, she told me with a satirical look on her face, 'I was good at needle-work. Of course, you didn't need to have anything much 'up here' for that.' She tapped her forehead.

Then she admitted she'd been good at Gaelic, too. I told her I'd read somewhere that Gaelic was the language spoken in the garden of Eden, the language that God used when speaking to the angels. I was never sure what my mother made of this kind of whimsical notion.

What was undeniable was that as my mother got older she took increasing pleasure in books. I think they enabled her to achieve a degree of emotional independence and equilibrium. She wasn't one for bodice-rippers or Aga sagas. She liked big themes and subtle writing. When my own first book was published and my plays began to be shown on television my mother was both proud and apprehensive. She acknowledged the skill but, from this close up, she saw that the very nature of the undertaking had something indecent about it, incontinent as the act of confession she'd loathed in her youth, reeking as it did to her fastidious nose of lies and self-indulgence. It entailed, if nothing else, a shocking level of self-exposure and, naturally, the closer to home it got, the more my characters reminded her of me, of her, of my husband, the more disturbing and indecent it seemed. Why did I write about such things? In a kind of nightmare scenario, my mother found herself taken inside my head, inside my heart, into my bedroom. My mother loved literature in private, literature that was safely inside the hard covers of books written by unknown authors. But she was uneasy about my telling tales – in all three senses of that phrase: fictions, lies, betrayals. Which is hardly surprising.

Who wants all that mess and stink on her own front doorstep?

On one of those nights when we were alone together in the sitting room after supper, a silence fell. Because my mother didn't tell her story chronologically, this evening – though we'd already long ago arrived at her maturity – we'd gone back to her early childhood and, as so often, to incidents involving my mother and Nancy. Sometimes it was as if these two little girls had been the only children in the family. I remember I was a little distracted. Tired. We both were. It was winter, not long after Christmas and New Year. We couldn't know it, of course, but this was to be our last evening alone together. In the silence we could hear the wind rattle through the garden shrubs. Maybe that sound and the bitter cold lapping the house reminded my mother of winters on Knigh Hill. Her face was suffused with a dreamy, slightly foolish look that sometimes came over her in old age. She told me how she'd got into bed recently, warm under the duvet, and thought, 'Thank God!' and then, 'Why do I thank God? I should thank David. He's given me everything.'

Soon after we had scattered my mother's ashes in the river, my father's life took on a new pattern. Generous and gregarious, he now played bridge two or three times a week, ran errands for friends and neighbours, and had an ever-increasing social life which involved a great many visits to 'Testicoes' (aka Tesco) to stock the freezer so that even when asked out to dinner he could always arrive with offerings carried in plastic bags: his own home-made marmalade, vegetable soup, some tiramisu. The plastic bags then came back home again, this time full of scraps for the foxes. My father was busy and to me, my mother's vigilant daughter, he looked happy as a dog let off its lead.

To die is to enter a great silence. The fear of being forgotten in that silence is as old as humankind. It's what much of religion has always been about. What the dead want most is to be kept alive in the memory of the living. But since the dead can't, in fact, want anything, even their *desire* to be remembered can only last so long as our memory of them. 'Remember me, remember me.' Dido sang those words whilst she was still alive. But Dylan Thomas added to that wistful desire another thought: 'Remember me, I have forgotten you...' The dead are at a disadvantage. The thought of forgetting my mother makes me panic. In the forgetting I shall lose her again, and in a more definitive sense than my first loss of her to the soldier who came home from the war. The very first betrayal of this story.

In the middle of the night I wake with a pounding heart.

Lying in the dark I'm helpless under the cold weight of my own physical decay: age and death are like a stink coded into every cell of my body. I have the sense that I can feel each individual cell turning to foul dust deep inside me. Life does death's work for it, in slow motion. Like having the wrong man pick me out across a bright, crowded room. The slow death of old age. Stasis. My work lies like stone in my chest, unspoken. Lying awake, I'm dimly aware that self-pity also has a life, and therefore a death, of its own. This is how my nights are.

But last night the dog fox woke me. His abrupt, cold bark ricocheted off the back walls so close he might have been in the room with me. It brought to mind my mother telling me about a woman who fell asleep one afternoon and woke to find a fox curled up on the sofa beside her. When the fox ran outside the woman didn't get up and follow him. Perhaps it was a decision she made, or perhaps she was just too lazy – or too frightened? There *are* people who are afraid of all animals. I don't know. I don't know where this happened, or who the woman was. Fragment of a story, like a dream that speaks to me of choices not made, of potential unfulfilled. Of instincts not followed.

Perhaps because of this story, last night, instead of staying where I was, tossing and turning, quietly I got out of bed and went down to the back door. It opened soundlessly on to the damp garden. It was later than I thought, and the sun already rising. The bark came again, close by, making the hairs on the back of my neck stand up. A young red fox came over the fence with something I couldn't identify in his mouth. So close, I heard his claws scratch on the wood as he jumped down. Seeing me by the door, he hesitated and moved his tail a little. He was so much at home I thought he must be the one who craps on my doorstep and leaves his stink hanging in the porch. I very much wanted to touch him. I wanted my domesticated hand to lie on his rough red coat, for him to leave his feral scent on my skin. But the fox – immune to such human confusion – tightened his elegant jaw on his kill and, with the weightless hop of a bird, went back over the fence and away, leaving a trace of blood on the paving stones. I thought of a passage I'd read somewhere in Isak Dinesen about the perfection of foxes: 'the fox does excellently well at being a fox. All that he does or thinks is just fox-like and there is nothing in him from his ears to his brush which is not beautiful and perfect, which God does not wish to be there, and the fox will not interfere with the plan of God.'

I go back inside and make tea. I recall how, not long after my mother died, my father had said to me, 'Your mother never really told me why she left Ireland.' With the sun on my hands, I look at the notes I have of our Monday evening conversations and start work on them for the first time. They're in a mess. I begin to arrange them both chronologically and according to themes: school, growing up, work and so on.

I do this early each morning, getting straight out of bed to go to my desk. I sleep well. Something inside me has been set in motion and it begins.

PART THREE
GOING BACK

1

'...and the children of Lir stayed in exile in their guise of swans until it came time for them to go back to where their father was with his household and all their own people. So they set out flying through the air lightly till they came to Sidhe Fionnachaidh where they gave out three sorrowful cries and Fionnuala made this complaint: 'It is a wonder to me this place is, and it without a house, without a dwelling-place. To see it the way it is now, Ochone! It is a bitterness to my heart...'
    – The Irish saga *Gods and Fighting Men* in a translation
                                                  by Lady Gregory*

Furze is in abundant bloom on this flat, upland area in the North Riding of Tipperary. A summer-blue sky is all around me, and flat-bottomed clouds whose shadows fall down through the air like shafts of grey sunlight. The little road is straight and empty, seeming to lead nowhere, and I walk until I reach the point where the old bogland begins. Here on the upland the light shifts like water over the heather-clad bog. I had thought this might be where my grandfather, John Kavanagh, walked alone that day, through air similarly ablaze with furze-blossom, coming to his decision to reject his inheritance, to leave home, to ask Kate Buckley to marry him. The scent of furze is warm and sweet. There's a light breeze and not a car, not a sheep, not another human being in sight. This upland scene is all golden expectancy, unpeopled because, although I'm here in search of my forebears, I haven't found them yet and even if my grandfather came walking towards me now I wouldn't recognise him.

On the desk in my rented cottage I've set out my maps and the notebooks containing my mother's memories, ready to match them against the real thing. But the real thing evades me. No one in Borrisokane, where my grandfather was born, remembers the name Kavanagh, nor can I find any trace of the 'darling little thatched cottage' where my mother recalled visiting her grandmother. I decide to reassure myself with a visit to somewhere familiar: the graveyard at Knigh.

Only, since I was last here, someone's been at work cutting the grass, trimming the edges and uprooting nettles. The white hawthorn that once marked my grandparents' grave is gone and I have no exact memory of its location. Here, by the west wall? Or over there by the ruins of the old chapel? I am unreasonably distressed by this lacuna. Old gravestones have been revealed and new headstones of shiny black marble have been erected. Certain names are engraved here more than once: Foley, McGrath, Grace. But no Kavanagh. Time has closed over them. I climb over the wall and begin to make my way up the steep lane towards the house on Knigh Hill.

It's a spring afternoon. The hillside is bright with sunshine and the dirt lane is thick with dust. On either side grows a profusion of yellow dandelions with remarkably large flowers and, almost hidden in the moist shade, lords and ladies with pale pink pokers, something I've never seen before. A pair of chaffinches is working the tops of the ash trees, gossiping as they go and littering the dust with the trees' flower buds. I know this is the lane the little girls came down with the donkey to fetch water. But I'm disorientated. A new line of giant electricity pylons strides up and over the hillside, and surely the ruined tower's in the wrong place. Most strikingly of all – though it didn't strike me last time I was here – there's no wood. Yet surely my Uncle Pat spent his working life caretaking Knigh Wood?

As I begin to make my way up the lane on my right, a curved driveway leads up to the shiny front door of a prosperous farmhouse. Behind it, a small grey house standing in ruins. Ducking under a line of barbed wire I go towards it, and in doing so I raise the owner, a youngish man named Quigley, who emerges from one of the outhouses wiping his hands on his shirt. When I suggest the grey ruin may be the house where my mother was born he looks bewildered, affronted even, then asks her name.

'Kavanagh,' I say firmly, but anticipating denial.

The man's face lightens. He points up the hill.

'The house is up there,' he says. 'It's well known. The fields on the left-hand side are still called Kavanagh's fields.' Adding gently, 'It was before my time.'

I walk on close to tears. A trace of them at last, the memory of a memory. 'It's well known.' These fields once belonged to my grandfather.

The house is in a state of bitter dereliction. Windows have been filled in with cement blocks, like eyes blanked out, and the yard my mother once looked down on shifts and rustles with sheets of black plastic. Liquid brown cow shit splatters the ground. This is where Mary Rose's wedding party took place, where my grandmother kept the gravel raked immaculate as any Japanese Zen garden, and where the flowers were an amazement to her neighbours. A great barn with an ugly tin roof now blocks the still-magical view.

105

Bewildered and clumsy, I clamber over unused farm implements and stinking sacks of old sheep's wool into the interior. A huge, rusting mechanical drill or harrow takes up most of the space. Here's where the family knelt to say the rosary. Amongst black patches of damp on the walls I find one little patch of colour. It's a strip of flowered wallpaper with, underneath it, several layers of paint: blue, green, and white. When I scratch the white it comes away like chalk: lime. Here is the blackened hearth with its wooden mantle. It runs almost the entire width of one wall. There's not much left in the way of an upper floor but on the back wall, like a stencil, runs the outline of a flight of stairs leading up to what would have been the main bedroom out of which doors once opened into two – possibly three – smaller rooms.

On the other side of the hearth, a door leads into a smaller room with a little fireplace set into the back of the chimney breast. I remember my father saying that when he visited he slept in a room on the ground floor. And in the wall opposite the hearth, a door leads through into what was another, narrower section of the house but which is now a tumbledown mass of ivy-covered rubble. Damp blooms everywhere on the walls. Beams and broken floorboards dribble yellow pyramids of dust on to the disorder below. A draught yawns a stale cold breath from the corners. The chill enters my bones like fear. I scramble in an idiotic sort of panic back outside. When I step away to look up, I see that the roof is in surprisingly good nick. But the low wall that once enclosed the narrow front garden, the garden itself, the trellised archways and the yard where my grandmother kept her pet guinea fowl, gone, all gone.

I walk on past the trees towards the brow of the hill. There I scramble under the fence and tack at a diagonal across one of my grandfather's steep fields to the circle of sunlit stones on the summit. A fox lies there curled in the warmth. Sensing me his head lifts, his ears, eyes and pointed snout fix me for a moment like an aimed arrow, then he cedes the cairn to me and lopes off, a russet-coloured stain slipping down through the grass. Like my mother before me, and mindful that this is a fairy ring – not a home of hobgoblins, as was once believed in England – I sit on one of the stones amongst the sheep droppings and the flowers, and gaze back the way I've come.

To the south I can see the purple smudge of the Silvermine Mountains where, I've learned, a number of English miners were massacred by Irish Catholics during the pre-Cromwellian rebellions of the 1640s. To the west, the Nenagh river – on whose greens banks Saint Patrick walked – coils through flat lowlands past the wool mill at Ballyartella to discharge itself at Dromineer into Lough Derg, a little peacock-coloured corner of which is visible from up here. One blistering afternoon in the 1920s, Dr Courtney – a fine all-round athlete and medical officer at Knigh Cross dispensary for forty-two years – swam the two miles or so from Dromineer to the other side of the lake. He did so not only because he could, but also to encourage the locals to take to the water, in which he failed.

To the north, Blind Lane goes on towards the ancient woods of Carney, and Claree, and on beyond that to the lowland bogs and Borrisokane, home of my Kavanagh forebears, a town described in 1845 as 'a poor, spiritless, desolate place'. It was in the needy environs of Borriso-kane that John Kavanagh's mother, my own mother's beloved 'Gammy', worked as a nurse, or, more strictly, a 'handywoman', as these unqualified nurses were known. In the fields and hedgerows she picked wild flowers and

107

leaves to make the herbal remedies for which, my mother had told me, she was well known. Herbs were best pulled on Mondays and Tuesdays, she used to say, not Sunday. According to Gammy, 'A Sunday cure is no cure.' As I recall this, my great-grandmother appears in my mind's eye: a small neat woman in black cape and bonnet, a red petticoat flaring at her hem, moving briskly away along the white lane.

Turning to look east I can see Lough Eorna, an innocent blue blink of water in which the two girls drowned when the ice gave way beneath them. And the ruined tower, known as Knigh Castle, looks from up here to be standing in the right place again, there on sloping ground just above the crossroad. The men who built this tower in the sixteenth century were the O'Kennedys and they dominated this territory for close on five hundred years. Their name – which they would give to a future president of the United States – derives from the Irish 'ceann eidig' or 'ugly head'. The tower was built of the rock it stands on: limestone. Grey limestone for the walls of houses and churches, white limewash for the interiors, grey powder of quicklime with which to fertilise the fields, lime gravel for my grandmother's garden pathway. Limestone makes water extremely soft. No wonder the Kavanagh girls were famous for their complexions. Sitting up here in the sunshine, this glorious chiefdom, spread from my feet to the far horizon, seems a place well worth living and dying for. And there below, just visible through the trees, is the grey roof of my grandparents' house, from here looking inviolate.

I'm sitting on a hard chair in the dingy lobby of the Nenagh registrar's office waiting my turn. I've chosen this chair rather than the vacant padded one because the padded one has a dubious-looking stain on it. Every so often someone emerges diffidently from the office, their business done, a little hatch in the wall opens, and the next person is summonsed inside. We're nearly all of us middle-aged or elderly women, quiet and patient, our body language clearly telling the world we mean to be no trouble to anyone. We have a right to be here in an anteroom of officialdom, but our right to the inner sanctum is something we passively hope for rather than assert. I can't see who it is who does the summonsing but it's a woman's voice, firm yet dulcet, very Tipperary. It inspires confidence in me that the registrar will be both efficient and sympathetic. I'm here to collect a copy of my mother's birth certificate and copies of my grandparents' death certificates. (When I asked my mother what her parents had died of, she shrugged and said, 'I wouldn't be surprised if mother died of TB and father just gave up.') As I wait I get more and more nervous. This move into a world of official records – a world my mother so hated – a world of facts written down in black and white, some of them facts she withheld from me, feels disloyal.

I have already seen some official records: my grand-father's birth and his marriage, both entered in the Borrisokane Parish records, but these records still seemed very much in the realm of the human. For one thing, they were in handwriting – almost illegible copperplate writing in faded brown ink – in leather-bound books kept locked in a safe in a corner of the parish priest's study. It was my landlord, Sean Egan, who, seeing my distracted air and the pile of books growing on my table, suggested I consult the local priest. It was perhaps the obvious thing to do but it wouldn't have occurred to me as permissible, and I didn't take the suggestion lightly: I am a good deal more used to TV producers and librarians than I am to Catholic priests.

Father O'Halloran was a big man in the prime of life.

The black skirts of his cassock swung just short of his ankles and his bare bony feet were thrust into a pair of unlaced trainers. I had arrived for our two o'clock appointment punctually though rather hot and untidy from clambering over Knigh Hill. Father O'Halloran, pale but patently inexhaustible, had just returned from a funeral. He took me into the little kitchen of his modern bungalow, one in a row of three grey bungalows standing in a cul-de-sac beside the new (c.1973) Catholic St Peter and Paul Church. A small, narrow kitchen table covered in cream-coloured American cloth, two hard little plastic chairs, and a used teabag drying like a tiny ginger scalp on the edge of the sink for further use. I wondered what to say if Father O'Halloran offered me a cup of tea, but he didn't. Beside the window a pair of formal black shoes were propped up to air, their tongues lolling. A little graveside earth clung to their soles. We both looked at them but nothing was said and Father O'Halloran did not move them. A small print of Leonardo's *Virgin of the Rocks* hung on the wall behind his head.

The man I now sat down opposite had a remarkable physical mannerism: a stare was repeatedly followed by a pause during which the eyes slid away. I recognised it as a power ploy, conscious or not, I couldn't decide. I'd seen it used by TV producers. But in Father O'Halloran there was no suggestion of the flesh, of indulgence in long lunches and expensive wine. Ironically, this Catholic priest brought to mind an image of the Puritan fathers. Where my landlord was liquid, charming, volatile, Father O'Halloran was stony, with solid flesh and veiled eyes – yet, different as they were, both were evasive. And I was shocked to experience the almost sexual charge of masculine authority in the relationship between a priest and his flock. I'm not speaking of the flesh, certainly not in the case of this man whose human powers were austere as granite, endowing him with the moral, physical and intellectual authority of the alpha male. Moses coming down from the mountain.

The parish record books lay, closed, on the table before us. From a court behind the church came the cries of boys playing basketball. The sun came and went, pulsing across the wall of the neighbouring bungalow. I had asked to see records for the birth of John Kavanagh in, I guessed, around 1870, and for his marriage to Kate Buckley maybe thirty or so years later. Father O'Halloran remarked that people frequently come to him with only the vaguest of research dates and he turns them away. He could spend his life, he said, going through the parish records on behalf of fourth-generation Americans with a passing interest in finding out about Auntie Mary. I sympathised. I took comfort in the fact that at least I'm not American. I'm English. But, in Tipperary, is that an advantage? The records are set out with the year written at the top of the page and beneath that the most basic of information: the month, the name, the place of baptism or marriage and the names of parents and sponsors. Father O'Halloran slowly turned the pages, working his way through the years from 1865, running one pale square finger down the margin.

And there it was: 1869, November 20th, John Kavanagh, born in the parish of Borrisokane. Four sisters and one younger brother were recorded here as well. The ease with which the task had been dispatched brought an almost palpable warmth into the room. Father O'Haloran relaxed. He turned the book around for me to linger over the record. I offered a contribution to the church. Father O'Haloran's pale brow creased in disapproval and gently he pushed my hand away. 'Now don't give out that you're a millionaire,' he said, with his first smile. He suggested that twenty euros would be appropriate. Our conversation moved on to his own history: ten years serving the Irish community in Cricklewood – where he co-founded the Cricklewood Racial Society ('It was still all right to make anti-Irish jokes in Cricklewood in the eighties,' he remarked. 'And everywhere else,' I added, speaking from my own experience.) – were followed by ten years in the slums of Chicago. Something had been explained. I was impressed, but not surprised. The only question was, if Cricklewood and Chicago, why Borrisokane? It was not a question I felt able to ask.

In the second record book we found the marriage of John Kavanagh to Katherine [Kate] Buckley on October 15th, 1899, here in Borrisokane. Their names are recorded in an elegant but fading hand. My grandparents must have spoken, the registrar must have heard their voices and written down dates, places, their names: John and Katherine, names associated with saints and with ancestors and with the baptism of children yet to come; dates which are associated with the unspoken act of conception; places which are no longer there. So, here is the proof that my grandfather got what he wanted. Everything is in order, and John and Kate are about to set out to make their life together. My mother is on her way.

Seeing what little I know of my grandparents' story confirmed in this way elated me. But sitting waiting in the lobby of the registrar in Nenagh I almost lose my nerve – what am I doing here sniffing things out, digging things up, making off with them like a fox with a dead chicken in its mouth? Then the hatch opens and I am called.

The registrar's face is as sweet as her voice. As we exchange a few pleasantries her dark eyes rest on my face and I'm very aware of my English voice. When she places

the certificates in front of me there's a gentle tentative-
ness in her manner as if anxious that what is about to be
revealed will distress me. I read that my grandmother,
Kate, died in March 1944, at Knigh, her condition:
married; her age last birthday: sixty-six; the causes of
death are named as anaemia, bronchitis and cardiac
failure. My grandfather died in January 1945, at Knigh,
his condition: widower; his age last birthday: seventy; and
the causes of death: bronchitis and cardiac failure. I notice
John Kavanagh died only ten months after his wife. His
name is spelt with a 'C' rather than a 'K'. The age given
for him is incorrect. In 1945 my grandfather would have
been seventy-six. And his profession is given as 'herd'. At
this, my brain goes numb. Gently the registrar suggests
that 'herd' means 'a herder of cattle'.

I nod and turn to my mother's birth certificate. Date
of birth: July 18th, 1911. Four years earlier than she had
admitted. Place of birth: Clashnevin. I am disorientated
again. I never heard my mother speak of anywhere except
Knigh. Next to 'Signature of Informant' is written the
name John Cavanagh, and next to that, his mark, 'X'.

My grandfather was illiterate.

2

When he was eight years old my great-grandfather, Patrick Kavanagh, came to Tipperary from County Mayo riding on his Da, Thomas's, shoulders. This Gaelic-speaking child was small for his age and light as a feather from habitual want of food, in spite of which he would be expected to work alongside other boys and adults in the potato fields. The boy could pick stones, he could carry. His Da was a devil with a spade: Thomas Kavanagh could dig a trench and throw up a 'lazy' bed in half the time it took the next man. 'Lazy' is a misnomer since the raised beds were dug by hand in the most hostile terrain, and Thomas was rightly proud of his skill and his strength. A man who knows what he's doing can dig a lazy bed out into the bog or up a mountainside where a plough could not go. It could give a better return than the plough. But nevermind a man's strength or skill, if the weather turns against him he'll be in difficulty.

Thomas Kavanagh was a Tipperary man who had followed a pretty face from the fair at Portumna back to Mayo, too dazzled by the western sun to notice the sly glint in her big black eyes. Now, in the autumn of 1845, Thomas was back, one of ever-increasing numbers of men coming east to look for work, driven by the hunger and privation of the rocky western region. When the Bishop of Kildare had been asked in the 1830s what was the state of the population in the west he replied, 'The people are perishing as usual.' Desperate enough to undercut the locals, the men from Mayo were willing to work for 4d a day instead of 5d. Not surprisingly, they were sometimes driven violently out of the county.

Violence was something of a Tipperary specialty. In the early nineteenth century it was described as 'the most crime-ridden county in Ireland, its very name conjuring up crimes innumerable and of the darkest dye'. In a pamphlet published in 1842 a magistrate of the county court claimed that 'many of the outrages committed in Tipperary are so heinous in their nature, so marked by cruelty, atrocity and barbarity as to equal if not excel those of the most savage nations on earth, excepting only the absence of cannibalism'. However that may be, the outrages of 1845 were provoked by a very particular set of circumstances.

In October of that year, storms of wind and rain alternated with periods of ominous stillness. Dogs barked for no reason, birds fell silent, and people were struck dumb with superstitious fear. Ferocity of competition amongst the poor for land had meant that, for generations, the plot most commonly rented was the notorious quarter ground; that is to say, a mere quarter of an acre. Too small to sustain a cow, these plots were turned over entirely to the potato: Red Americans, Ash-Leaf kidneys, English Reds, Cups and, most common of all, the watery Lumpers. By the 1800s, it had become almost the *only* foodstuff amongst the poor, and the chief reason for this was that from just *one acre* – should you be lucky enough to have so much – you could support a family of six. On average, the adult male labourer ate up to thirteen pounds of potatoes and four pints of buttermilk a day. The leftovers went to the pigs.

Looked at from a woman's point of view, this meant if

you had a husband, six children and your mother-in-law living with you, you had to scrub and boil around fifty to sixty pounds of potatoes every day. On the other hand, scrubbing and boiling potatoes required no specialist skills and, eaten in the quantities described, it provided a tolerably healthy diet. The Irish were strong and their infant mortality rate low. Imagine your own children and think how easy it could be. A belly full of fresh, hot potatoes, flavoured with mustard seed or buttermilk, and then back out into the open air, filling your lungs with it, with the soft rain on your face, and berries in the hedge for afters. This was the bounty of Tipperary that Thomas Kavanagh remembered from his own youth.

The trouble with growing your own potatoes was twofold. Firstly, Ireland's climate, particularly in the west with its perpetual light rain and mild breezes, is ideal for the spread of blight. The years 1845 and '46 were exceptionally wet. Secondly – and this is trouble of a different kind – the high cost of fertiliser. The cheapest way round this was to use ash got by 'skinning' and burning the land itself, a method which – initially – gave excellent results. Long-term, however, burning was one of the chief ways of perpetuating the poverty of the Irish countryside, a feature much remarked on by foreign visitors. It was a method favoured by the poor for two reasons: it was cheap on their own rented plots and labour-intensive on their landlord's.

A Borrisokane landlord set on improving his land – a man 'exceedingly unpopular and obnoxious to the peasantry' – was murdered for forbidding the practice. One man was hanged for the crime; two hundred others gathered in silent protest to skin, burn and sow his potato ground. Amongst those two hundred were my ancestors.

Walking back into Tipperary with his son on his

116

shoulders, Thomas was not to know that 1845 was the first year of what came to be called the Great Famine. In October the first signs of blight were discovered in the crop. Overnight, fields turned black as soot. As Patrick and his Da walked the lanes the stink of rotting vegetables soured the air. In one of the larger fields, they saw a priest scurry along the rows, one white hand clamped over his nose, sprinkling holy water.

Little more than a hundred years later, my mother stands at a small yellow Formica table with her back to a door open on to a sunlit garden: red canna lilies stand tall as a man's shoulder, and young banana trees fan leaves of a florescent green, their phallic fruit clustered above a brownish-purple hood. This is at my parents' home in Jahore Bahru and my mother is putting the finishing touches to a chicken curry, following a recipe dictated to her by her Malay servant, a young woman who sometimes comes to work with her baby on her back. When she does this she's almost tearful with apologies, but the baby lies on the verandah and doesn't make a sound, his eyes, like black plums dipped in water, fixed on the light dappling the ceiling. Perhaps he's soothed, too, by the liquid sound of hidden brown birds in the garden. My mother slices half a cucumber into paper-thin rounds. She puts her own home-made mango chutney into a little bowl. She adds lime juice and finely chopped coriander to the chicken. She works quietly and calmly but sometimes she has a fag stuck in her mouth and we tease her that cigarette ash is her secret ingredient. She tests the rice again and decides it's ready. She has an unnecessarily large dish ready to hold it. She ladles steaming white rice on to only one-half of the dish, and on the other half she places a mound of plain-boiled potatoes. This is because she would never

117

dream of serving a meal without potatoes. I don't know what sort these are but they're yellow, waxy looking, and fragrant with butter. Without knowing I'm looking, my mother forks one of these into her mouth and stands looking out at the garden as the potato's creamy flesh melts in her mouth.

As the extent of the disaster became plain, brutal calculation broke down the old rules of hospitality. Cottagers turned strangers from their door empty-handed. Just a few weeks earlier, that would have been unthinkable. So, like a pair of tinkers, Patrick and his Da aimlessly walked the roads around Borrisokane. Lying on the bank of Lough Derg one heaven-sent sunlit afternoon they watched as three barges laden with grain slid silently by, on their way from Dromineer and thence to England. Accompanying it along the path went a line of armed policemen. The Kavanaghs shrank like hares deep into the grass until they had passed. Posted on a farm gate they saw a notice neither of them could read, but they understood well enough the coffin and the skull and crossbones with which it was illustrated:

'Thomas Garvin, take notice to sell your potatoes at no more than 5s per barrel. If you do not, or if you hold them back, I will call to see you on my rambles. I mean to make an example of all such Oliver Cromwells as you are. Signed: Captain Thunderbolt'

For a couple of days, Thomas and Patrick found work along the ditches of one of the big estates, clearing trees brought down by the storms. On the Kavanaghs' third morning, rumour came that there was going to be trouble. A mob of men was coming to intimidate the estate

118

steward for not employing every able-bodied labourer of the neighbourhood. Not being 'of the neighbourhood', Patrick and Thomas feared for their lives. They were in any case scarcely strong enough for the work. They left after receiving only one day's pay: 4d for Thomas and 2d for the boy. The threatened intimidation did not in fact take place. Instead, the following morning a pay clerk, travelling to Borrisokane by pony and trap, was set upon by armed men. He was brutally beaten and the day's pay taken.

Thomas knew he was being incapacitated by fear and hunger. He and Patrick took to sleeping by the back road into the Sopwell estate, sheltering under massive old Spanish chestnut trees. On the first night, Patrick, believing the mansion to be on fire, crept across the lawn to one of the windows. Inside the huge shining room he saw hundreds of candles burning mid-air. In their light sat a woman with bare plump shoulders, vulnerable as an egg, and not quite human to the boy – no more than he, a stinking bag of skin and bones, would have been human to her.

When the storms returned, the trees under which they took cover terrified Patrick. Back in Mayo there were no trees, nothing to deserve the name. There were rocks, and lochs, and heather. At first, Patrick had been in awe of the mighty Tipperary trees. But when the wind made them groan, threshing their branches and straining at their roots, he believed they meant to break free and crush him. For several nights they were drenched by torrential rain. Thunder and lightning shredded their nerves. It was the storm and Patrick's shrieking that finally drove Thomas to seek shelter with his aunt.

The woman whose door they knocked at hesitated to open it. Margaret Dunne (née Kavanagh) had only just

119

accepted the fact that she was pregnant for the sixth time. Tears of rage still pooled in the hollows of her eyes. Margaret also knew there was yellow fever in the district. But when no second knock came she leaned into the silence and then, driven by curiosity, opened the door. She had time to think she'd made a terrible mistake before recognizing her nephew. His trembling child, white as a pulled root, she took to be four or five years old. All bones and big black eyes. His mother's eyes. No one had ever actually said that Thomas had been 'spirited away' by the woman from Mayo, but Margaret's first instinct was to reject the little boy as an alien, fairy creature. Instead, she pushed a stool to the fireside and brought her shawl for the boy's shoulders. When her husband got home he recognised an opportunity – cheap labour – as much as an obligation. Work was made available on the Dunnes' fifteen acres and at night man and boy bedded down in the straw in one of the outhouses, which was no hardship since neither Thomas nor Patrick had ever slept on anything else. For nearly a year Patrick was mute.

Margaret's husband, Daniel Dunne, didn't actually own his fifteen acres, nor did he have them on a secure lease. He rented them 'at will' – his landlord's will, that is – at an annual rate of 20s per acre. In his turn, Daniel sublet two acres in eight different lots, at 10s per lot, providing eight poorer neighbours with a 'quarter ground' on which to sow their potatoes and himself with a modest addition to his income. In good years, twelve acres were enough to provide for his family and recently, mindful of the privations his parents had suffered in times of dearth, he had put an acre to turnips, an acre to cabbage, and two to barley. His wife, Margaret, kept a goat and some chicken she wintered indoors in a coop that formed the lower half of the kitchen dresser. Some of the Dunnes' neighbours grew a few lines of carrots and turnips, too, but they used them – as their landlords expected – for rent, not to eat. Daniel, however, was determined his family should know the taste of such delicacies and grew enough to ensure that they did. It was these small advantages that would see them through the approaching calamity.

Six months after the Kavanaghs blew in on the west wind 'like the weather', as Daniel put it, Margaret's baby was born. The birth was easy and the baby – their first girl – docile but delicate. Luckily for her, she was born in summer and to a mother whose milk was rich with butter and carrots. Mary, as she was named, might otherwise not have survived. But the sight and sounds of a newborn baby made Thomas restless. When Margaret breastfed the child, he had to leave the room. His change of role from poacher to gamekeeper was also difficult to bear. He was obliged to take turns with Dunne in guarding the fields and seeing off the starving with stones.

On occasion, reluctantly, Thomas took Patrick with him to the market at Nenagh. There they saw milling crowds, come in from God only knew where, bringing with them their piteous pleading, their filth and foul, hunger-related diseases. They heard them described as vermin. Boys fishing for eels in a stream nearby found many dead, poisoned, it was supposed, by excrement draining from the workhouse. But the streets of the town were no better, notorious for the cesspits at every door, cesspits deep enough to drown a man and rumoured to have done so. It was reported in the *Nenagh Guardian* that in Galway city, at the express desire of the local authorities, each soldier in the 68th Regiment fired twenty rounds of ball cartridge for the purpose of purifying the air and expelling

121

cholera. Rather more efficaciously, as soon as they were home – before entering the house – Thomas and Patrick washed their hands in their own urine. They did not tell what they'd seen.

Meanwhile, the fields alongside the river continued to wave with ripening wheat. In the great landowners' enclosed pastures cattle and sheep continued to graze peacefully, fattening for their destination on English dinner tables. Only sometimes, like a fox at work in the dark, a starving man might slaughter and drag away one animal and maim the rest. The aristocracy continued to ride to hunt, to give house parties, but also to be more often absent in England, and at such times their massive grey houses went dark. This brought one advantage to their tenants, including the Dunnes: those vegetables normally given as part of their rent were kept back for their own consumption. In Daniel's case, this meant a surplus, which he sold on at exorbitant prices. That winter was especially cold. Thomas saw great white bosomy clouds come to rest on the western horizon amongst broken sections of rainbow. Intense cold was accompanied by thick fog. Ice covered the rivers and streams. God showed no mercy. Nor did man: in spring, the price of seed potatoes and foodstuffs trebled, and in September the soup kitchens closed.

Patrick, ten years old, was growing into his bones – Kavanagh bones, long and strong. He had learned how to make a trap of twigs to catch blackbirds. His father knew how to bring down crows with a stick. They took few fish. Poachers were imprisoned, and in any case, the streams on the Sopwell estate were said to have been emptied of trout. Margaret gathered nettles from the graveyard at Uskane. Sometimes, accompanied by Patrick, she did this at night. Then they would risk the landowners' fields to take blood from the warm necks of cattle, sealing the vein afterwards with a pin. At home, Margaret mixed the blood with milk, or salted and fried it. Patrick watched and listened. He learned these new skills quickly and easily.

When the spring thaw came, Thomas looked at the carrots – a vegetable his wife had never tasted – the eggs, and the goat's milk in his aunt's kitchen and he decided to go home.

'I didn't know you for that sort of a fella,' said Dunne.

'What sort is that?' Thomas asked.

'The sort to move on as soon as the dog starts wagging its tail,' Dunne replied – which was the closest he ever got to expressing any kind of feeling for his wife's nephew.

Thomas left his son Patrick behind when he set off alone to walk back to county Mayo. Whether or not he ever reached home, or found his wife and children alive, I don't know, but he never returned to Tipperary.

Daniel Dunne, moving quickly, now acquired the lease on twenty acres vacated by a family whom poverty had forced to emigrate. One other entire family died of hunger and disease that winter. But their desirable house, which Dunne had long had his eye on, couldn't be taken by new tenants. Fever was believed to stay in the walls, in the thatch and the dung-heaps. The bodies were left to be dragged away by dogs, the house was knocked down and anything that was left was burned. Then the land was dug over with lime and, come spring, Dunne put it to use. His little empire was expanding.

Now began the mass evictions. From that area of bogland between Borrisokane and Nenagh two hundred were evicted. Many were actually 'screaming with hunger' but their screams brought no mercy. Others lay already dead, unable to benefit from the £1 gratuity given to those who were prepared to knock down their own homes. Deaths and evictions enabled Daniel Dunne to continue, hand over fist, moving up into new circumstances. Over the next few years, three families who were Dunne's fellow tenants were evicted, the reason given being their bad management of the land. These evictions were carried out by the landlord's agents, but Daniel didn't speak out against them. Indeed, one took place at his suggestion because the man – protesting at his miserable wage – refused to work for Daniel at a time when he was most needed.

The fact was, Dunne couldn't afford labour problems. Conditions had been imposed on him by his landlord, including the proviso that the land must be dunged, not burned, and at no time was the area under potatoes to exceed that under green crops. Dunne was glad of it. He perfectly understood the benefits of this system. Before the Famine, Daniel had been amongst men who had posted threatening notices on the gates of blood-leeching landlords. Ten years later, he would no longer have felt able to afford such a gesture. It was through caution, hard work and ruthless opportunism that he acquired the lease on forty acres of land instead of fifteen, on four cottages instead of one, and turbary rights in a vast area of sweet-scented bogland where one day my grandfather, John Kavanagh, would walk dreaming of a woman.

Between 1854 and 1878 the price of livestock rose by 81 per cent, oats by 58 per cent, butter by 86 per cent. Dunne was able to sell his produce for three times the price of an ordinary year. He sold and he saved. In 1865 – along with others of his kind – he placed a considerable sum in a savings deposit with the Savings Bank in Nenagh. He had a toehold on the land, on the ladder to respectability and prosperity. Here, with men like Daniel Dunne, begins the future Ireland: conservative, bourgeois, rural.

Naturally, Daniel had ambitions for his daughter, Mary, now twenty years old. For several years he'd been weighing up the local men with regard to their eligibility and though, of course, none was good enough for Mary, mentally he had drawn up a shortlist. Status and wealth were his priorities – in particular, good land – and he'd gone so far as to turn the soil in fields belonging to one keen suitor in order to check its quality. Daniel had no intention of forcing his daughter into a marriage that was disagreeable to her. At the same time, this pretty, sweet-tempered girl – the apple of her father's eye – wasn't expected to make her own choice.

Patrick Kavanagh meanwhile had continued to work on the Dunnes' land as a labourer, nothing more, and with no prospect of more. Now twenty-nine years old, his situation was exactly the same as when he'd arrived out of the storm as an eight-year-old child. There were two Dunne sons in place and one in the graveyard. Patrick was one of the family and yet he was apart: he ate with them, but he slept in the outhouse. He did not work with the livestock, nor in his great-aunt Margaret's vegetable garden. And he seems never to have lifted his eyes to look beyond the earth he worked, as good a man with a spade as ever his father was. He showed no interest in either women or drink, but he had a mean streak, a gene that was to pass on down through the generations: mean, stubborn, narrow, unlike Mary, who was gracious and sweet-tempered, and who all her life had been fascinated by her cousin's fathomless black eyes.

As a child, she liked to follow him when he sang as he worked out on the boundaries of the farm. Patrick sang in Gaelic, his voice true enough but without any art. Now, as a grown woman, it would be more than Mary's life was worth if her parents saw her trailing after her cousin. But still, sometimes she does. Patrick ignores her. Then one day he turns suddenly, his eyes warning her off. Mary puts a hand on his arm – the first time they've ever touched – and as she does so, I realise that this is of course my great-grandmother: Mary Dunne is my mother's much loved 'Grammy', and her father, Daniel, in all his brutality and ambition, is my great-great-grandfather.

I imagine the young couple forced her parents' hand in the most obvious way possible (illegitimacy was both fiercely disapproved of and rare in rural Ireland). Their first child, John, my grandfather, only just scrapes in at seven months: the marriage took place in the Catholic chapel – Patrick signed with his 'mark', Mary didn't even do that – in Borrisokane in February, and John was born in September. By then the couple had moved into a two-bedroomed cottage which, with its single acre, belonged to Daniel Dunne, and there Patrick Kavanagh continued as a labourer in the employ of his father-in-law. This is the 'darling little cottage' of my mother's childhood memories. And I think I've found it, a mile or so outside Borrisokane in a townland called the Curragh.

Curragh means a marshy or boggy place. Named the Scohaboy, this bogland stretches south for three miles or so, flat, dark, treeless. Sweet-scented it may be, still this is the stuff of folk tales, ambiguous as quicksand. Here the light insinuates itself between earth and sky like something slinking just out of sight so that you find yourself constantly turning to see what it is. Nothing. Its presence a kind of absence that's nevertheless as powerful as a forest or a sleeping beast. It's here I come across a tiny cottage, standing with its back to the Scohaboy, facing

green meadows – but also within sight of the Borrisokane workhouse. Long deserted, the thatched roof gone,
enclosed by a little stone wall and with a wind-dwarfed
apple tree beside it, the cottage is like a child's drawing.
This is where Patrick and Mary came to live when they
married in 1868.

Along with the house, the acre, and one of her mother's
goats, Mary brought her husband turbary rights in the bog.
Turbary rights meant they could cut peat for their own
use, or sell it, as they wished. It was a precious resource.
But no other advantage came to the young couple from
Mary's embittered and humiliated father.

Whether the marriage was happy is at best uncertain.
Mary Dunne is absent from the census forms for 1901
– or rather, a little note at the bottom of the page states,
'Mrs Kavanagh slept in Borrisokane.' This may have been
in the line of duty since by then – in the teeth of Patrick's
furious opposition – Mary had become, as my mother had
remembered and described, a nurse. Often as not unpaid,
still, Mary carved a considerable life of her own outside
the home.

I had assumed that Mary attended mostly on women,
that she dealt with pregnancy and birth. In fact, many of
her patients were men, 'old boys living on their own.' As
often as not these old men were suffering from 'a sore
heart', and the cure for that wasn't in Mary's bag, though
'lichen was the next best thing.' Of course Mary knew
the priest disapproved. Her remedies weren't just popular
but, amongst those who clung still to the old beliefs, they
were considered to be more effective than the priest's own
blessings. Father O'Brien didn't actually prevent Mary
from going about her business, but she believed his disapproval had an inhibiting effect on her patients' recovery.
Unlike the priest, she didn't much believe in the value

of suffering, nor did she make his distinction between body and soul. Some of Mary's nursing took her to the workhouse, and it may be that's where she was on the night Patrick closed his dark eyes for the last time since, on his death certificate, it's not his wife but his daughter who is recorded as 'present at death'. Maybe the marriage had been a 'career move' on Patrick's part, or a romance that had gone sour. There's a Scots saying: 'As loveless as an Irishman'.

My grandfather, John, was the first of five children; three girls and one other boy, Daniel, who, in the 1901 census is still living at home and is described as 'deaf and dumb'. The description comes in the column headed 'Deaf and Dumb; Dumb only; Blind; Imbecile, Idiot or Lunatic', and with the direction, 'Write the respective infirmity opposite the name of the person afflicted.' Under 'Rank, Profession or Occupation', Daniel is described as a tailor. I picture him working at a bench set up under the thatch. Alone in the house I imagine he would have felt the vibrations of a stranger's footfall. Which must have been how he sensed the curlew, as a vibration, sometimes becoming aware of its call before his brother did and putting a hand on John's arm to stop him working. Out on the Scohaboy Bog the boys would stand side by side, very still, washed in the smell of heather and thrilling to that eerie, heart-stopping cry that some people believed was a banshee. No one knew what Daniel thought it was. An approaching thunderstorm, long before it had darkened the sky, drew the light out of both the gorse and Daniel's face. This was the sort of thing my grandfather got to know when his teacher thought he should have been in school learning another order of things altogether.

By the time my grandfather was born, free basic education was on offer to every child in the country. In

John Kavanagh's home town of Borrisokane there was a national school he might have attended. No doubt he went along those few days in the year he wasn't required to work. But, until 1892, there was no legal compulsion for him to do so.

I'd always supposed that, by the time of John's marriage, old Patrick Kavanagh was dead. In fact, he was still very much alive, which makes me realise my grandfather didn't exactly *choose*, as I'd previously imagined, to reject his inheritance, breaking his widowed mother's heart in the process. With his father alive, to stay on in his parents' house would have been an option only if he'd resigned himself to celibacy. Many of his generation – and generations to come – did so: in 1911, a quarter of middle-aged Irish men and women had never been married. But John had fallen in love, and with Kate, a woman who wanted life on her own terms. Besides, the house at Curragh had so little land. Even by the standards of the day it was hardly an economic holding. My grandfather had little choice but to leave home and make his own way. He was his mother's son. Behind his gentle exterior there was a quiet will, and a streak of daring that helped him to move out into the unknown.

But what did John hope for? When he walked out there on the Scohaboy, waiting in a torment of uncertainty for Kate Buckley to come to him, what did he believe he could offer this woman? She might be coming to him 'with her arms swinging', that is to say, empty-handed, but Kate's hands were both strong and beautiful and she possessed a natural refinement which was immediately apparent in her bearing and in her speech. What would make this marriage worth her while, beyond the promise of John's love? In the year he married, 1899, 32,000 people emigrated from Ireland. On their marriage certificate John is described as 'labourer' and Kate as 'spinster'. Both bride and groom 'signed' with their mark, an 'X'. John's cross is large and straight. An honest, straightforward mark. Kate's mark is smaller but with a little flourish, the strokes crossed like fingers. Emigration was surely unthinkable for this young couple, so ill-prepared for exile, but probably no more unthinkable than for many of the 32,000 who did leave. When my grandfather turned his back on his inheritance, all it amounted to was a cottage, an acre of land and turbary rights in the bog. It can't have seemed difficult to improve on. What John and Kate had in abundance was youth and strength. Of course what they hoped for was a better life.

In my rented cottage I am alone in luxury, with three bedrooms to choose from, a pretty kitchen, and a stable door. Some of my reading time is spent pacing the floor. Often I go to the door and throw the upper half open, sometimes on to a sunny morning, sometimes on to a starlit night. In the dark I can hear the companionable sighing of the horses in the paddock. In the daytime I can see the grey rooftops of the workhouse and the Fever Hospital. Both are now in the process of being demolished, keeling over like blank-eyed drunkards imploding on their terrible, anonymous pasts. Sometimes I cross the field, go through the line of trees and stand looking away, towards the bogland. The utter stillness of this vast, dark terrain silences my inner noise.

I never once heard my mother mention either the Famine or 'the Bad Times' as it was referred to, as if to use the words 'famine' or 'hunger' was to tempt fate to repeat itself. Nevertheless, I now know that in 1840 the lane up Knigh Hill had seventeen inhabited houses where twenty years later – as now – it had two. I now know it may be the ghosts of dead children that give this unpeopled landscape its air of having been abandoned.

Or maybe it's all a trick of the light. Maybe Ireland always has had an inherent nostalgia, a way of seeming to stand with its lovely back turned and its attention on something far off, something you can't see. Consciously or not it must have entered the young Agnes's soul. Certainly my mother's character was tinged with a melancholy similar to that of the countryside she grew up in and knew so well. A child, like a monk, is celibate, communal, self-centred, ignorant of the wider world yet engaged daily in a search for the meaning of existence and its own place in life. A little animal on a spiritual quest, forming itself out of the surrounding elements like coral forming itself from calcium in the sea. Whether or not she knew it, my mother was born into a land more populous with ghosts than children, with derelict cottages, and ruined chapels crumbling beside grave-yards set mysteriously in the middle of fields.

Sitting at the table in my cottage I unfold the copy of my mother's birth certificate. Date of birth, July 1911 – not the date I knew. Place, Clashnevin – a place I'd never heard of.

3

'This is where your mother was born,' says Maureen Mounsey, parting the branches of the whitethorn and stepping delicately between wet cowpats dropped like tins of fresh brown paint into the grass. 'This is "the back of the Birds"'. Sure it's a pity there's nothing left for you to see, but this is where the little place stood, here. Well, there were three of them, joined together in a row and above them, there' – she points across the field – 'was the Mass Stone.'

She adds, superfluously, that she believes the walls of my grandparents' house were made of stone. There's no trace of a building, nor of the Mass Stone now. It's more than twenty years since the houses were demolished, the Mass Stone removed – most probably broken up and incorporated into a wall somewhere – and the field cleared and put to grass for cattle. A field like any other in Tipperary, green and damp and sweet.

In the first ten years of their married life my grandparents moved home five times. Their first child, Mary Rose, was born at a town address near the old Fever Hospital in Borrisokane in 1900 (a decent full fourteen months after their marriage). Their second child, Pat, was born in 1902 some ten miles away to the south-east, at Ballinree. Eighteen months later their third child, Thomas, was born in Druminure, a townland back near Borrisokane. Josie and Dan were both born at a place nearby yet mysteriously isolated, out on the bog and known as 'the Island'. Most likely it was here that Mary Rose swung her little brother Pat round and broke his leg against the hearthstone. Journeying between these places the family travelled by donkey and cart. Damaged or not, Pat, as the first son, always sat up on the box beside his father. Often as not, they sheltered from rain under a shared piece of sacking. This is when, cocooned in scented privacy, my uncle Pat was told the stories that John himself had been told by *his* father, Patrick, stories from the Bad Times.

All this moving around can have happened for only one reason: since leaving his father's house John Kavanagh had been the lowest of the low, a labourer to hire, one of the 'untouchables' of rural Irish life. But, by the time of my mother's birth, they'd turned their backs forever on the boggy uplands, on the furze, the heather and the curlews. From the Island they would have crossed the remaining half-mile or so of bogland and gone down a track alongside young beech trees, the pale manor house of Sopwell in view, then out on to the rather lovely road that dips, graceful and tree-lined, down to the Ballintotty river valley and the lush damp meadows of Clashnevin in the parish of Ballymackey. And it's here in this one place that, over the next five years, four more daughters, Bridget, Cathleen, Agnes and Nancy, would be born.

My grandfather had found work with a landed family, gentlemen farmers named Cross. James Cross owned six hundred acres, enough both to rent out several substantial farms and to need outside labour. My grandfather became one of the lucky ones, employed not on a casual basis but kept in regular work, and sufficiently favoured to be given living accommodation on one of the rented farms. The Mounseys, related to the Cross family by marriage, have rented this farm – the house and the land – on secure lease for six generations and Maureen told me that, when she came here as a young bride in the 1970s, at least one of these labourer's cottages was still standing.

Although the Mounseys were kind enough to show me where my mother was born, neither of them ever met her or my grandparents. Roger and Maureen are my age, or a little younger. They know the Kavanaghs by name only. If they met them, say, walking down the lane from the church at Ballymackey, they'd no more recognise them than I would. Maureen nevertheless went upstairs to dig out a small, damp-stained suitcase from the wardrobe. Her husband doubted she'd find it, but she insisted she'd seen the case there only a few months – or was it years? – before, and hadn't they been telling one another they should find a better home for the contents, for surely they were irreplaceable.

The rusty clasps opened silently, but the lid creaked as it was lifted and the case exhaled a faint musty breath. Inside were the work records Roger's father, grandfather and great-grandfather had kept of the men employed at Clashnevin, including pay-books dating from the late nineteenth century. We worked our way through the books until, arriving at the first decade of the twentieth century, we found the names: O'Meara, Duff, Ryan, Healy, Bird, Shanahan. Kavanagh. Spelt with a 'K'. In this way it was verified that my grandfather was one of seven men who worked and lived here, 'at the back of Birds'' (the 'Birds' I now understand, were a family by that name). But after June 1913 his name no longer appears.

These handwritten records continued until the 1980s when they were transferred on to the computer I'd already noticed set up in a cold, shambolic outhouse. This is where the dogs are housed at night, and the white bench-desk is splashed with brown streaks from their food. Above it, notices are posted on a corkboard that looks like its corners have been gnawed by rats. A single-storey, dark room, unceilinged – that is to say, open to the roof rafters – giving the room height, but there appears to be no chimney, so I guess the space would often have been thick with smoke.

Maureen showed me into this damp and chokingly vile-smelling room and as quickly showed me out.

'This will give you some idea, Maggie,' she was saying, 'of what the Kavanaghs' little house was like and there, you see, is where the fire would have been, with the mantle above—' when she broke off, blushed furiously, and marched me back outside. She gave a little moan. 'Maybe I shouldn't have shown you,' she said, 'but you know, we've let the place go....'

Later, when I consult the House and Building Return for 1911, I understand the reference Maureen had made to 'stone walls'. There's a column on the census form in which the enumerator is directed to enter 'O' if the walls are made of 'Mud, Wood or other Perishable Material'. The house in which my mother was born had stone walls – damp, no doubt – a slate roof, earth floor, three windows and just three rooms. Three rooms for, at the final count, eleven of them. The house just squeaked into what was categorised as 'second class', 'fourth class' being the lowest and consisting of a windowless mud cabin with a single room. Fifty years earlier, *nearly half* of Ireland's rural population had lived in this class of house and this half had certainly included some of my Kavanagh ancestors.

However, by the time my grandparents arrived here at Clashnevin, the government had rehoused a quarter of a million people. A good number complained the new houses were 'bird-baskets', the chimneys smoked, the walls were damp and the hearths weren't big enough to take their pots. When I found the House and Building

Return in Nenagh Library, I exclaimed in shock, 'Only three rooms! And can they really have been so small?' But the young librarian gently reminded me, 'It was the same for everyone. They had nothing.' He smiled. 'They expected nothing.'

That evening, back in my own cottage, I open a magazine called *Household Hints*, published in 1899. Maureen had come across a little stack of these magazines at the bottom of the suitcase containing the Mounsey family records. Some of the pages are stuck together with mildew.

I learn that at the turn of the 19th century the Dublin elite got itself into a fine old panic over the rural poor. The irony is that, by the time the authorities sat up and took notice, the poor of Ireland had already begun to 'improve' themselves: either by dying, or emigrating, or by 'consolidating', that cure-all for Ireland's crisis of land. There were, however, still appalling levels of poverty, child mortality and TB, and the authorities appear to have had little difficulty finding someone to blame: Irish *women*. In an article from the 1899 magazine – the year my grandmother started out as the wife of an insecurely employed labourer – I read:

> '*In the family life each mealtime should be looked forward to as a time of pleasure – a rest and refreshment for the body and mind. The woman of the household should set the example of always sitting down at the table neatly dressed, and of having the room, whether it be the kitchen or another room, where the meals are served in perfect order...all jarring subjects of conversation should be set aside.*'

As late as 1911, the year my mother was born, teachers were being instructed to put it before their girls that 'we in Ireland are very backward indeed'. A couple of years later, in the same popular women's magazine, an article entitled 'Are Mothers the Ruin of Ireland?' suggested it was hardly surprising men drank and beat their wives; it only wished 'they would beat them a good deal more until they served better meals and kept the children in order.'

It was an unusually hot, wet July when my grand-mother's eighth child, Agnes, was born. When she didn't draw breath immediately, the woman who attended the birth put a touch of poteen to her lips, remarking as she did so, 'Won't that get it roaring in no time?'

Which it did. The baby continued to squall through the first three or four months of her life as if, the poteen having once got her going, she didn't know when to stop. As if outraged that the option *not* to draw breath had been taken away from her. Agnes was the first of Kate's children to cry so much, but at four months the storm subsided and the baby's temperament changed. She grew into a quiet, observant child whose grasp on life was as strong as her seven siblings, most of whom ignored her as much as her mother did, except for Josie and Bridie who occasionally squabbled over her, patted her, rocked her and lugged her about with powerful indifference to her comfort. Agnes stayed passive as a sack of potatoes but her black eyes took in every little thing her brothers and sisters did and got: every morsel that went in their mouths, every clout they put on their backs, she made note of. Her hands were large, with long fingers, always reaching out for things. 'Greedy' her mother called them, but her father had his own word for them: 'seeking'.

My grandfather hadn't been brought up to herd animals or in any other way to look after them. There were his mother's goats, but they were roped and unlovable:

137

mean-tempered and blockheaded, with lemon-coloured eyes as dead as gobstoppers. John would gladly have sold the skin of those goats to the old man in Portumna who made drums. But the land he came to at Clashnevin, in a valley between two rivers, was rich meadowland where the wind turned the grass this way and that, parting it like a comb in a fine head of hair and, by the time my grandfather came there at the turn of the century, it was intensively grazed by cattle. It turned out he had a way with them, with the cattle, the dogs and the horses. His employer, James Cross, soon noticed and put Kavanagh with his seventy-year-old stockman, or 'herd', to be trained up in the herding of cattle and the breaking of workhorses. He chose my grandfather over John's fellow labourer, a man named James Foley, who lived with his family about seven miles away in a house on Knigh Hill.

There was no need to tell my grandfather that an old boy like Leary, in his filthy suit with cuffs barely reaching his grime-encrusted wrists, an old boy who gave the passer-by no more than a shy nod, was full to the brim with knowledge. You couldn't put a value on what he knew. He was able to judge the age, the health and the character of his animals at a glance, able to calm them with a word. He tended them in sickness, injury, and birth. He was mother to animals whose mothers either died or failed in their duty. He found animals that were lost and when the time came, he drove them to market, many animals over many miles. He negotiated a price, knowing to the shilling the value of each animal. He judged the desirability of a bullock, looking for bulk in the hindquarters where the best cuts of meat come from. He knew never to buy cattle from Mayo – that country in the west out of which John's father had emerged – for they, far from flourishing on the rich grassland of Tipperary, would fail, even die. The old man had the skill, which John soon learned, of calculating the weight of an animal to within a few pounds just by looking at it.

This old stockman had worked for Mr Cross for the past thirty years, with never a day off for sickness. 'I took a day off to get married,' he used to say, with a wink. 'And didn't that cure me?'

Recently, however, the old man's wife had died and his eyes had begun to cloud over with glaucoma. Sometimes he stumbled when he went after the cattle and his face froze with terror if he sensed an animal he hadn't seen was suddenly close by him. He believed they knew, might even take advantage of his weakness, and a young bull ox was an unpredictable creature. A young stallion, too. 'And why wouldn't he be?' the old man would say. 'What other pleasure does he have? Why should he sing to the boss's tune?' My grandfather was not one to take advantage, but nor was he above seeing an advantage might come to him.

Like his mentor, my grandfather came to believe that horses were the king of beasts. It was here he learned to walk horses in the dew. All his life he believed in it for closing up the cracks in a horse's foot or in a human foot, come to that. He never struck or spoke harshly to the animals in his care. Never mind they were nominally under his command, didn't he have to bow to their necessities and their natures, like a child tending a row of beans – or like a man with a woman?

The woman in question, my grandmother, had only one claim to distinction – apart, that is, from her natural distinction of person – which was that her father had been coachman to the Bishop of Killaloe. But I'm amazed by her strength. Kate, now thirty-seven, had eight children, a cottage with three rooms and, naturally, no running water. The floors were swept clean twice a day and there was no dung-heap (other than her neighbours') within sight or smell of Kate's front door. All three windows in the house were opened at least once a day, an exercise so chilly, draughty and – so it was generally believed – injurious to health as to be the next thing to blasphemy. It was Kate who cut twigs from the oak and splintered them into toothpicks. She told the story of how, as a little girl, she'd sat high up on the box beside her father when he drove the Bishop's black coach alongside the shining magnificence of the Shannon river. But if ever the Bishop himself came on board, so Kate said, she was set down in the dust. In her child's mind it was as if the pairs of elements – bishop and commoner, male and female, rich and poor – must forever be kept separate. Forever and ever. Amen.

My grandmother's one great pleasure was to sit in the field in the long grass just out of sight there beyond the Mass Stone, her hands folded on her lap, taking the sunshine. At such times, even Pat knew not to disturb her. If anyone dared ask what she was doing there, she would answer with great relish: 'Nothing'. One summer afternoon she heard a mysterious twanging, the sound of tennis being played on a court out of sight beside the big house. When it was explained to her that grown women were batting a ball back and forth across a net, Kate laughed. Sometimes she sat too long in the damp grass, getting chilled before she went inside.

I realise I can't imagine what the inside of my grandmother's house was like. That is, I can only list what isn't there: no cushioned armchair, no hot bath, no radio. No pencil and paper. No upright piano. During this Victorian era, the great era of *things,* of possessions – and in spite of my mother's memory of brass lamps and copper pots – my grandparents possessed next to nothing. No doubt, as the young man in Nenagh Library had suggested, they expected nothing. It was here at Clashnevin that Kate began to cough.

Sometimes, judging her moment, the oldest child, Mary Rose would ask how it was that Grandpa had come to be the Bishop of Killaloe's coachman and Kate, after considering a while, would reply as if for the first time: 'The Bishop fell into a faint at our door and my father drove him home in the cart, gentle as if he'd been a sleeping baby, gentle enough that the drop didn't fall from the end of the Bishop's nose, and when he came to his senses the Bishop said God had sent your grand-daddy to be his coachman.'

Kate always allowed herself a little snort at the end of this story and then, for hours afterwards, Mary Rose and Pat (with the iron on his leg already) enacted the scene, galloping around the field so rumbustuously that a good deal more than the drop on the end of the Bishop's nose fell off; his legs fell off, his arms, his head and his other parts until the Bishop of Killaloe, dismembered and unmanned, lay scattered across the field and the children's laughter faded down a slide of exhaustion and the long grass hid them, and even the infant Agnes, crawling in grim-faced determination this way and that, couldn't find them.

But of course, most of this can only be in my imagination. This is where my mother was born, in the parish of Ballymackey, between the Ballintotty and the Ollatrim rivers. A green and pleasant place, but not one she ever told me about.

*

London, 1988. The violinist gets to his feet, cradling the fiddle and standing like a man cheek to cheek with his beloved, facing the audience. There is a pause. Then a

141

cascade of icy notes. My husband, my parents and I are sitting in St John's Smith Square, Westminster, part of a well-heeled, quietly attentive audience more familiar with the habits of concertgoing than of Christian rites. It's winter, Christmas. I look towards my mother, hoping to catch her eye, but she's hypnotised by the music, by the place, the powerful sense of occasion. I recognise that dazed, slightly disbelieving look on her face. The musicians are very young. They make of this overfamiliar music something so fresh it's startling. Cold, passionate, clear. The sound ricochets in flying volleys around the baroque interior. I become confused as to which season we're in. Does the music represent winter, or spring? Those shivering chords must surely represent ice, but is it forming, or melting? My surroundings become insubstantial, no more solid than the music streaming around and over us and which, like a wafer becoming flesh, has taken on such dense physicality I feel I could climb up on it, up towards the icing-sugar cupola and dissolve into the blue air. Then applause erupts on all sides and I'm brought back to earth. The moment of being adrift in time and space is over. My mother turns her face towards me. We're here. Now. There's a crackle of programmes and the soft animal rustle of clothes and limbs being rearranged. A salvo of coughs. 'Winter' is over and we are about to hear 'Spring'. I think to remark on this to my mother but she has leaned forward a little, her face rapt, lips parted as if preparing to drink the music in. I've lost her again.

4

I have a mental image of the Mass Stone that once stood in the middle of the Clashnevin fields, offering Kate her rare moments of privacy. During the time of the Penal Laws (late seventeenth to late eighteenth century – also in England through the seventeenth century) the practice of Catholicism was proscribed and 'priest-hunting' treated as a sport. Priests said Mass out in the open where, paradoxically, they were hidden, hidden in fields and on hillsides away from their official places of worship, surrounded by the natural world like their pagan ancestors. Here on the Mass Stone the priest set out the tools of his trade: missal, rosary, Eucharist. These priests and their shivering congregations were 'the secret people'. In this way the Irish people came to be bound especially close to their priests – some of whom became folk heroes because they had been persecuted in the name of their faith.

The spirit of Catholicism was strengthened, but its physical fabric suffered: chapels, abbeys and monasteries, many used for worship since the Middle Ages, fell into decay. At the turn of the nineteenth century these ruins were a great tourist attraction. Parties drove out from Dublin, travelled from England and Europe to visit ivy-clad heaps of stone which were seen as representing the wild and the romantic, at that time highly fashionable concepts. No doubt they averted their eyes from the rural poor – or else looked at them in the same spirit as equally wild and romantic. Later Victorian tourists included the still-ruined Irish chapels on their itineraries, posing amongst crumbling walls with their servants and donkeys to have their photographs taken – just as I had posed my own daughter under the ivy-covered archway of the crumbling chapel at Knigh that summer when, in another life, we were passing through on our way to Donegal.

This is the chapel I'm looking towards now as I hesitate with my hand on the gate. Today I understand its dereliction, still I'm reluctant to go wandering amongst ghosts and stones in the graveyard again. Across the road is a substantial, whitewashed farmhouse. Looking at it, I realise this must be the home of the Clearys, the family from whom my grandfather used to borrow the tram cart. It was Rody Cleary whom my mother put down as the most dashing man she could ever imagine, a 'strong' farmer with a watch on a silver chain. Stones and books can't satisfy me any longer. I need flesh and blood. Or at the very least, a cup of tea. I dive across the road towards the house.

The iron fence and the gate here are white, too, and the latch of the gate is stuck in paint. I go round to a side entrance. The prosperous, bourgeois appearance of the front of the house gives way to a working farmyard. The disused stables running along one side house rusty pieces of machinery, some broken furniture and bales of hay. A gate into the fields is fixed with rope and a cat slinks away at my approach. I stand at the back door contemplating a blackened saucepan which, in some minor domestic emergency, has been dumped by the drain. A curtain is drawn across a small window and the sound of a television blares out. The five o'clock news with a bulletin on the war in Iraq. I tap on the door several times.

The woman who finally opens the door to me is not the bent old lady I'd unconsciously been expecting and, I suppose, hoping for: a figure from the past, an archetype, an old woman from a folk tale. True, the figure standing in front of me is a little stooped from the physical demands of her work, her face is weathered and her cropped hair dyed a reddish-black. But her hands are wonderfully unmarked, she wears a pair of battered jeans and grey trainers, and is, I calculate, five or so years older than I am. She looks at me with her head cocked on one side and questions in her bright eyes. I apologise for disturbing her. I tell her that once upon a time my family lived on Knigh Hill.

It turns out that Joan Cleary is from 'away', from Limerick, and that she came here to Knigh only in the seventies when, as a 'not-so-young bride' she married Jim Cleary, Rody's son. She doesn't herself remember any of the Kavanaghs but her husband, God rest his soul, was born and raised in this house and he knew them. She herself had gone to my uncle Pat's funeral, here at Knigh Cross. Hearing Joan say 'your uncle Pat' sends a frisson through me. But I'm confused. Pat was still alive in the *seventies*?

'Oh, he was,' says Joan. 'I'd say it was the eighties that he died.'

I stare at her in shock.

'Why did you go to his funeral?'

Joan laughs.

'And why wouldn't we, when it was just here in the graveyard?'

Joan considers me a moment, then stoops and picks up the greasy pan.

'Will we go in and find my address book?'

Joan's address book proves to be exactly like my own: a bundle of ancient pages bound together with elastic bands inside a split, marbled cover. Every inch of every page is covered in indecipherable runes, some in pencil, some in biro: red, blue, green. She's searching for the address of a woman called Catherine Ryan, now living in Cork.

'She'd be able to tell you about those times, all right, your grandparents and so on,' she tells me. 'Everyone else is gone.'

But what's an unknown woman living in faraway Cork to me? I feel my heart slow and sink down in my chest and Joan perhaps senses this. She puts a hand on my arm. She speaks that universal word of comfort.

'Tea,' she says. 'We'll have a cup of tea.' As we move from the hall into the kitchen she apologises for the state it's in, saying: 'The cows must always come first. And there's your grandmother kept the floor so clean you could eat your dinner off it! She was known for it.'

The kitchen is indeed an amazement of disorder: pots and pans, papers and bills, biros, the weights to a set of scales, loaves cooling on a rack and dishcloths wrung into damp knots littering the work surfaces. This dark room is illuminated by just one small window and by a red light burning beneath the Sacred Heart on one side and a blue light beneath the Dove of the Holy Spirit on the other. A little wigwam of brickettes smoulder in the cave-like hearth. There's a seductive smell of baking and peat and tea with a homely bass note of cow shit coming in at the open window and I yearn to be taken care of, to be, in a word, mothered.

Some hours later, after half a home-made loaf with jam and butter, two slices of fruit cake and several pots of tea, I've learned that Joan has been running the farm virtually single-handed for the past twenty years. When she first came here her father-in-law, Rody Cleary, was still alive. Rody Cleary owned this land, and land elsewhere, and had been a prominent man on the local council during the 1920s and '30s. Joan remembers hearing from him that Pat Kavanagh was 'trouble'.

I recall my mother saying, 'Perhaps Pat drank it all away?' But I'm finding it difficult to ask the obvious questions, to proceed as if I am an interrogator here on some kind of official business. Besides, Joan – a woman with fields of cattle who has just got up to fetch a plastic bottle of supermarket milk from the fridge – has already moved on to talk more generally of farming, motherhood, and the greater world. I notice that when she smiles, she favours the side of her mouth that has a couple of teeth missing.

'And whose daughter is it you are?' she asks.

'Agnes's.'

'And where was Agnes coming in the family?'

'One but last. Nancy was the youngest and only Pat stayed.'

And so we sit on, like two badgers in a den, supping our tea and chewing the fat until, on the third attempt, I finally get to the door to leave. I'm both thrilled and appalled to have so abused this generous woman's hospitality. Catherine Ryan's address, being far away in Cork, slips forgotten to the bottom of my bag. But directions to both Billy Foley, caretaker of the graveyard records, and Danny Grace, a historian and teacher, neither of them more than five minutes away, are committed to my memory like magic formulae.

'Call on them now,' Joan urges. 'Evening is a good time to find people in.'

But as I walk towards my car a massive orange-coloured moon is sailing up over Knigh Hill and looking

147

at my watch I see that it's a quarter to nine. Too late to call on anyone. Besides, I'm desperate for a drink. The four roads leading away from the cross are empty under the moonlight. Opposite me stands the tiny little house where generations of the Graces (Danny's relations) lived and worked the forge, where generations of doctors held a weekly surgery from 1858 until 1991. It's where I'd always imagined my grandfather came running looking for help when Mary Rose broke Pat's leg, but I now know the accident must have happened when they were still living on the Scohaboy Bog, which probably explains the delay in treatment that left the little boy crippled for life.

Now the Graces' house, which I see has been given the name 'The Dispensary', is up for sale. And here, beside my car, is a stone I've taken little notice of before but I now walk round to read, by moonlight, the inscription. It's in Gaelic, so all I can understand are the names: John and Thomas O'Brien, and the date: 1920. My mother would have been nine years old at the time of whatever event the stone commemorates.

In the village I stop to buy a bottle of Guinness. The bar turns out to be a very small, very dark cupboard where, for some reason, my request is utterly incomprehensible to the sweet-faced girl behind the bar – and to the three men rooted to it. They stare for all the world as if I've just asked to be given the Holy Sacrament and then the men, half-rising, lean a little towards me, swaying in unison, so that I have to sway, too, in order to see past them to the shelves behind the bar and, swaying together, we have a few moments in which we might as well be trying to land a man-sized jellyfish or manoeuvre a mattress down the stairs, until finally I spot a bottle of Guinness and triumphantly point to it. The faces around me are illuminated

148

with something like joy and the girl exclaims, 'A bottle of Guinness is it?' – at least, I suppose that's what she says, because it turns out I can't understand her either.

In the cottage, I kick off my shoes. Tired but restless. I'm often restless on these long evenings alone. A tad bored. I also frequently drink a glass or two too many and then I read less of the journal of the Borrisokane Historical Society than I'd intended and watch the tele instead. Like tonight. Always the Irish station, and these programmes are usually in the Irish language. To me it has an odd sound, soft but muffled, as if the speaker's scarf has got stuck in his mouth and he, too, has had too much Guinness or whiskey to notice. Tonight we're in a pub somewhere in Cork, and there's a lot of bulky human bodies shifting around across the screen and the general din of human conviviality, all disorganised and aimless, then the camera lurches to one side, finds a group of musicians and locks attention like a dog with a cat in its sights. Then a woman begins to sing, a voice so pure and true it makes your heart turn over and your eyes sting, a voice so much her own that it sings for everyone: the first voice ever, and me the first and only listener. When the song ends I go and throw open the upper half of the back door and lean out into the moonlit night, tearful, hungry, elated. Am I at home, or away?

5

At sight of me, the woman claps her hands together.

'Well and aren't you a Kavanagh!'

I've found the little girl who used to come over the hill to the Kavanaghs' with a jug to borrow milk; the little girl my mother and her sisters used to pick up in the donkey cart and give a ride to school. Annie O'Brien is still small but now she's eighty years old, a little stooped, and wearing a confident dash of bright orange lipstick. Small she may be, but she has natural authority: an X-ray look, a voice that's easy on the ear and an air of barely repressed amusement. A woman managing and enjoying her own life. Taking my hand she exclaims, 'Such a look of your grandmother you have!' – which probably surprises her less than it surprises me.

It's with Danny Grace I've come here to the O'Briens' little house at the back of Knigh Hill, the house where Annie and her brothers were born.

I imagine everyone has a similar first impression of Danny. Energy, warmth, vigour. These qualities make him seem bigger than he is. His strong voice booms from a barrel chest and his head, with its thatch of thick fairish hair, is slightly too large for the rest of him, giving him a still-boyish look though he's a man in his fifties with a craggy face and the hefty body of middle age. For all his cordiality, Danny is very observant, very much a listener, revealing little about himself except to say of his books,

'The research is fine, it's the writing that's difficult.' With a laugh, 'And in summer, isn't there always the temptation of tennis?'

Born in 1948, one of eleven children, Danny was raised in a small house not so very far from the O'Briens'. Knigh Hill, the Cross, and the woods were his childhood playground just as, a generation earlier, they'd been my mother's. But whereas my mother upped and left, for Danny, Knigh has remained the centre of his world both physically and intellectually: 'a home bird', as his wife describes him. A graduate of University College Dublin – and I of University College London – Danny is also, like me, a writer concerned with the past.

When Danny answered the door that afternoon, I introduced myself in the usual way:

'My family were at Knigh. I'm Agnes Kavanagh's daughter.'

The look in Danny's eyes intensified.

There was a pause.

'Then what in God's name are you doing standing there on the doorstep?' he demanded. 'Come on in.'

Which is how it has come about that, on the following evening, with the introductions over, Danny and I take our places at Annie O'Brien's table. The walls of Annie's dark and high-ceilinged living room are papered with a design of grey bricks, the floor covered with a lino which, at first glance, looks like wood. The O'Brien father was, as my mother had remembered, a carpenter. The dresser is his work. Also the table, which Annie has covered with a cloth but in her mother's day was kept bare and scrubbed white. The old chairs, eight of them she remembers, five at the table and three there along the wall, they would have been her father's work, too. But, 'There was no comfort in them! No one thought of comfort in those days.'

A red light burns under the image of the Sacred Heart. As Annie goes about laying out teacups, a plate of bread and butter and a packet of Jaffa cakes, her humorous eyes move like a conjuror's hands, quick and sassy. Annie spent thirty-five years of her life 'away', but hers is a very different emigrant story from my mother's.

When she was already a not-so-young woman, Annie went to live in Dublin, leaving her mother to manage an otherwise entirely masculine household. One cold wet morning in Rockwall she saw an advert for California, a poster that might have been a child's drawing, with sunshine and a golden bridge, and she went there like a girl dancing after the Pied Piper. But she couldn't settle. She was lonely and out of place and took the first opportunity to go to New York. There she found herself a job as a waitress for a big financial company on Wall Street.

When the tables had been laid up with stainless-steel cutlery from Sheffield and linen napkins from Ireland, and the men had not yet arrived to eat their steaks and their ice cream sundaes, Annie, neat and chipper as a sparrow, would stand at the windows on the eleventh floor to watch the pedestrians on the street far below darting through deep shadow like people in a narrow mountain canyon, and sometimes she would think of her brothers out on the hillside watching their sheep. But Annie loved the big, brash, noisy circus that was New York in the fifties and sixties. She roomed in a house in the Bronx, the Jewish quarter, which doesn't surprise me. There's still something not just Irish American, but Jewish American – Jewish New York to be precise – about Annie: confident, wisecracking talk, fast as an express train.

Yet, when she was sixty-seven, Annie, unlike my mother, came home, to this little cottage on the hillside above Lough Derg, to live with her only surviving brother,

Jim. Although she tells me their parents' marriage was happy, and that they were happy children, none of them followed their parents' example and married.

'The truth is,' Annie is saying, 'many of the fellas couldn't afford to marry and by the time they could, they were too old. And me,' she adds with a gravelly laugh, 'I carried a torch for a man I couldn't have.' She looks from me to Danny. 'You've a very tolerant wife,' she observes. 'Allowing you to go out at night with a woman.'

Danny's eyes roll.

'Well I'm married to an actor,' I say. 'So I have to tolerate more than that.'

Annie laughs and exclaims, 'Oh yes, he'd be kissing them too, wouldn't he?'

This is the moment Jim O'Brien chooses to slip quietly into the room, returned from a funeral, in his dark suit like an old photograph of the rural Irishman come to life. At the little window, wild stock – or 'poor man's flowers' Annie calls them – show their pale faces like spirits of the long dead. As we came into the house I'd noticed their spectral presence, their innocent yet luxurious scent. When I remark on them, Annie says, 'Your grandfather liked to take a sprig for his buttonhole on a Sunday morning – and my mother liked to give it to him!'

My grandfather's sudden appearance sends a flush of excitement through me. He's here at last, through the eyes of someone who saw him, spoke to him, heard his voice.

'What was he like?'

'Blue eyes,' says Annie immediately. Then she has to think a moment. 'He wore a hat,' she says. 'Always a hat. John Kavanagh was a gentleman.' And Agnes was his favourite. Out of sight of Mrs Kavanagh, it seems my grandfather gave the children cigarettes, sweets, if he had them. It was Agnes who got the most and according to

Annie what she did then was to put them in her knickers and shin up the apple tree so she could look down on the rest of them. Yes, Agnes was her daddy's girl.

'And you know, I expect, Maggie, that it was Paddy could do no wrong in his mother's eyes.'

'I do.'

As a child, Jim had thought Paddy the proper little gentleman with his knife, and nicotine stains on his fingers, well out of school when he wasn't much more than twelve but already as tall as his daddy and never mind his limp, working the woods and the vegetable garden. With a somewhat intimidating nod to me, Jim makes the following observation:

'Your family lived better than we did.' His voice is unexpectedly light, thrilling, giving the odd impression it's not he who's speaking but someone else. 'Isn't that so, Danny? Didn't they live better than your grandparents?'

'Indeed they did. They were the ones had the pig, the cows, the vegetables.'

'No fish?' I ask, thinking of the torture of boiled fish that every English child, Catholic or not, was once routinely subjected to on Fridays.

'Fish!' exclaims Danny. 'No one in Tipperary would have known a fish if they'd met one walking up the lane. No, it was bacon we were made of.'

'The stuff with bristles!' exclaims Jim.

Danny claps his hand to his forehead.

'Hairy bacon'! Don't remind me,' he groans. 'Yes, your family lived better than we did.' With faint, not entirely benign amusement, Danny adds, 'The Kavanaghs had notions.'

'Will I tell you,' offers Annie, tapping the back of my hand, 'about the day your family first came here to Knigh Hill? This is how I know it from my mother:

154

'It was November 1913. Cold but dry. The family who'd lived there in shape-shifting form for as long as anyone could remember had been put out from both house and job. They scattered into local cottages and, to be true, my mother was glad they were gone. She was hopeful of a new young family to make friends with, and curious as a cat.

'Your grandmother was a young woman in those days. She came up the hill with a bundle on her back and a babe in her arms, walking strongly out front, with her eyes fixed on the house, a house with six windows and a good slate roof. A long way behind her was coming a man driving a donkey and cart and in between, a string of children, all of them dark-haired save one little girl like a fairy with fair curls and white legs, and that was your aunt Josie who grew up and married a man who ran away to Canada. So your grandmother went on up to the door of the house, but then she stopped, and looked back the way she'd come. So the children all pushed past her to run around inside. They shouted and called out: "Mam, there's a grand big fireplace!" and "Mam, there's three grand big rooms upstairs!" One of them stuck her head out the window and called down: "Mam, it stinks up here!" Because you see the house was sound enough but filthy. For a long time your grandmother just stood there, looking back. Then she went down on her knees and kissed the doorstep. She did! She put her lips to the doorstep and the little one at her skirts – Agnes, it would have been – let out this great wail.'

The first thing my grandmother did was to drag everything out of that house and burn it to ashes. Then the walls were limewashed, inside and out. When it was done, Annie's mother saw Mrs Kavanagh smile for the first time, and she covered her face with her hand to hide

155

the fact she'd nothing much left in the way of teeth.

Soon the place which had been a midden for years was clean as a dog's bone. Only there was no privy. Privies were seen as unhygienic. It was a question of habit. Remember, there was no running water until the 1960s and it was usual to do your business in the fields. But Mrs Kavanagh insisted on having a privy in the smaller of the two outhouses, so my grandfather dug a hole in the ground, put a seat over it and set beside it a bucket of lime. He made a little door into the back for it to be cleaned out and that was the tinker's job once a year. Jim corrects his sister. 'Twice a year,' he says, which provokes laughter. Twice a year with his horse and cart the tinker took the soil away – by now a rich compost – to spread on the fields or the school garden. And that way he earned a few shillings. Months later, my father confirms the system was much the same in some of cottages in the Sussex village where he grew up – but for the helpful tinker.

'Let me tell you something about your grandmother,' says Annie. 'At the time we're speaking of – when she was still a young woman – she wouldn't have a priest in the house. She told our mother she'd never have the Stations in her own home and the rest of us willing to kill for the honour! It made Nancy cry her little heart out. But Mrs Kavanagh said if ever she got the house clean enough in the first place, would she be able to *ask the priest to take his shoes off before he stepped inside*? No she would not! And him crossing the yard with his hem gathering up the muck! It had turned her stomach, she said, to see it below at Clashnevin, and the one time that farmhouse was clean enough to welcome a fly was for the priest. Every other day of the year you put your life in God's hands just by going in at door. 'And God,' your grandmother used to say, 'is not averse to death.'

156

This is the first time I've *heard,* as it were, my grandmother's voice. It's not her independence of mind that surprises me but her somewhat mordant wit. And I get the distinct impression it's not just farmyard dirt my grandmother was anxious about but some more abstract contamination from the priest himself.

'And Agnes?' I ask. 'Did she cry too when her mother wouldn't have the priest?'

'With Agnes it would be more difficult to say what she was feeling,' says Annie. 'She may have felt the embarrassment of it, you know. Only she would never have a word said against her mother.' We have sat on into the semi-dark. I've begun to notice what Annie means about the chairs having no comfort in them. Now, perhaps moved by the same feeling, Annie – with a faint groan – gets to her feet, turns on the light, and fetches a bottle to the table. She fills our tumblers with generous slugs of sweet sherry the colour of peat. The heat of the drink in our bellies, the glow of alcohol along our veins is delicious and we drift a while in silent reflection.

The Kavanaghs have arrived. Although I still don't quite see how they've done it, here they are, in the world of my mother's memories. They have the land and its produce, the house and the privy. But the house itself is empty. My grandmother apparently has nothing but her 'notions' – not even her teeth – and, as often as it's been said my family were decent, hard-working folk, no one has actually said they were liked. As if reading my mind, Jim, without looking at me, remarks:

'The Kavanaghs had a reputation for meanness.'

'How so!' I exclaim. I turn to Anne. 'Annie, my mother remembers you going up there to my grandmother with a jug for milk.'

Annie laughs.

157

'And so I did! Your grandmother would offer butter, too, and apples. But you see, Maggie' – there's a hesitation – 'none of that was theirs to give.'

This has to be spelt out to me.

'You explain to her,' Annie says, with a nod to Danny.

'You know,' says Danny, turning to me, 'that your grandfather worked for the Crosses at Clashnevin. Now the house at Knigh, that place was the Crosses' outfarm, so, when the family were turned out...'

And of course, by the time Danny has said this, I've understood. The man whose family had lived on Knigh Hill was James Foley, the young herd my grandfather had displaced at Clashnevin. My grandfather – 'a powerful worker' and 'honest as the day' – had taken both the man's position and his home. The house Kate was so happy and proud to be in went with the job. Of course nothing at Knigh had belonged to my grandparents. The house was never theirs, nor even the lease, for any of their sons to inherit. No doubt the Kavanaghs had a right to most of the produce from the garden they created, and they would have owned the pig. But the cows, the sheep, the carrots and the hay from the fields, all of these belonged to the Crosses, never mind the fields are still remembered as 'Kavanagh's fields'. The irony of the Kavanaghs' 'notions' is that, whereas the Graces and the O'Briens had lived here as self-employed craftsmen for generations, my grandfather, an outsider, came from a long line of labourers. And the ousting of the family who had lived there before them – including James's sister-in-law, Margaret, the almost legendary 'Mud' Foley – not only underlined the insecurity of their position, but had perhaps sown seeds of enmity between the the Kavanaghs and their neighbours.

Sensing my discomfort, Annie lays a hand on my arm.

158

'Your grandfather was a lovely man,' she says. 'We knew we could rely on the Kavanaghs. Daddy's only complaint against them was you could stand a long time at their door before you heard anything worth hearing. And never a bad word between them.'

As well as his work at Knigh, my grandfather travelled the seven miles or so back to Clashnevin to work there, as before. Seven days a week. The Graces at Knigh Cross knew the time of day by the rumble of Kavanagh's pony and cart coming down Blind Lane, turning left towards Loughourna and then fading away towards Rathaleen along the road that crosses the railway line from Nenagh to Dublin, the line that was built in 1862 and was to carry away all but one of John's children. Then, at seven o'clock every evening, the Graces would hear the cart go rattling home again where, as Jim remarks with a grin, 'He had to take his boots off before ever he was allowed in the kitchen. Your grandmother was very particular like that.' He laughs again. 'Poor Mrs Kavanagh!' And here it comes, as automatic, as irresistible as a sneeze: 'She kept that floor so clean you could eat your dinner off it.'

'Such a grand sight!' exclaims Annie. 'With the door stood open on a summer evening you could see the big mirror she had there and in front of it, on shelves, rows and rows of glass jars, bottles and jam jars, all sparkling clean like crystal. Poor Mrs Kavanagh, she had those jars down and washed every week. Every week without fail!'

So there it is: the crystal my mother had remembered so fondly was only jam jars. I ask Annie if my grandmother used them for anything. Flowers, maybe?

'She did not!'

'But my grandmother did *grow* flowers, didn't she?'

In the second it takes Annie to draw breath I've had time to fear the loss of one of my best-loved images.

159

'Dear Lord!' Annie exclaims. 'You could go up there in December and she'd have flowers about the place. Oh yes, she was a great one for her garden. She had it all laid out in beds with stone edging and little paths.'

And in summer, people from miles around went up the lane especially to see and smell the flowers in Kate's garden. It was a picture of paradise. Sometimes my grandmother would come out to the gate and tell them the names. Annie still recalls them: roses, gladioli, fuchsia, wisteria, and lilies. Nothing common. She remembers there were begonias growing in a black pot by the door. Exotic as parrots in the gorse.

And in the pause perhaps we all think of it the way it is now, in a state of desolation, shifting under sheets of black plastic.

'Poor Mrs Kavanagh,' says Annie, on a sigh. 'She was delicate.'

'She was thin,' adds Jim. 'Thin as a heron.'

In my mind's eye, it turns to winter. The steep track from the house is slippery. Icicles drip from the slate roof and my grandmother's cough sounds from the outhouse where she stands long hours, deftly twisting wreaths with the winter foliage. From the kitchen, a lamp glow suggests a warm interior.

'My mother remembered a brass lamp,' I say. 'A lamp on a chain that Kate would lower to do her sewing.'

'And so there was!' says Jim in his thrilling voice. 'The lamp came down to your grandmother's shoulder and it made a pretty tinkling sound when she moved.'

Only now do I learn that it was my Dunne ancestors who, with their newly acquired wealth – which sat on them as awkwardly as lizard-skin shoes – first came into possession of the treasures my mother remembered.

At that time – in the 1860s – Thomas George Stoney,

of Kyle Park, near Borrisokane, was declared bankrupt. The declining gentry endured considerable hardships – most things are relative – and many decamped to Dublin, or back to England. But in Stoney's case, a factor in his financial crisis was certainly his expenditure on famine relief. When Kyle Park went into receivership, my great-great-grandparents, Daniel and Margaret Dunne, were amongst those newly prosperous small farmers who went along to the auction. In a thrill of prescient consumerism they bought several distinguished pieces and a stack of bric-a-brac for their new house in the Curragh.

Which is how it came about that, one day in April 1914, not long after my family had arrived at Knigh, a loaded cart came up this track from Borrisokane. The children ran out to meet it. The old man, Patrick – who'd not spoken to his son since John left his house to marry – had died. His widow, Mary, could do as she pleased, and it was her pleasure to gift her favourite son with those pieces that, in just the same way, had only come to her on the death of her own estranged father. She chose carefully. The house at Knigh was large, it would take some of the bigger items that had crammed her cottage like a tight-packed ship's hold: a bed, a clock, a mirror. A set of yellow plates in the French style. And a brass lamp on a chain. These things must have been beyond even my grandmother's notions.

It's true to say, however, that by this time the circumstances of most people in Ireland had improved. Every woman owned a blouse and a suit, grey or navy probably, though it would only be for a wedding or whatever. Otherwise 'it never got an airing'. But a hat, yes, by this time, when a woman went out she always wore a hat. She had the suit and the hat in place of the shawl. The Kavanagh women, even Kate herself, were amongst the first in Puckaun to take up the new fashion.

161

As we've been talking, my picture of my grandmother has undergone constant revision. For all her neighbours being unable to resist having a sly dig at her, one thing seems certain: she was as formidable as she was 'delicate'. Annie agrees.

'Yes, I'd say your grandmother was classy. She didn't blab on the way I do, but she could pin you down with a word. She spoke quietly and to the point.'

I tell them my mother used to say Kate was hard.

'She used to say, "Daddy was a sweetheart, but mother was hard."' Annie modifies 'hard' to 'strict'.

'You have to remember,' says Danny, 'in those days – and to be sure it was the same in my own time – if a child didn't toe the line it got a clip and no questions asked.'

Well, I remember my own mother giving me the occasional slap, and at least once chasing me round the kitchen with the broom. But I got occasional kisses, too, quick, shy pecks, but kisses nevertheless. Did my mother ever get kisses, I wonder? My suggestion causes some mirth. Kisses? Our mothers weren't so free with their kisses, suggests Danny. Still we were loved, remarks Annie. Some of us.

Annie taps my knee.

'But then Agnes was number eight, wasn't she? There's many a child in a big family like that felt she didn't get a fair shake of her mother.'

I'm travelling to Egypt on a P&O liner with my mother. Just the two of us, sharing the neatest little cabin imaginable with our hairbrushes laid side by side on the tiny dressing table. It's 1951 and we're going to join my father in Fayid. My mother is wearing a lovely green Horrockses sundress with big buttons along the shoulders. I have just won the children's fancy-dress party dressed as a

Hawaiian lovely in a grass skirt with a flower behind my ear. I hadn't wanted to take part. I never did want to go to parties. My first instinct as a child (and as an adult) is always to say 'No'. I have to be dragged towards the balloons and the jellies, the panicky games and the fake adult smiles. But apparently I'm 'lucky to be asked', so go I must. Once there I always enjoy myself – too much – and by the time my mother comes to collect me I'm usually red-faced and showing off, a sight which so disgusts my mother that, before we're out of the gate, I get one of those clips around the ear. Today I've had an especially thrilling time and only avoid a smack because we're in public. I'm feeling extremely pleased with myself when I'm stricken by stomach pains more appropriate to a paid-up member of Hell than to a cocky but otherwise innocent nine-year-old child cruising the Med at the expense of the British Civil Service. I make it, just, to one of the below-decks lavatories before my gut explodes noisily, revoltingly, and above all, humiliatingly. This rush into the engine-throbbing entrails of the ship happens over and over again. My mother becomes irked with the grinding tedium of it, and irritated by my persistence in the face of the impossibility of there actually being anything more in my guts for me to squirt out so unpleasantly and embarrassingly into one of the immaculate white lavatory bowls whilst the wives of other civil servants or army personnel powder their noses at the lilting mirrors. She seems determined to make little of it. What a fuss over a stomach upset! Whatever changed her mind, finally my mother calls the young ship's doctor to see me. He is quietly but unambiguously angry at not having been called earlier. I'm already dangerously dehydrated and for a couple of days I lie in the ship's white infirmary, in a white gown, with a white plastic tube in my arm, sweet smelling and infuriatingly smug, pleased with myself again and much preferring the role of intrepid survivor to that of the Hawaiian lovely. Arriving at Port Said, I am carried down the gangplank to my waiting father who is astonished, having expected it to be my mother suffering from the ravages of seasickness, whom he'd have to coddle. But my mother had left seasickness behind at the Bay of Biscay and, a woman some months short of her fortieth birthday, properly 'abroad' for the first time, has been having the time of her life. She has eaten at the captain's table and danced under the stars. We are to spend our first night in Egypt staying with my father's superior officer, Colonel Postlethwaite, and his wife in their rather grand house in the married quarters at Fayid where the palms hang with dates like amber ticks. When the front door opens, my father's first words are to ask for the lavatory for his daughter. My mother must have been mortified.

5

As a child, my mother never heard the word 'famine'. It was never talked of in her family, she never read of it in books, and at school – Annie O'Brien confirms this – all they were told, with little explanation, was that there'd been 'a massive drop in the population in the mid-nineteenth century'. The reason the children didn't know their own history was that, from the foundation of the National Schools in 1831, the school curriculum had been decided in Westminster, England. Every care had been taken with the syllabus to omit anything that might arouse a spirit of nationalism. No Irish language or Irish traditions were taught. In the music manual there wasn't a single Irish air. Some of the founding myths of Ireland were allowed in almost fairy-tale form in *A Child's History of Ireland*, but it was as if the teaching of history in English schools were to end with the myths of King Arthur.

What at first sight seems even more surprising is that these National Schools were, as my mother recalled, strictly non-denominational. Even in my mother's time, when the re-established Catholic Church had achieved such all-pervading power in Irish society, inside the National Schools no religious emblems of any sort were displayed, and Catholic children were inculcated with the catechism *at* school but *outside* school hours. Religious education as such was forbidden in schools. In both schools and homes, the Bible was rarely seen. Father O'Haloran (the priest at

Borrisokane) tells of a priest who died in the 1970s who had a considerable library which included prayer books, breviaries and several volumes of religious commentary, but no Bible. Unlike Agnes, Annie O'Brien hated having to learn the catechism; the tedium of it, all those rules that made her feel like she was tied up in string. But she has never lost her faith in prayer and always puts a few pence in Saint Anthony's box. A friend of Annie's asked her recently:

'Did you ever fall out with God?'

'Oh sometimes I do,' said Annie. 'But then I fall in with Him again.'

Prescriptive as the school syllabus was, however, not only was Ireland a long way from Westminster but the majority of schools were a long way from Dublin. Teachers in rural Ireland had, in theory, a degree of autonomy. They could, if they chose, teach subjects outside the official curriculum, and some did. Had Mrs Griffin chosen she might, in an alternative reality, have given the girls a lesson in history they would never forget.

In the cold, ill-lit classroom there hung an ancient map of Ireland like damp blooming on the whitewashed wall. This is where Mrs Griffin might begin by pointing out to them that Ireland is an island, an island which furthermore seems to have turned its back on England and to be reaching out – see here, its limbs and fingers – stretching westward into the Atlantic, towards America. 'Children,' says Mrs Griffin, 'we are not an English people. We are Gaelic. For hundreds of years Ireland was strong but divided. Waves of rebellion washed continuously back and forth over the country. Even the English invaders failed to establish single kingship and the rule of law.' For centuries her motto has been, 'England's difficulty is Ireland's opportunity.' And in every crisis in English history Ireland has seized the moment of weakness to stab her enemy in the back. In any way possible. In 1916, Roger Casement was found guilty of trying to secure German aid in the struggle for Irish independence. He was hanged in Dublin.

The year of this history-lesson-that-never-was is 1917: eighteen months after the Dublin Easter Uprising, and a year before three-quarters of a million British troops – amongst them tens of thousands of Irish men – failed to come home from the killing fields of Europe (close on thirty thousand Irishmen died). The Moran sisters, sitting here covertly blowing on their fingers to keep them warm, have their father away fighting for England. There is a sudden sharp intake of breath as Mrs Griffin lifts her big black bag up on to her desk. Her fingers stroke its clasp. The girls are mesmerised.

'It took the brutal violence of a monster to conquer Ireland.' With her hand on the clasp, Mrs Griffin allows the tension moment to build before she clicks open her bag and from its dark interior she lifts – not the dead baby the girls are expecting – but a head. Just that: a severed head. 'Oliver Cromwell!'

Here was the ogre of Irish history, the man who, in 1649, had arrived at Drogheda, thirty miles north of Dublin, with massacre on his mind. It was the third of September, Cromwell's 'lucky day', as it came to be known. He came with a war purse of £70,000 and a force of twelve thousand Roundheads. When twelve days later he set off to march south to Wexford, he left three thousand Irish dead. As the head swings round the children see a broad, thoughtful face with not quite closed eyes and the warty skin of a toad.

I've come to the library in Nenagh, the reference section. This is a pleasant space, quiet, with little groups of men at one of the low tables reading the newspapers and gossiping. Next door is the Convent of the Sisters of Mercy, once the county gaol. A class of primary school children comes in – white-socked girls with wags of shiny hair swinging down their backs and boys with the names of football clubs on their T-shirts – they flit along the shelves and dip into books where the names of Cromwell and O'Connell are writ large and chapters on the Great Famine are illustrated with brightly coloured pictures of the starving and the dispossessed. When I ask if I can take out membership in the library I'm self-conscious about my voice again, that is to say, my unmistakably English accent. With the sweetest manner imaginable, the librarian says, 'Of course you can,' and when I remark that I'm here for two months she smiles and exclaims, 'Now isn't that grand?' Cromwell was here for nine.

By the summer of 1652 more than half a million Irish had been lost to the sword, pestilence, famine or exile, reducing the population to 500,000. Which is to say, Ireland was conquered, and the way was clear for a massive scheme of land confiscation. What Cromwell had achieved was not unity, but a traumatised submission to English domination. In 1640, it was Catholics who owned 90 per cent of the land of my mother's parish in North Tipperary. Thirty years later, as a result of the Cromwellian clearances, the figure was 16 per cent.

When I joined my parents on holiday in Ireland in 1993, one of the places we visited, along with all the other tourists – many of whom, no doubt, were 'of Irish descent' – was Cashel in South Tipperary. Having admired the rock and the ruin of the abbey we walked through the little town to visit the castle. There, as we went slowly down the treasure-lined Long Gallery, my mother said wistfully, 'We weren't told about this side of things at school, we never learned about the history, or that there were such beautiful things in Ireland.'

When she moved on, my father said quietly to me, 'What she doesn't realise, of course, the sad thing is, all these beautiful things would have belonged to the Anglo-Irish, not to the Catholics.'

In compensation for his loss, John Kennedy of Knigh received 353 Irish acres in County Galway, half the acreage he had owned at Knigh and of dubious value being either rock or bog. 'All that war had ruined, fled or was driven into Connaught.' The west, rocky and inaccessible, facing out over the vast Atlantic – looking, as Mrs Griffin pointed out, to America – 'received wave after wave of refugees and went its own way, taking with it the faith of its ancestors, the Irish language and the love of its country. Having once entered Connaught the Irish Catholics were penned there like sheep, forbidden under pain of death to pass the borders.'

As the bitter curse has it, 'To Hell or Connaught!'

Even those Catholic estates that survived were dismembered. Penal Laws directed that, at the death of a Catholic owner, his land was to be divided amongst all his sons, unless and only if the eldest became a Protestant. This clearly affected not just large estates, but smaller holdings, too. Over generations, Catholic holdings became smaller and smaller until the notorious quarter ground was commonplace and the margin enabling the great mass of the poor to survive became narrower and narrower. As its name suggests, the Great Famine wasn't the first: for example, between 1816 and 1842 there had already been fourteen potato famines.

Loss of land was the first hammer blow.

The second was the nature of the new aristocracy. Protestant, English, and opportunist as ash in the bog, it proved itself to be an alien race, in large part indifferent to and contemptuous of the native Irish (an attitude still sometimes apparent in the upper-class Anglo-Irish and English residents today). In the mid-1830s, the French writer, Gustave de Beaumont, visited Ireland. He formed the opinion that 'a bad aristocracy' was the prime cause of 'the inveterate leprosy of misery' covering Ireland. Was it surprising that, under these circumstances and in a country where the ruling class lacked moral authority, lawlessness and a contempt for the 'official line' should soon establish itself as part of the Irish pattern?

Those men who, at the time of my great-grandfather's arrival in Tipperary, were posting threatening notices on the gates of strong farmers, they weren't a new phenomenon. For close on a hundred years there had existed secret societies whose anger had been fuelled by enclosure of common land and by high tithes. During their nocturnal attacks they murdered or mutilated both people and animals. Victims were as likely to be Catholic as Protestant, as likely the labourer agreeing to work for low wages as the master exploiting him. The essential nature of the associations was twofold: violent and secret. Unsurprisingly, Westminster's school syllabus didn't cover these aspects of the children's history either.

Meanwhile, between 1779 and the 1820s the population of Ireland increased by 172 per cent to eight million, two-thirds of whom were dependent on agriculture. With no industrialization to support it, Ireland's economy was fragile indeed. When the Great Famine hit, it was partly the sheer size of the problem, the numbers involved, that was overwhelming. England's first response may have been a cry of sympathy, but the policy of the British

170

government towards the Famine was laissez-faire and, as the tragedy grew into mind-numbing proportions, there was a tightening of the Treasury purse strings – like the reflex tightening of a sphincter muscle.

The 'massive drop in the population' Annie referred to was this: nationwide, a million died, a million emigrated and half a million were evicted from their homes. For nearly half a century to follow, emigration would remove up to half of each generation. The year my mother was born, 1911, the population of Ireland stood at 4.4 million, reduced from 8.4 million in 1846, the year of her grandmother's birth. Those who died were mostly the poorest of the poor. Those who emigrated were generally from the 'better class'. My great-great-grandfather, Daniel Dunne, who wasn't quite either, stayed and prospered.

'Children!' Mrs Griffin might have continued. 'Your Irish climate is mild but infamously damp. The further west you go the more the terrain is either rock or bog. There are no orchards, no turnip fields in Clare, or Mayo. The bog sustains nothing but cotton grass. There are snipe, but the poor did not own shotguns. Had they done so they might have been as likely to shoot the landlords as the birds. You ask (the children had not breathed a word) why did the poor not eat nettles, hips, grass? They did. Indeed, the nettles, the berries, edible roots and cabbage leaves disappeared from the countryside, and children and old people lay down beside the road to die of diarrhoea. You must remember, children, that the majority of deaths came not from starvation but from hunger-related diseases.'

It did not cross the children's minds to ask why their forebears had not eaten fish. Herring occasionally formed a very small part of the Irish diet, but the western coastline, famous for its beauty, is also notoriously treacherous, both

171

the ocean itself and the rocky landfall. In 1846 there were no railways in the west of Ireland, there was a poor road network, and no means of refrigeration. The pace not just of transportation but of communication was fatally slow. The severe winter of 1846—47 that made relief difficult made fishing impossible. In 1846 the British government declared officially that 'no deaths from starvation must be allowed'. In private it was a different matter.

Another thing the little girls at Puckaun School, my mother amongst them, weren't taught was that at that time in the English press their lost forebears were represented as pigs, or as Cecil Woodham Smith tells us, as 'Neanderthals, the missing link between animal and human. A once stalwart people had been reduced to an anonymous teeming mass, entirely without the means with which to turn away the catastrophe howling towards them. They were abandoned to their doom.'

When Mrs Griffin spits the children out into the damp evening air a new sound, the sound of marching, goes along the village road and into the field behind the school. My mother's last memory of the school in Puckaun is playing in the yard, forming a ring with the other girls as they move backwards and forwards chanting:

We've come to see Janey Joe, Janey Joe, Janey Joe,
We've come to see Janey Joe, how is she now?
Janey Joe's washing, she's washing, she's washing,
Janey Joe's washing all the day long

and so on through all the household tasks until,

Janey Joe's sick, she's sick, she's sick,
Janey Joe's sick all the day long

172

and finally,

Janey Joe's dead, she's dead, she's dead,
Janey Joe is dead all the day long.

But little do the children know – nor indeed does Mrs Griffin herself, though the sound of marching feet may have alerted her to it – that there's more history to come. The birth of the Irish Free State will be preceded by some of the bloodiest chapters in Irish history yet. The first Sinn Fein club in Puckaun has just been founded. So far as the children are concerned, the club is little more than an extension of the pub, a place where their fathers get swallowed up in a dimly lit interior where they talk, talk, talk – only to have the organization suppressed the following year. But in a field at the back of the school a company of the IRA, C Company 1st Battalion, consisting of thirty-one men, carries out illegal drilling on Sundays and this obviously arouses a lot of interest amongst the boys, some of whom, within a couple of years, will be drilling amongst them[1].

Soon the idea of a government force, to be raised in large part from disbanded ex-soldiers, unemployed and brutalised by war, will be conceived in the mind of Lord French, the viceroy of Ireland. This force will come to be known as the Black and Tans.

Mrs Griffin in fact never opened her monstrous black bag. She never taught her children about Cromwell, or the Penal Laws, or the obliteration of the Irish language. Nor did she ever read – as I have her do – from Cecil

---

1. *My grandfather may never have owned a gun, but 'By early 1914... about 250,000 men in Ireland were enrolled in some kind of paramilitary organization' Roy Foster 'Vivid Faces' Allen Lane 2014.*

Woodham-Smith's *The Great Hunger* (not published until 1962). Nevertheless, it was because of all these things the children hadn't been taught that, when my mother finally stood up to recite the verses she had by heart, the poem that fell from her innocent lips was Tennyson's 'The Brook':

> *I come from haunts of coot and hern,*
> *I make a sudden sally,*
> *And sparkle out among the fern*
> *To bicker down a valley.*

An English brook running down an English hillside described by a thoroughly English poet. On that summer day in 1920, this was still typical of the Westminster-decided curriculum in Irish schools. But all that is about to change.

PART FOUR
TEACHERS AND SOLDIERS

1

Maybe being eight years old has something to do with it and watching the road ahead come at you between they grey ears of the dear old donkey instead of having to toil all that way, summer and winter, on foot along the Mass path. But mostly this happiness, leaping and dancing in Agnes's chest like the flames inside her mother's crystal, is because she's at a new school. It's a smaller school, in a different village, and instead of a dragon waiting malevolently at the door, there's a calm, cheerful woman – often as not with a baby on her hip – moving amongst the children in a large airy classroom like a woman contemplating a pleasant scene.

The three little girls take turns at the reins and the donkey, when freed of the traces, spends the day in the blacksmith's yard where on summer afternoons buddleia bushes pulse with butterflies. On cold mornings the children vie for the honour of lighting the fire for Mrs Keane, of having her smile and say thank you. She bestows this honour most often on the coldest, hungriest child, the one who looks as if he'll be asleep before the morning break. Her monitor is a handsome young man of seventeen. At Carney School there's only one classroom, which means the boys are in with the girls, but because the oldest boy is only eleven their boyness is diluted in the large mixed class.

At Carney each of the older children has their own desk

on which every morning the monitor places a clean chalk and clean slate. The smooth slate is a call to perfection which Agnes finds irresistible. There are no more spelling mistakes. No more sums that look as if they were calculated during a fit of convulsions. But perfection takes patience. Agnes works slowly, and in doubt she freezes, unable to make a mark without being certain it's the right one. On their second day at the new school the Kavanagh girls were asked if they had a favourite subject, and which of the shared chores they would prefer. Agnes neither contributed nor asked anything. Mrs Keane noticed this. She noticed the child's clean neat dress and anxious expression, and she didn't comment or reprimand her in any way. Then one day, without being asked, Agnes stands and from her austere mouth there falls, without pause or error, the poem she'd learned by heart at Puckaun but refused to deliver up to Mrs Griffin.

Although my mother never mentioned it, the day she chose to come out with Tennyson's poem was soon after the start of Ireland's War of Independence. This 'little war', as Lloyd George called it, began in 1919 when six IRA men ambushed a party of police at Soloheadbeg, Tipperary. Two of the policemen were shot dead. Soon after, Sinn Fein was suppressed in Tipperary. In open defiance, Nenagh's Sinn Fein Court sat for the first time in the summer of 1920. Rody Cleary, the Kavanaghs' neighbour and a prominent Sinn Fein councillor, served as a judge alongside a young priest named Father Fogarty. Before long these courts and the Dáil Éireann – the elected parliament of Ireland – were declared illegal. Martial law was imposed.

This is the time when the Black and Tans[2] first began to

---

2. *In their bicoloured uniforms, they were named after the black and tan dogs of the famous Tipperary hunt, whose purpose – and pleasure – was to chase foxes from their coverts and rip them to pieces.*

be seen in Puckaun. The irony is that it was to the Black and Tans my mother owed her happier and better education.

The Black and Tans had – still have – a deservedly repulsive reputation. At the height of the Troubles there were seven thousand of them. Most were Englishmen[3]: some were crooks, ex-prisoners, unskilled labourers, men on the run, but most were ex-First World War veterans brutalised by years in the trenches and, as auxiliary RIC, being paid ten shillings a day when they could get nothing at home. They terrified even those they had been recruited to help (the RIC). One of their habits was to drive about the place in open-top lorries firing at random, sometimes into the air, sometimes at poultry, occasionally and sometimes fatally, they fired for no other reason than sport at human beings. These were the men whose sour breath and cruel teasing my mother recalled, the men she feared and hated and whom she'd heard described as 'scum' even by the people who took their money.

In Puckaun, the Black and Tans found themselves perforce rubbing shoulders with Sinn Feinners as much as with the Royal Constabulary, with the Gaelic League as often as with Catholic priests, with ambitious new tenant farmers as much as with covert members of the IRA. My mother recalled that it was Rody Cleary who intervened when the teasing of Kavanagh girls in Kennedys' had gone far enough. Cleary's deadly smile and air of authority, the silver watch chain glinting on his chest, daunted before it provoked. With some easy throwaway remarks he led the girls off homeward, and it was only Nancy who ever looked back over her shoulder, regretting the lost sweets.

---

3. *More recently it's been calculated that 20 per cent were Irish Catholics.*

My grandmother decided to move her girls to the school at Carney.

When the winter term begins, the Kavanagh sisters go via the O'Brien house to pick up Annie and give her a lift in the cart. Every morning she's there at the gate, her mother beside her, her fair skin – which flushes easily – shining with gratitude and the cold-water scrubbing it's been given. Already in awe of the sisters, Annie can only widen her eyes in wonder when they tell her Mary Rose is courting. She stares even harder at the donkey's ears which, familiar as she is with donkeys, tell her everything about his state of mind: cheerful – rarely; irritable – often; and sometimes keenly interested in things no human can pick up on: a sound, a scent in the air, a fleeting glimpse of a she-donkey standing amongst stones in a distant field. Then, almost halfway on their journey, they come upon something unexpected. A tree, a huge old ash, has fallen across the lane and blocks their way. Should they turn back and go home? Or tie the donkey to the tree and continue to school on foot? If they go home Nancy – having wised up on such matters – predicts they'll 'get an eating' for having missed their lessons. And Agnes refuses to desert the donkey. Besides, wouldn't someone take a fancy to him and steal him? 'Someone would take a fancy to the cart more likely,' says Cathleen. 'But,' says Annie, speaking for the first time, 'a cart's no good without a donkey.'

Afterwards, Agnes reluctantly accepts responsibility for a decision which in her memory – even seventy years later – was arrived at by some kind of shared inspiration denied by the others. They turn the donkey's head around and set off for school by a different route, one they recall quite clearly from the days before they detoured to pick up Annie. It's downhill under the trees. Yes, yes, they remember. In a spirit of high adventure they set off, the donkey's feet pattering and a sun-warmed breeze idling over their faces.

When they've turned left at the crossroads and the sun is at their backs again, even Agnes knows they're pointing in the right direction. But the road is unfamiliar and becomes more so. It's straight and treeless and flat. Not a cottage nor a human figure to be seen, only a few cows in the distance and partridge scurrying like mice through the gorse. When this has been going on for much too long Cathleen lets the reins go loose and Annie begins to cry. The donkey slows to a halt and puts his grey muzzle down to the grass that forms a soft spine down the centre of the road.

A faint sound – a sort of thin whine – takes the girls' attention. They twist on the seat of the cart to look back. On the horizon there appear, as if rising out of the bog itself, three people on foot, one behind the other. Agnes remembers stories of 'the hungry grass' that swallows anyone who dares set foot on it. Within a few moments the children can see the figures are a man and two women. Moments after that they can see it's an old woman in the company of a middle-aged couple. All are dressed in black, or an approximation of black, dark brown in the case of the man's coat. And they're wearing new hats which, to Agnes's mind, give them an untrustworthy look. The man raises an arm as if to detain them, but the children aren't going anywhere anyway. Nailed to their seat, they watch apprehensively as the strangers leave the faint track they've followed across the bog and step up on to the road.

Only now does the old woman stop complaining. Close up they look quite ordinary, really, and the women lift weathered faces full of quite ordinary curiosity. The girls all find their voices at the same time. They explain that they were on their way to school in Carney when they got lost. Upon which, without waiting for an invitation, the three climb nimbly aboard. There follows much shifting of broad bums and little bums on the seat, a good deal of muted blasphemy, and a liberal sprinkling of blessings on the girls' heads. The adults argue like crows over the best route through the web of lanes but soon they're trawling slowly past familiar fields. When the children drop their passengers on the edge of the village they've still not been told their business. But there's no need. With a nod from the man and a fidget of gloved hands from the women, the strangers join a stream of mourners filing slowly past the priest and into the graveyard: they have come to a funeral.

The Kavanaghs aren't the only ones to arrive late at school. In fact, four of the boys don't turn up at all. When the girls have been at their desks for half an hour a twelve-gun salute from the graveside detonates the quiet air. Mrs Keane's reaction is muted. Unsurprised. Instructing the children to stay seated, she tells them that a young man is being buried today, a young man who 'had dreams of fighting for his country'. That's why there are soldiers, Irish soldiers, by his grave, firing into the air to honour him, to remind the authorities there are more young men like him. One of the boys holds up his hand:

'Was he an IRA man?' the boy asks in a voice squeaky with excitement.

There is a brief silence.

'He was,' says Mrs Keane in a tone that forbids more questions.

Then she claps her hands together to indicate it's work as usual. At the same time she doesn't entirely succeed in disguising her unease which is underlined by the monitor's state of agitation. He keeps going to the door and looking out into the road, his eyes shining vacantly with what's not yet out there for him to see. Eventually, however, he's rewarded by the sight of a group of men with rifles over their shoulders going along the road to Dwan's Bar, followed by four grinning, strutting boys: Mrs Keane's missing pupils. But what makes Agnes start up in a panic is the sight of her brother Tom following along behind. Tom, of course, has no rifle. No black beret. He should be at Clashnevin, working alongside his father on the Crosses' farm. Instead, he's here, and his sixteen-year-old face is lit up with an alien thrill.

Then an argument breaks out amongst a group of male mourners in Dwan's yard. The girls recognise the bellowing voice of their passenger. Fists are raised and oaths exchanged before an older, heavier man gets his hand on the fellow's collar and shakes him like a dog. Mrs Keane closes the schoolroom door.

The priest might have stepped in and put a stop to the altercation but, having blessed the mourners, Father Fogarty didn't choose to go with them to the pub. This wasn't because he disapproved of the politics of the man he'd just buried. Not at all. When Father Fogarty stood in the pulpit he spoke in a soft voice but with open republican fervour. His sermons were disliked by Canon O'Meara, but the Canon accepted that, in a man forty years his junior, 'modern' opinions were only to be expected. The women of his congregation were great admirers of John Fogarty and, having seen his photograph, I suspect this was as much for his looks and gallantry as for his political conviction. Something about this mild-mannered yet authoritative young man, with his gentle features and dark curls, suggested romance, idealism. Danger.

Some months earlier, the IRA had attempted to blow

up the Royal Irish Constabulary barracks in Borrisokane. No lives were lost but bloody mayhem was created and in its aftermath the volunteers, some wounded, scattered away into the surrounding countryside. One of these, Michael Kennedy, was carried to Puckaun where he was left with Father Fogarty. The priest hid the man in the chapel until the roar of police and army vehicles fell silent. Then, under cover of summer darkness, but still at risk of his own life, Father Fogarty drove the wounded man to his own home in Nenagh, seven miles away. (Michael Kennedy later died of his wounds.) Though the two men passed silently along the lanes, anonymous as a dim stack of shadows, the sound of the trap's wheels, the clip of Father Fogarty's pony – she had a little swing out to the left with her foreleg, creating a distinctive music with her hooves – were well-known sounds and no one, ally or informer, would have been in any doubt as to who it was. That night there were no informers. 'Oh we all liked Father Fogarty,' my mother told me.

It was because of Father Fogarty that Tom – to his mother's disgust – became a regular churchgoer again. It was in Puckaun chapel one evening in November that he noticed a smattering of strangers in the congregation, amongst them two young men, one of whom Tom especially envied for his smart haircut. When the offering plate came around, Agnes had dropped her penny coin and it had rolled into the aisle. The young man with the smart hair had picked it up and handed it back to the little girl who bobbed her thank you. When Mass was over Tom heard talk of another IRA ambush. Earlier that afternoon a British intelligence officer, motorcycling back to his barracks in Nenagh, had been ambushed and killed.

Tom, who'd grown into a nice-looking boy with an easy air about him, had taken to hanging out at Knigh crossroads, even in winter, especially at twilight and after dark. This may have had something to do with a girl, but at this time in his life Tom was no doubt as vulnerable to his heroic impulses as to his sexual ones. On this particular November night, having a great admiration for Rody Cleary, he went down there to the Cross when he shouldn't have done, that is to say, not only at dead of night but with an idea got from somewhere that something was about to happen, something that would endanger Cleary. Pat knew what his brother was up to and thought him a fool. My grandfather, sitting up by the fire, also knew something was afoot.

The Graces' little cottage, already darkened, stood at one corner of the crossroads. The Clearys' whitewashed farmhouse, some yards further on towards Nenagh, was on the other side, facing the graveyard. A light still showed in one of the farmhouse's upper windows. As Tom stood shivering in the November dark a distant sound, starting like a pulse inside his ears, swelled steadily into a dull roar as, accompanied by a double beam of light, it came towards him along the road from Nenagh. Tom shrank back into the dark under the trees.

2

Tucked in out of sight of the road, a pair of bicycles were leaning up against the white wall of the Cleary farmhouse. They belonged to two young men who had cycled out from Nenagh to 'Devotions' at Puckaun, then on here, hoping to sleep the night at Knigh. They were twenty-four-year-old Thomas O'Brien from Nenagh, and his cousin, John O'Brien, aged twenty-one, an American citizen – it was John's smart haircut Tom had noticed in the chapel earlier. They came to the Clearys' because Thomas O'Brien was sweet on a young woman living there named Josie McGrath.

It is also true that both boys were members of the IRA. They had taken the oath of secrecy but had not yet seen action. However, from the usual pattern of events they knew the military could be expected to exact reprisals for the killing of the British intelligence officer in Nenagh, and the O'Briens were among a number of people who had quietly left town for the safety of the countryside. But the safety of the Cleary house was questionable. Rody, himself a known target for the Crown forces, had already slipped away to spend the night elsewhere.

Shortly after midnight, watched by Tom from the shadows, a touring car, a Garford car, and a heavy lorry draw up outside the Clearys' farmhouse. With the metallic drumbeat of hobnails on tarmac, twenty or so men jump down into the road. Inside the house,

Mrs Cleary – surprised to find she'd fallen asleep at all – immediately awakes, fearing the worst; the worst being that these men come looking for her husband are Black and Tans. Going to her bedroom window, at first she can make out only that a band of armed men stands at her door, but she quickly recognises them as men of the regular British Army (they were, in fact, men of the North Hants Regiment).

'We liked the army lads,' Joan remembers her mother-in-law telling her. 'But not the Black and Tans.'

With the army lads tonight was a man in civvies whose identity was disguised by a home-made mask. When the two women – Mrs Cleary and Josie McGrath – went down and opened the door, the young officer's face was expressionless. 'I'm sorry to disturb you,' he said, perfectly at ease. 'We're looking for Mr Rody Cleary.'

He pronounced both names in the English way – 'Roddy' and 'Cleery'. Mrs Cleary told him that her husband was away in Dublin, on business. Rody was in fact sleeping soundly a few fields away at Loughourna. Josie McGrath meanwhile had kept her eyes fixed on the man in civvies. Now she sprang forward and tore the mask off his face. With an exclamation of disgust she recognised him as a local policeman. The man flinched, but he said nothing.

A quick search of the farmhouse uncovered the O'Briens, in bed asleep. The English officer suggested it was strange that they, not part of the Cleary family, should be here on this of all nights, the night one of his colleagues had been brutally murdered on the Nenagh road (open attacks on British soldiers had at that time been authorised by the IRA HQ, and reprisals, authorised or not, were certainly carried out by the Brits). The O'Briens protested their innocence, but admitted they had left Nenagh because they were afraid of trouble. They were ordered to dress.

They were then hustled out of the house. Mrs Cleary was later to say that, yes, the English soldiers had behaved 'most courteously' throughout the raid.

Tom had understood immediately what was going on. What he didn't know was that Rody Cleary wasn't there. When two unknown youngsters, backlit by the hall lamp, tumbled out of the front door, he was for a moment both relieved and confused. Then he recognised them. He watched in impotent horror as the O'Brien cousins – without handcuffs so far as he could tell – were shoved down, side by side, into the well of the lorry. Quickly, silently but for the clip of boots on tarmac, the soldiers dispersed between the three vehicles. Twenty soldiers, two of them with fixed bayonets, accompanied the O'Briens. One of the officers climbed into the cab of the lorry with the driver.

There was a long pause, an incomprehensible yell, and then the silence was shattered by the simultaneous starting up of three powerful engines. A cold stream of light bathed the bare trees. At the crossroads, the touring car hesitated, then, through an opening fan of its own headlights, swung left and headed off down the Ballyartella road towards the lough. The other vehicles followed. Tom stepped out of hiding.

It was an exceptionally dark night, with neither moon nor stars. The headlights of the convoy created an eerie corridor. Above the pounding of his own heartbeat, Tom fancied he could hear voices. There was a diminution in the roar of engines and a curious stretching out of the corridor of light, as if a distance was opening up between the vehicles. There was no doubt now about the voices, raised, staccato, like the barking of dogs. *Was* it dogs? No, the barking turned into all too human screams. Tom's veins ran with ice. The screams were grotesque,

188

screams of terror, of agony. Then came a volley of shots. It seemed to go on forever, but probably only lasted forty-five seconds. And then the lights went out.

Tom turned and ran away up Blind Man's Lane. As he went in through his home gate, Pat lunged at him out of the shadows, whispering, 'Not a word now!' But Tom wrenched free and burst into the house still cursing and panting. His father was still sitting up waiting and Tom poured out some sort of version of the events he'd just been witness to, the sounds of which must surely have been audible up here at home. In the room above, my grandmother raised her head from the pillow, listening. Then she came down, barefoot, her hair in skinny little plaits. She took Tom by the shoulders and turned him round to face her.

'I will not have this filth brought into my house!' she hissed.

No doubt Tom was swearing a blue streak; maybe that's what my grandmother meant by 'filth'. On the other hand, lift your head above the parapet at such times and it's liable to be shot off. The Kavanaghs wanted nothing to do with the business of liberation, of fighting oppression, of standing up for yourself; of falling into the abyss of dirt, terror and death.

My mother was nine years old at the time of this incident which she claimed not to remember. She did, however, remember the row. It was the first time she'd overheard such a bitter argument at home and she was shocked, disbelieving, that Tom would dare upset their mother so.

I was the same age, nine years and seven months, when, in 1951, swept up in the agitation of the Egyptian nationalist movement, my mother and I – along with the other women and children – were evacuated from Fayid

189

(the British Army were at that time stationed in the Suez Canal Zone to protect Britain's financial and strategic interests). In the warm dark at the airport she wept over this unexpected separation from my father, the first time I had ever seen her cry. It rather surprises me that, when we were safely home, my mother gave an interview to the *West Sussex County Times*, but she did:

'In Fayid,' she is quoted as saying, 'the people were lucky, for they saw no signs of trouble or fighting, and although the withdrawal of Egyptian services and supplies made things difficult, they were in a well-protected position. It was only to make room for families evacuated from Ismailia that the Wadeys had to give up their £15-a-month private bungalow to W. D. authorities. However, Margaret and her schoolmates had armed soldiers travelling with them on the school bus –' [actually, an army truck, which was, on occasion, stoned]'— and a guard accompanied the mothers when they went to the NAAFI to shop. Neither were they allowed out after dark.' And difficulties for the housewife mounted. Mrs Wadey told us: 'The first thing that happened was that our "safragi" (their cook and general servant) left us. The local people,' she said, 'were terrified, having been told that if they did not clear out the British would kill them. The dhobi (the laundryman who called three times a week) disappeared, and then all the tailors and shoe-repairers. All the tradesmen piled up their belongings and left; the shopping centre was closed. Fruit, vegetables, eggs, disappeared, and all shopping had to be done at the NAAFI.'

In spite of it all, Mrs Wadey and almost every wife, wanted to stay with her home and husband. The social life had been wonderful, and they had many friends there. She is confident that conditions will settle down sufficiently for her to return soon. In the meantime, she and Margaret

190

(with new hot water bottles bought here to combat the sudden change in climate) are settling down in Horsham and hoping for good news.'

In fact, only a few months later, King Farouk was overthrown and, by '56, all British troops had been withdrawn from Egypt. Until, that is, in November of that same year they returned as part of an Anglo-French assault on Suez, its aim to secure the canal for European interests.

Violence and terror had been an undercurrent in my mother's childhood: she was a child of the Troubles. But I was a child of troubles, too. My personal view of English history wasn't so much gleaned from *Our Island Story* as from the experience of being kicked out of one country after another. In the atlases of my childhood, large parts of the world were coloured pink. But all through my youth, the pink bits were becoming hotspots that in due course changed colour as Britain's dominance was overthrown. It was the death of the Empire, of which Ireland's struggle for independence – all unknown to me – had been a part. Ironically, in Egypt, Cyprus and Malaya my mother and I stood together shoulder to shoulder on the side of Empire. Or did we?

In Cyprus one sweltering afternoon I got caught up in the fringe of a furious crowd being cleared with tear gas. Enosis had recently been banned, in speech and print. In July Britain had withdrawn from Suez. Self-determination for Cyprus was simply 'not on'. The crowd, demonstrating against UN support for the British position, was mostly schoolboys with soft hair like a brush of charcoal on their upper lips, hurling stones and bottles. One I recognised as the son of our dressmaker. The force clearing them was of course the British Army: soldiers in khaki and steel helmets. Some of whom I knew.

I was twelve years old. Alongside my feral life on the streets was another life, one I was equally in love with. In this other life, wearing immaculate white knee socks and a circular green skirt with matching waistcoat, I danced the Gay Gordons with young national service men in the officers' mess. I swam with Brigadier Manfrey off the rocks at Dekehlia and was allowed to do so wearing his cap. My pubescent passion for 'Pretty Pridom', a tall young captain from Surrey, was, happily, unrequited. When I recognised him amongst the soldiers clearing the rioters, my heart was set pounding with unwelcome emotions: fear, outrage and revulsion. I'd seen something I wasn't supposed to see, something primal and very ugly. Emboldened by my companions' fury I hurled a few weak insults of my own. The crowd bumped shoulders, laughed and swore, then, eyes streaming, we turned and raced away. Whose side was I on?

One evening as we were leaving Annie O'Brien's, Danny had asked me a surprising question: 'But were you brought up entirely English?' I was somewhat taken aback. I may have been christened Margaret – as many little girls in that decade were – after the English princess, but as a child I didn't read *Winnie-the-Pooh* or *Swallows and Amazons*, and the beach where I spent my long summers wasn't Bournemouth but Famagusta, and my friends were French, Greek, Cypriot-Greek, Turkish-Cypriot, Armenian-Jewish and just one English girl. I'm not quite sure what I thought *I* was, but my tribal loyalties were confused. I'd already lived in eight different homes in three different countries and was at my sixth school. Half-English, half-Irish, daughter of non-believers, I was happily attending the

French Catholic convent in Larnaca where my five close friends were all of different nationalities. Little wonder that afternoon on a sweltering side street in Larnaca I recoiled instinctively from identifying with the colonialists. It could have been a passing emotion, and certainly it was something I didn't theorise about at the time. But the instinct has never left me. I am not a pacifist, but Egypt, Cyprus and Ireland have made it impossible for me to believe that might is right and that the booted foot – of whatever nationality or persuasion – can go where it likes. The answer to Danny's question – if there was one – is complicated.

In Egypt, Cyprus and, later, in Malaya, my parents and I – along with so many others – were caught up in the massive collapse of empire, a collapse which only peripherally affected the pleasant round of our lives. All I can remember being said on the subject took the form of rumours and jokes. King Farouk of Egypt was not only a libertine, forever 'on the prowl for large blonde women' – as Gore Vidal would have us believe – but his favourite recording was of a dog being run over, this last rumour being much loved by the children. His Beatitude Archbishop Makarios, a shrewdly brilliant man – leader of the Cypriot Greek Church (the most senior of the Greek and Russian Orthodox churches) and, as such, entitled to sign his name in the scarlet ink of Byzantine emperors – and a powerful campaigner for Enosis, was humorously referred to as 'that geezer from Scotland, MacArios, who's causing all the trouble!' And so on. These were the voiced orthodoxies of the day, as prevalent as the political correctness of our own.

Later, when demonstrations, riots, pipe bombs and killings had all made their mark, a state of emergency was declared. Perhaps inevitably, the army used torture to elicit information from suspected terrorists. But by then we had left Cyprus. My parents were in Malaya and I was far away learning to become a lady in an English boarding school.

What did my mother think of all this? I don't know. Whenever reference was made to 'murderous bloody imbeciles' I remember only her silence, that way she had of becoming very still with a faraway look on her face, eyes downcast, or rather, a little to one side, an expression I associated with her reaction to anti-Irish jokes.

A few weeks after the killing of the O'Briens, Father Fogarty's house at Puckaun was raided by – as it was reported in the *Nenagh Guardian* on Christmas Day – 'men unknown', a journalistic euphemism for the Black and Tans. The house was searched and documents were taken away. But Father Fogarty was not arrested, neither then nor on any other occasion. Rody Cleary, however, who'd spent the rest of 1920 on the run, was arrested shortly before Christmas and held in the military barracks at Nenagh for a fortnight before being released, unharmed. His family took his Christmas dinner in to him from Knigh. Two months after that, in February, in a field beside the Ballyartella road, a workman from the wool mill 'stumbled across a body…the face blindfolded and the hands tied with cord behind the back. The victim had been shot at close range, twice in the head and twice in the chest.' He was identified as John Carroll, a thirty-four-year-old policeman who had been visiting his sick father. When he set off to cycle back to Nenagh he was abducted and killed by local members of the IRA.

The results of the inquest into John Carroll's murder were reported in the *Nenagh Guardian*. There was no inquest into the deaths of the O'Briens at Knigh. At the subsequent military inquiry the sentry admitted that he had bayonetted one of the prisoners. When asked why he did so when there were twenty armed men in the lorry, he lamely replied he didn't know. His fellow soldiers had then fired thirty-five rounds of ammunition. The NCO jumped down to stand in the road by the cab of the lorry. He informed both his senior officers that the prisoners had tried to escape and had been shot. One prisoner had apparently struggled with a sentry whilst the other had got his leg over the side of the lorry. For some reason, the young captain did not go to the back of the lorry to inspect the bodies. Medical evidence showed the O'Briens had died from both bullet and bayonet wounds. Only a censored version of this inquiry was published in the local press.

Tom Kavanagh was left to play and replay that night over and over again in his mind. Could he have raised the alarm in time and averted the death of those two young men? If he had tried and failed, what might his own fate have been? In confession and conversation with Father Fogarty he received some comfort. But that comfort was to be short-lived. A glorious summer of 'phoney peace' ended when, in London, Michael Collins signed a treaty which brought peace with England at the price of splitting Ireland in two: the Free State and the six counties of Ulster. The Church, in general and in particular – including Father Fogarty – supported the treaty or, as many saw it, 'chose to go with the winning side'. Tom's sense of betrayal and disgust knew no bounds. 'Aren't they the same as the Garda, just part of the fecking establishment?' he was heard to say. Somehow his views became known to his Anglo-Irish employers, the Crosses, and he was dismissed. This meant further trouble with his mother.

More, Tom was shocked rigid by how close he'd come to causing his father's loss of job and home. His parents placed him under a strict curfew. He was mentioned every evening in the family's prayers until at last the agitation simmered down and Tom, whom everyone loved, was forgiven. Indeed, with that reward peculiar to repentant young sinners, he was loved more than ever.

In the weeks to come, I looked for an opportunity to ask Jim O'Brien what political views – Tom aside – did the Kavanaghs have? Jim slapped his knee.

'Politics?' he guffawed. 'They had none! As we did neither. What difference did it make to the likes of us?

Tom's dismissal turned out to be good luck in disguise – just a few weeks later he found a position working with horses – with whom, like his father, he had a natural affinity – in the employ of a man who kept his opinions about de Valera, the treaty and the Church discreetly to himself. Meanwhile, Ireland erupted into the horrors of the civil war which, in the way of such wars, was to produce more killing, cruelty and bitterness than the war with the enemy that had just ended. My mother, who never spoke of the war with England, never mentioned the civil war either.

It was one day during this turbulent and terrible time that Mick Gavin walked down the lane that was white with dust and, arriving at the Kavanaghs' door, stooped to remove his boots before daring to enter my grandmother's kitchen. Mary Rose's courtship was played out against the backdrop of the Troubles and, writing this, I recognise it as a recurring theme in this story: ordinary life, youthful innocence and happiness, played out against a background of violence.

Still, whatever the three little Kavanagh girls may have known or not known about the civil war, it was the *courtship* they were mystified by. Where had this man come from? Why was he allowed to walk out proudly alone with their sister, arm in arm? And why, above all, why was the man so *old*? Now, all these years later, I have a chance to put the same question: 'Why?'

3

And so, one evening at Annie's, I ask, 'Was Mary Rose's marriage to Gavin an arranged match?'

'Oh it was,' says Annie, immediately. 'That was the standard thing in those days and many of them turned out well enough. "Romance" was an unknown word. Sometimes of course a girl would let a fella catch her a few times too many but that's another story. Most times the men got together over a whiskey and a deal was made.' I try, and fail, to imagine my grandfather doing this. 'Usually the girl had something, she didn't come with her arms swinging. Mary Rose had nothing much, but she was young, and Gavin was old. I saw him once when I went with my brothers to turf and there was a bent old fellow there cutting the peat and someone said "there's the man Mary Rose Kavanagh married."'

'Gavin knew a thing or two about peat,' offers Jim.

But what I want to know is this: if my grandmother was so ambitious for her daughters, how come she accepted such a marriage for Mary Rose, who was perhaps the brightest of her children? With the sense that I'm stepping out on to the ice, I ask, 'So why? Why Mick Gavin?'

'It was Mud Foley,' says Jim.

And the story, as they were told it, is this: late one warm afternoon Kate Buckley sat with her daughters in the sunshine by the open door. Mary Rose was reading to them from the *Messenger of the Sacred Heart*. Perhaps it was the time when she read that the *Messenger*'s intention for the month of April was to 'convert China'. Whatever it was, Mary Rose had a lovely voice, calming as doves, and soon the girls had fallen into a dream. Even the mother paused in her sewing. Below them the trees stood very still. A sense of peace, completion, and fulfilment lapped over them. Innocent as the Garden of Eden. Then Kate, although she'd heard nothing, turned and saw Mud Foley coming up the hill towards the house. In her pocket, she had Mary Rose's future.

Mud Foley's sister had recently died, and straight after, her sister's husband had gone, too. His name was Gavin, and their eldest son, Mick, now a man over fifty, had finally come into his inheritance. It was the day after the old man's wake that Mud came up there to the house on Knigh Hill.

The two women went inside and, leaving the girls sitting outside like slit-eyed cats in the sunshine, closed the door. Mud Foley was all honeyed sweet talk about her nephew. The poor man, now so lonely and he 'a dacent good-looking fella with land enough to raise an army on'. She rattled on for some time in this vein, drinking one good strong cup of tea after another, and only when she seemed on the point of leaving did she reach inside her jacket pocket. My grandmother expected to see that stinking old pipe of hers come out but what emerged was a spoon. It glittered in the old woman's dirt-grained fist. Then, briefly, she allowed Kate to test the weight of the thing in her hand, to feel its silky gravity.

'There's plenty more where that one came from,' said Mud as she slid it back into her pocket. 'Along with the land that bought them.' she added, as if this was a small matter they might have forgotten. She patted her pocket. 'And isn't it a mortal shame the dear man has no wife to shine them for him!'

As we ponder this image, Annie taps my arm.

''Twas a shame,' she says, 'that with six daughters your grandmother had only the one big occasion, because you can't count your uncle Paddy's wedding.'

I'm astonished.

'Uncle Pat married?'

'Oh he did! He married a girl from Nenagh and they had four children. But it's Mary Rose's wedding none of us will ever forget.'

It had taken the best part of a week to clear up after Mary Rose's wedding. Then Mrs Kavanagh took to her bed. The thin curtains were drawn across her window and the children went around on tiptoe.

'Your mother is tired,' said their father.

Agnes sensed there was something else. She waited on her, taking up cups of tea and bowls of bread broken up roughly into warm milk and sugar – a remedy she went on believing in all her life. At the taste of sugar, a faint smile came on to her mother's face. Agnes wondered if she might not be able to settle very carefully on the foot of the bed and talk to her. But she didn't, and they didn't speak. That July was the coldest, wettest July in living memory. Agnes's birthday came and went without being remarked, even by the child herself. In spite of the weather, July is a grand month for weddings and Kate spent day after day out in the damp outhouse, standing on the bare concrete floor, preparing bouquets. Her strong hands were red and roughened from work, but the fingertips were permanently white: 'dead fingers', she called them. In spite of which she worked deftly

200

and decisively, moved as much by the shapes she was making as by the colour and scent of the flowers, all from her own garden, supplemented with greenery from the hedges, touches no one else would have thought of: wild grasses, ferns, and ivy. Even from inside the house the others could hear their mother coughing.

It so happened that in the summer of Mary Rose's wedding, when the girls had been at Carney School for three years, Mrs Keane was mysteriously away for several months. She returned speaking a tongue the children had never heard before. She told them she'd been to summer school in the Gaeltacht, in Donegal, where she saw the sea for the first time. This new language wasn't new at all but ancient, the language of the old kings and poets of Ireland. It was their true language: Gaelic. Gaelic had in fact been virtually extinct in north-west Tipperary since 1815 and many an otherwise qualified teacher spoke not a word of it.

Agnes quickly discovered a natural feeling for this new/ancient tongue. She was drawn to its soft, somewhat monotonous sound, which seemed to her like the sound of wind moving through the trees. She enjoyed the new verse and songs they were taught. Mrs Keane told Mrs Kavanagh she believed Agnes would benefit from going on to the convent in Nenagh. Nothing was said to the girl herself but Agnes, who hung on her teacher's every look, picked up on the idea that she was intended for the convent and this had its effect. She had no very realistic picture of the convent, but the word conjured an idea of privilege and refinement.

Watching Agnes attack her homework, her mother could see she was exhausting herself, her legs in knots and lips moving as she went over and over the vocabulary she'd been set to learn. Agnes was the only one of the children who had this fretful will that pushed her to over-reach herself, wanting the impossible: perfection. Kate recognised herself in this and a new idea of her daughter's possibilities began to form in her mind. Catching her mother's look, Agnes was gratified. It encouraged her to work even harder.

For many young teachers and pupils this was a time of hope and inspiration, a time of national pride and of romance. The children were told their future was not as second-class British citizens: Ireland was Irish now, the country belonged to them and they should be proud to be part of the rebirth of their motherland.

On May 24th, 1923 the civil war came to an official end. In the new Ireland, attendance at school, and with it literacy, increased dramatically. Outside the Gaeltacht, however, and in spite of the best efforts of the Gaelic League, Irish did not become the people's first language. Few of the children would find Gaelic of any practical use whatever. Indeed, most of them, even those who, like my mother, felt a natural empathy for it and enjoyed reading the old myths and poetry, never spoke it again, anywhere. Gaelic became a language of self-conscious nationalism, used in the Dáil and engraved in public places – a curious echo of the use of Latin in the Catholic services.

One of those places where the Irish language was used was on the stone memorial at Knigh Cross. I had noticed the inscription that moonlit night after leaving Joan Cleary's farmhouse, but had not thought to ask anyone its meaning. It's worth remarking now that my mother, as a Gaelic speaker, would have been in no doubt about who was remembered there and why. Naturally enough, the story of the O'Brien cousins made me especially conscious of being my mother's English daughter.

One day in November 1925 there was great excitement at Knigh Cross.

There was a crowd milling around down there and Annie, with the three youngest Kavanagh girls kicking their heels after Mass, got caught up in it. Some kind of ceremony was going on. Someone hushed the children: didn't they know a memorial to the O'Brien boys was about to be unveiled? There were musicians playing brass instruments and a lot of people hanging out on the fringes: almost without exception men, but young and old, local and people from elsewhere, and the excitement – if that's what it was – was kept just under wraps by a very different mood at the centre of the crowd: a mood of intense sadness and solemnity. But it was the band the girls were interested in, a brass band making a sound such as they'd never heard before. Rude, raucous, comic and melancholy, it delighted and agonised them. In spite of the severe looks they got, they couldn't stop themselves laughing and clapping their hands to their mouths. The novelty of it was heady stuff. The girls went running excitedly up the lane to home, wondering why the others hadn't come down because surely to God the band must have woken the dead. But it was probably what happened next and not the ceremony at the Cross that forever set that afternoon in the girls' memory.

Running into the house, they found Mary Rose, sitting with their mother, holding her pale, almost transparent hands out to the fire. Kate got up sharply and shooed the girls away, but Mary Rose, who kept up a steady whine of complaint, didn't even seem to notice. At least, she didn't turn to look at them. Then the door closed the girls out. This had never happened before. Having raced up the hill in a frenzy of excitement, it took some time for them to cool down and accept that their own story was dead in the water. They sank down on their haunches outside, their backs against the wall. Inside, the almost inaudible voice of Mary Rose went on and on. The girls were silent a long while before Cathleen said, ''Tis a lovers' quarrel, so.' Something to that effect, and the others might have been reassured, only just then a wail started up inside that made the hairs on the back of their necks start up.

'Let's go back down to the Cross,' said Cathleen, in a different tone

of voice.

But the last pained notes of the band had already sounded, and the crowd could be heard quietly dispersing, just the shuffle of their feet, no voices or laughter, for all the world like cattle going along the lane between bare hedges. On the hillside below them, the girls heard the Slatterys' door slam shut.

By the time they went to bed, the children understood that Mary Rose had run away from her husband and nothing – not even Father O'Meara in an unrecognisably granite mood – would persuade her to go back. After a couple of hours of low-keyed bullying, Mary Rose had slammed out of the house shouting, 'I wish to God I knew as little about marriage as he does!' Agnes wished the same, because once Mary Rose couldn't hide her face any more they all noticed something wrong with it. The rest of her was skin and bone, but her face was fatter, swollen-looking. Caked with white powder and wearing a martyred expression, she had the look of a ghoulish plaster Virgin.

204

The following morning, with Mrs O'Brien and her daughter, Mud Foley and old Mrs Grace all in place offering what comfort they could, Mick Gavin came marching into the house without taking his boots off and with the fingers of one hand gripping his three-year-old son's shoulder. His son was a pint-sized version of himself topped with a few bruises and a mouse-coloured fringe.

'He's all yours,' said the proud father.

'There's more than the boy is mine!' cried Mary Rose in a thin, high voice.

'Then you can whistle for it,' said Mick. But in the doorway he stopped and added with a grin, 'I'll be generous now. You can have the piano.'

'Now she must cut her coat according to her cloth,' said Mrs Kavanagh, indicating to the children to go away.

After that she said nothing on the subject whatever. But Agnes could hardly fail to draw a lesson from this. The phrase her mother used may have reminded her of her sister stooping anxiously over the kitchen table cutting the creamy white stuff that had been a marriage gift from the Ballyartella Mills. Agnes knew her mother wasn't speaking literally. But of course, when you're a child you can't always read the meaning of things.

Before anyone could shake a leg, Mary Rose had thrown off the role of martyr. It was a role which, frankly, she seemed born for. But within a year, she'd not only regained her health – both physical and mental – she'd left home, left Ireland and gone to England, to Manchester. She became the person I'd known her as all through my childhood: 'Manchester Mary'. She left behind her little son, Sean, to be brought up by her parents. When visitors came, Annie remembers my grandmother pushing him forward for inspection, saying, 'I make sure he's clean.'

205

A chilling remark my mother had, in fact, told me, but which I'd chosen to forget.

*

Hackney, 2005. My daughter and I are sitting in a pub called The Eclipse, in East London. A cold night. We're both tired, she from being the mother of two small children, I because I've been working hard and, as they say, I'm 'not as young as I used to be'. There's a fire in the grate and a cat asleep on a shabby armchair in the corner. Chic old-fashioned. The pub, on the road where my daughter lives, is a small middle-class enclave in an area of extreme, largely black, poverty. A month ago, on the street a hundred yards up from my daughter's front door, there'd been a shooting incident in which an eighteen-month-old child was injured.

We have been talking about 'Manchester Mary'. 'So what happened to little Sean?' my daughter asks. 'At some point he was packed off to England and brought up by his uncle Tom.' 'You mean he didn't go to his mother?' 'No. She was a working woman, of course.' 'Did he never see his mother again?' 'Not so far as I know. An abandoned child.' 'And then?' 'I hear he became a singer on cruise ships. Crooning. "If I were a blackbird." That kind of thing.' 'Gay,' my daughter says immediately. This makes me smile. 'I don't know about that. He seems to have been entirely devoid of character – like opening a book with blank pages. Only that he was mean as sin, like his father. The only time he ever went back to Ireland was to sniff around to see if his father had left him anything.' 'Had he?' 'His father was too mean to leave anyone a regret, let alone a silver spoon.'

Whilst we've been in the pub, the rain has turned to

206

snow. We've been watching it fall against the backdrop of the darkening street, the soft whiteness covering up the grime to give a romantically Dickensian look. As we leave, there's a group of young black boys on the corner laughing and exclaiming, opening their mouths wide to swallow snowflakes that disappear between their dark chocolate and pink lips like sweet confection.

I stand by my car to watch my daughter step inside her door, back home with her partner and her sleeping children safely tucked up under duvets. Then I drive away across the virgin snow.

PART FIVE
THE WORLD

1

At first the sheer size of the convent of the Sisters of Mercy in Nenagh intimidates Agnes. Its high-ceilinged gloom and marbled floors are as cold and clean as her mother's butter pans out in the freezing outhouse. Whilst wearing their convent uniform the girls are not allowed to run, not even when they're outside in the town. They're not allowed to swing their arms or raise their voices and they're expected to curtsey on sight to the Mother Superior, a figure so remote and boney, her white face so like a skull, as to seem scarcely human. Their personal grooming is to be immaculate at all times. Agnes is naturally quiet and clean, a fact which had previously distinguished her from her fellows but here – in this one respect – she's the same as everyone else: a neat, well-mannered girl. She desperately wants to do well. She's happy to be in a school where there are no boys. Still she feels out of place.

For the first time in her life she's without Nancy. True, Cathleen is being put through her paces somewhere in this great mausoleum, but she's in the year above Agnes and pretends not to know her. Nancy has a year still to go at the school in Carney, and without her Agnes feels exposed, like someone missing a layer of skin. Without Nancy she feels dull and misunderstood. Her little gestures of humour miss their mark. I recall my mother telling me that in order to go to the convent no one expected you to be an *'intellectual'*, you just had to show yourself capable of benefiting. But when she pictured the convent offering her privilege and refinement, Agnes had forgotten she'd be surrounded by girls to whom privilege and refinement – or something like it – had been given at birth: daughters of 'strong' farmers, girls who took piano lessons and lay in bed reading novels printed in England. Agnes is shocked by their assertive breasts and vaselined lips. It's the nuns who put the idea of Vaseline into their heads by expressly forbidding it.

To judge by the colour of her brows and eyelashes, Sister Brigit of the Annunciation must be fair, but not a single hair of her head shows from under the white wimple that frames her face and is surmounted by a blue-grey headdress. The headdress is made from the same heavy serge material as the robe that falls in graceful pleats from her waist. From her leather belt hang two sets of keys and a string of rosary beads, black, but with a dark purple tassel which strikes an incongruously dashing note. Sister Brigit's face is a perfect oval. Her skin, what little of it is on show, is parchment-white and of the type that lines early, but that hasn't begun yet. Sister Brigit is nineteen and, though her calling may require her to contemplate death, though she may even – as her prayers command – be preparing herself to be embraced by her Heavenly Bridegroom, like her pupils she still believes she's immortal. Life throbs in her blood and shines in her eyes and no amount of God can stop it. Agnes sometimes speculates on the possibility of the nun's hair being red, like the Irish saint Brigid, that 'ever good woman' whose story Agnes has recently read. There's also a poem about another Brigid, one who's neither a sister nor a saint, but in Agnes's mind the poem is addressed to them both:

Brigid's kiss was sweeter than the whole of the waters of
Lough Erne; or the first wheaten flour, worked with fresh
honey into dough; there are streams of bees' honey on
every part of the mountain, there is brown sugar thrown
on all you take, Brigid, in your hand.

The real Brigit's hands are plump and smooth as a baby's.
Her voice is the most ethereal in a choir made up of
ethereal voices, nuns' bodiless voices, that rise in angelic
purity to Heaven, their eventual destination. When they
step outside the convent the sisters murmur, 'Averte
domine oculos meos,' and the Mother Superior adds, 'Ne
videant vanitatem,' and so they set off cheerfully into the
worldly temptations of Nenagh, which is after all a busy
market town with a splendid courthouse and a population
of four thousand, all of them sinners. Not that the Sisters
of Mercy patronise the shops. Like the others, Sister Brigit
has no personal belongings other than her prayer book,
missal and rosary. Even her name isn't her own but a
name God gave her when she entered the convent.

Sister Brigit has a little group of swooning devotees
amongst the girls, but Agnes isn't one of them. That is to
say, her devotion is secret, even almost from herself. She
doesn't realise that when she's with her, her eyes never
leave the nun's face. The first time Sister Brigit, faintly
enquiring, turns her calm blue on Agnes, the girl takes
several seconds to absorb the disquieting fact that, like a
cat on the wall, *she can be seen too*, that she herself is an
object of scrutiny and appraisal.

Before the end of the first term Agnes has made two
friends. Real, close friends, so you don't mind if a blob
of their spit lands on you by mistake, friends who get the
giggles with you during Mass, friends whose eyebrows
you envy but you feel superior to because there's only two

of them and they've no brothers. Friends whose maths is even worse than yours. Together they swelled with silent, and not always kind, laughter, like dough rising, until they burst. When she and her friends walked through the streets together they went arm in arm. As friends do.

Una and Mary Brophy were born eight months either side of Agnes. The sisters were confident and pretty, brown and stocky as pit ponies. Most afternoons when school was over the three girls went back together to the Brophys' public house on the corner of Pearse and Kickham Street. The only entrance into the Brophys' living quarters was through the shop, through the bar and up the back stairs in a fug of beer and cigarette smoke. When the mother asked for a side-entrance to be made so the girls could come and go without having to push their way through the men doing their drinking, the father had said, and surely to God, woman, wouldn't he be losing half his trade who were only there to get a smile out of his daughters?

Mrs Brophy, an older, stockier version of her daughters but with a satirical cast, was a countrywoman from Kerry, which meant she had a reputation for boldness. As a cook, however, she was unadventurous. She had a shop full of fancy ingredients and her daughters often pointed this out to her, but she resisted their allure. Agnes liked to linger in the dim, paraffin- and boot-polish-scented interior to look along the shelves: tins of apricots, Spam, packets of jelly, macaroni – whatever that was when it was at home – ready-made jam and, even more shocking, cake mix. 'Dear Lord!' my grandmother exclaimed when she was told. 'What kind of woman uses cake mix?' A woman like Mrs Brophy was the answer. But Mrs Brophy was majestically confident in her own skills, both culinary and economic.

'Potatoes with butter!' she would announce triumph-antly banging the dish down on the table. Or, her smiling face wreathed in steam: 'Bread with milk and sugar and who would be arguing with that, God bless it!'

When Ellen Brophy wasn't selling fancy goods in the shop – she rarely pulled a pint, saying, 'Will you be expecting me to stand there all day listening to a load of men gossiping?' – she lay on the sagging sofa upstairs with one cat on her tummy and one under each arm, reading English murder novels and working her way through a bag of liquorice allsorts. When Agnes had become a familiar feature around the place, sometimes, torn between fascin-ation and disapproval, she would perch briefly beside Mrs Brophy, reading over her shoulder whilst pretending not to. It didn't escape Mrs Brophy's notice what an asset Agnes would be in the shop.

Aged fifteen, she has reached nearly her full height of five foot six and a half inches. Her back is straight and her bearing, now that she's on the verge of womanhood, has a proper pride. Already she's not the sort of young woman to be taken lightly. She also usually has her own small supply of Woodbine cigarettes in her pocket. Sometimes the girls go out the back for a shared smoke, sitting on the cold cellar step in a square of winter sunshine the colour of urine, with as much warmth to it as a nun's kiss. They've no sooner perched their bums than the yard-boy appears and sidles over to beg a puff. The girls refuse. The boy – sent into their father's employ from the Brothers' institution for orphans in Limerick when he was thirteen – has deprivation and ill treatment written into every line of his body. The girls show him no compassion and are mildly averse to his company, repelled by his drab hair and blotched skin.

Today, however, his long raw face, the awful potential

of his absurd masculinity, strikes them as the funniest thing they've ever seen. Offended, basking in the attention, the boy folds his skinny limbs and slides down to sit leaning against the wall, picking at his thumbs. Agnes looks over at him, gasps, and breaks up with laughter. The sisters look at her from under their black eyelashes, long shrewd looks that make her laugh even more. It ends with her getting hiccups.

My mother always told me that, as a young woman, she didn't trust men. Her explanation as to why was vague. She had decent brothers, after all, and a particularly loving father. What she said was, 'You heard things.' Adding, 'The Brophys were town girls. They knew more than I did.' It was the Brophys who gave her what are called 'the facts of life'. She was certainly never given them at home. As Annie exclaimed when I raised the subject with her, 'We knew nothing! Nothing!' My grandmother didn't even get around to telling her daughters the facts of menstruation. The only thing Kate ever said on the subject was what she said to all the girls as they hit puberty: 'Mind yourselves now! Don't let the boys touch you or you'll be sorry.' And Agnes, not even to her dearest friends, not even during those scandalous afternoons when the Brophys communicated all and everything, not even then was she able to confess that her own 'monthlies' had already started. A couple of weeks before the afternoon just described, Agnes had spent two days with her knickers stuffed with any old rags she could find before sister Bridie, giving her a pitying look, had said, 'You'll need these,' and threw her a half-empty pack of sanitary towels. Without showing her how to fix them or, in a house full of men, how to dispose of them.

'Tell mother you'll be needing a shilling a month from now on. She'll know what you mean.'

And though Agnes eventually steeled herself to tell Nancy about her periods – (which is all she did for me) – she never disclosed anything else. The other 'facts of life' remained, literally, unspeakable.

There is a painting of Saint Agnes hanging above the long dining table in the convent refectory. Accompanied by her lamb, the saint is standing amongst lilies to symbolise her purity, and holding a palm to indicate her martyrdom. When Agnes first arrived at the convent this painting, with AGNES written in black capital letters across the bottom, was a source of fascination. Agnes was dazed by the sight of her own name at the foot of such a beautiful image. Noticing her interest, Sister Brigit one day gave her the saint's legend to read. It was a much-thumbed little booklet with graphic illustrations in a childish style of both the saint's swooning beauty and her torments. On the frontispiece the reader is told that Saint Agnes, who has a church in Rome still dedicated to her, was murdered in 305 AD. Agnes didn't want to read on but found herself powerless to stop:

'When she was twelve or thirteen, Agnes took the eyes of a Roman prefect who had seen her coming home from school. He begged her to marry him, but she told him she was already engaged to be married – to Christ. Choosing Christ over the son of a Roman prefect had its consequences. The law gave Agnes a choice: either she could be a Vestal Virgin and make sacrifices to Roman gods – to Venus, Mars or Jove pictured about to hurl a thunderbolt – or she could be exposed naked in a brothel. Agnes chose the brothel but was miraculously saved from the "most shameful of fates" by death: she was stabbed in the throat by one of her "disappointed suitors"'.

Stories of the saints were fortunately not the only stories Agnes was introduced to at the convent. The girls

217

were given the 'high' literature of Ireland, too: the poetry, the sagas and the folklore. They were encouraged to read some of this in Gaelic, some in Lady Gregory's English translation. This glimpse of another, higher order of being inspired her, offering a heady freedom from the tyranny of the mundane. Agnes responded with almost excessive delight. The essays she was set for homework consumed more and more of her time. Her favourite amongst the sagas was the story of Fionnuala and her brothers who, in the shape of swans and after many years of exile, return to their home which is now nothing but a green hillock, without a house, without a fire, without a hearthstone. Cycling home towards her own house on a green hillock, Agnes spoke aloud to herself the words of Fionnuala's complaint, words she couldn't imagine she would ever forget:

'It is a wonder to me this place is, and it without a house, without a dwelling place. To see it the way it is now, Ochone! It is bitterness to my heart. Without dogs, without hounds for hunting, without women, without great kings; we never knew it would be like this when our father was in it.'

One still summer evening, having toiled slowly up the hill, Agnes grinds to a halt, then, standing her bike up against the fence she leans watching her brother as he works a young chestnut horse that belongs to his employer's daughter. Tom's grace and strength had been with him even as a little boy, a way of moving as individual as a fingerprint. He works on the animal with a gentle but implacable will and finally the horse acknowledges that the man is his master – or perhaps that, like two dancers, they are equal, engaged in a shared enterprise. When asked what it is he loves so much about working with horses, Tom replies, 'Horses know they're alive, but they don't know they're going to die.'

The air, thick with gold dust from the hayfields, is sweet and heavy. Sweat has made dark patches on Tom's shirt. His rolled-up sleeves expose an inch or two of milky-white skin above his dark forearms. A man made for this place, this moment. But Agnes knows this perception of her brother is deceptive. Tom's not what he seems. The bright hard surface of things, their lovely impenetrability, no longer deceives her. After all, she's a young woman now, and she's not quite what she seems either. More or less subconsciously, a sad note has sounded in the core of her being.

As she wheels her bike on up to the house, Agnes can see the front door stands open, as it always does in fine weather. Not a leaf nor a petal in her mother's garden stirs. 'It is a wonder to me, this place...' Agnes can hear her sisters' voices, but for the moment she doesn't want to go inside. Once inside, it would be difficult to keep the words of the poem in her head. She doesn't want to see her mother who at five o'clock in the afternoon has no choice but to be there, inside, working. And Sean, Mary Rose's little boy, now aged six, will be there in his clean grey suit, kicking his heels against the settle. Agnes doesn't even want to go out the back with Nancy to smoke on the sly and laugh over nothing, over everything. She would like to be solitary, invisible as the wind moving over the green hillside. She would like to be the young fox moving cautiously amongst the cows in the field, on tiptoe, his brush sweeping across the damp grass behind him like a coat-tail held up out of the muck, nose high and showing his white chops.

2

The following summer, the summer of Agnes's sixteenth year, a dance master with the nickname 'Britt' began to walk out from Nenagh to the surrounding villages to give dance lessons. Not traditional stuff, which the people knew well enough for themselves, but the quickstep, the foxtrot and the waltz. There was a craze for dancing. This was partly down to the pictures. A cinema had opened in Nenagh. It showed Buster Keaton films, and Gladys Cooper in *The Bohemian Girl*. The music, the comedy, the close-ups allowing undreamed-of intimacy, kept the audience mesmerised. The world was coming to call and people were losing their innocence, becoming self-conscious, comparing themselves and one another with film stars. The classes took place in Paddy Dwan's barn in Carney, opposite the public house, and Britt – an excellent man on the flute – provided the music himself, helped out sometimes by a man on the accordion. Britt had small brilliant eyes and narrow feet in patent shoes. The timing of his arrival depended somewhat on the weather. In order to earn their dancing pennies, Nancy and Agnes delivered the wreaths their mother made, or took eggs to market at Borrisokane. It might have been as well if Mrs Kavanagh had kept to the habit of doing these chores herself, the only chores that got her out into the world, but no one was to know that at the time.

The two youngest Kavanagh sisters dance with one

another. Agnes has responsibility for Nancy. Nancy isn't just younger, smaller, prettier. She has no common sense – this has been an article of faith in the family ever since the day that Nancy, all of nine months old, tipped herself out of the tyre in the field and rolled into the ditch. But sometimes when the Devil gets into Nancy he gets into Agnes, too. She can feel it coming on. Her skin prickles. Then every nerve in her body goes slack and liquid with the loss of will to resist, like the moment before falling asleep, only she doesn't fall asleep, she doesn't even look the other way, not at all. What she can't resist is watching Nancy get up to mischief. It's not that Nancy is malicious or even wilful – Agnes is the wilful one, 'pig-headed', as their mother calls her. In fact, Nancy is biddable to a fault, trusting, and inclined to bend with the moment, to give in to her lively sense of the ridiculous. To speak when she should be silent. No one can understand where these traits come from. So being responsible for Nancy is no light matter. Still, Agnes would do anything for the sake of dancing. They all would. It's like a biological need, a force inside them demanding satisfaction.

Sometimes when Nancy's dancing she can't keep a straight face – can't keep a straight back either, doubling over and shaking in an agony of laughter. Agnes doesn't laugh. Every ounce of concentration is in her feet. Sometimes, one of the very few boys makes a clumsy offer, but the girls turn him down without even looking. They're not here for the boys, and the boys only ask because Brit's told them to. Besides, they're still wearing their boots and their hands are none too clean. So girls and boys go through their paces separately, just as they did at Puckaun School, and in this way Britt's classes avoid the worst censure of the priest who occasionally drops by to put to memory the

221

names of those who are present and to make the remark – much quoted by Nancy – that 'the Evil One is forever setting his snares for unwary feet'.

On one of these summer nights, Mud Foley takes her pipe out of her mouth and remarks to Britt, 'You've a fine crowd present.'

'I have,' says Britt. 'But when I start collecting it will be small enough.'

Dan is a notorious offender in this respect, slipping away when the time comes to pay. One night Mick Meara sets his dogs on him as he darts off, weaving in and out between the newly arriving adults and away down the lane. Not that the dogs do anything much when they catch up with Dan, only lick his hand, knowing him as they do and having nothing against him personally. Having received a few caresses, they return to their owner bright-eyed and pleased with themselves.

Amongst those just-arrived adults is a young man who always turns up in time to watch the last waltz. He steps inside and ducks his head to light a cigarette. Agnes often has to tell Nancy off for encouraging the boys – 'I DON'T!' – 'You DO so!' – 'What is it I do?' – 'You know!' – so at first, seeing from the corner of her eye how his head turns to follow them, Agnes supposes this pale-faced young man is after her sister. She pulls Nancy protectively closer, bosom to bosom. But from that same corner of her eyes she also manages somehow or other to notice that the young man has black hair and that his eyes are bluer than they ought to be. Something tells her she's the one he's looking at, not Nancy, and her heart does a flip. The young man's name is Jim Cooney. She hears someone call him that. A nice, plain name. He looks a nice, decent fellow, but then, isn't brother Tom a nice 'decent fellow'? Even Dan probably seems that way to

222

someone who doesn't know him. But Agnes doesn't trust men, no matter what they're called.

As the Kavanaghs, the Graces and the Kennedy girls walk home through the twilight, the sound of music fades behind them, and the sisters love this mysterious moment almost as much as any other. Ahead, the track goes in a long white curve around the hillside, with here and there a dark tree standing, still and silent. Once out of sight of the village Agnes takes off her shoes and walks barefoot, enjoying the intimate wet lick of clay between her toes. Sometimes the young people sing. In darkened cottages along the way, older people and children already in bed hear their voices, not the words, just the singing, the girls it would be, coming closer, passing, and then moving away into the summer night. At Knigh Cross they might stop a while, laughing and talking in low voices before parting, the men looking back over their shoulders.

Nowadays, the long white road back to Knigh makes for rough going, almost impassable in places. When it enters the acre or so of ancient woodland that still stands near Carney, it's easier to come off it and take the narrow road that runs past Annie's place.

I'm calling on the O'Briens to ask about Jim Cooney. But when I raise his name my companions look blank. I mention the fact that my mother had spoken as if her parents had reservations about Jim Cooney, not that he wasn't a decent lad, but that he was a humble farmer's son – and as we all know my grandmother had 'notions' – or was it more to do with the black beret my mother remembered him wearing? This, Jim agrees, could have given the Kavanaghs reservations, for the black beret certainly had a political meaning, though Jim is ambiguous as to what that was: Yes, possibly the IRA, but a black beret was just

223

as likely the Blue Shirts, an organization at the opposite end of the political spectrum. No, no, Annie corrects him, the Blue Shirts came later, in the '30s. And that's as far as it goes. Neither Jim nor Annie remember this young man who'd taken my mother's fancy. What they *do* recall is her reputation as a dancer. A grand dancer. Yes, it was well known. And Jim is suddenly bursting to tell me something.

'Will I tell you a story about your mother?' says Jim. 'I had it from the man himself, a man in his sixties when he told me but remembering well a time when he was a lad. Agnes was maybe fifteen or sixteen years old when she was walked home from a dance – a ceili it was, here below at Knigh Cross – by the first boy she ever danced with, a local boy called Mick Flynn, a boy she'd known all her life. It was still only twilight because she would be expected home before dark. They went slowly up there under the trees and Mick put his arm around your mother's waist. She didn't complain and Mick thought he might have been in luck with a kiss if only the road had been long enough. But as they neared the brow of the lane, the door of the Kavanagh house went, and they guessed it was her father coming out to see where his daughter had got to. Mick decided to scarper and hid behind a bush from where he overheard John Kavanagh say to Agnes, "Are you on your own?" "Yes," your mother replied, all innocence. "Did none of those young men have the manners to walk you home?" your grandfather asked indignantly.'

The following summer, if Agnes wears her new high heels – cast-offs of Josie's, actually, but new to Agnes – she's as tall as the dance teacher by all but a whisker. She's begun to stay on for the adult classes whether her parents like it or not. It's whilst dancing the foxtrot with Jim Cooney for the first time that he asks her, is she still at school? No! she counters, does it look like it? The truth is, she's leaving school in July, in a few weeks' time. Sooner than might have been expected. Agnes hasn't done well at the convent. The fact is, when she sits down to write an essay her feelings and ideas get all muddled. What was clear and fresh in her head turns to mush on the page. Her last school report confirmed this. The nuns wrote that her needlework was excellent. They recognised her unusual sensitivity to the Gaelic language and to literature. They praised her as a good worker, but she was not clever. Agnes had never imagined she was. And she's finding it shockingly easy to avoid reading the disappointment on her mother's face.

Since the first evening she followed Britt's steps, since then Agnes has known – and to be honest, half the girls in Paddy Dwan's barn feel the same – that she's a dancer. And now she's part of a dancing couple, their relationship defined – and limited – by a series of moves she has by heart. In my mind's eye I see them, Jim and Agnes, their two black heads, black as coal both of them, and their feet going smoothly and easily, effortlessly in harmony. This is what Agnes lives for: the almost mechanical pacing of their legs, broken every so often by an immaculate slow spin on their toes, the occasional warm fan of his breath on her cheek, the guiding pressure of his hand on her back.

Having left the convent, Agnes keeps herself occupied and earns a few shillings 'helping out' at the Brophys'. Of course helping out in a grocer's shop isn't much, but it's preferable to what Nancy's doing. Agnes certainly thinks so. Nancy, who not only didn't follow Agnes to the convent but left school just before her fourteenth birthday and is employed as housemaid at the Protestant glebe house in Puckaun, working for the Reverend Burroughs whose sons (the boys who'd been at Puckaun School with Agnes and Nancy) are now, like the Kavanagh sisters, almost-but-not-quite grown up. The sisters have their first serious row when Agnes accuses Nancy of thinking too little of herself. Of being lazy and stupid. Ending: 'And don't go out of this house looking like that with your hair all over the place and Josie's old shoes on you!'

Nancy goes. Looking 'like that'. Halfway across the field, following the fox's diagonal path, she halts and scrabbles in her pocket. When she walks on, Agnes, leaning in their bedroom window, sees a little puff of smoke go up like a retort above her sister's head. But it's still Agnes Nancy comes to, never their mother. Nancy is forgetful, trusting. Careless. Agnes is none of these. Which is why, watchful and somewhat intimidating, she has come to take Mrs Brophy's place amongst the dim shelves in the shop. Agnes learns what macaroni is and she's stepping out with Jim Cooney.

No, my grandmother's children are not turning out the way she'd hoped. True, the previous year both Tom and Dan had been away at Ardnacrusha, employed on a scheme for the 'electrification of the Shannon', work which had caused the level of Lough Derg to rise, drowning several small islands, the Corikeens, which Kate Buckley had visited as a child with the Bishop of Killaloe. Tom, a mild-mannered young man, had come home with a loud voice and money in his pocket. He wears two wristwatches, one on each wrist, one telling the time in Tipperary and one – so he says – the time in New York. He walks out with two girls. He has gone back to work with horses, but his mother can see he's not satisfied. The work on the Shannon, the men he met there and the stories he heard, have infected him with restlessness and discontent. Dan, on the other hand, has to be kicked out of bed every morning, seeming unable to believe easy money won't come looking for him.

Pat, of course, is a different case. His place is secure. Not only his mother's blue-eyed boy, he's the eldest son, and is therefore expected – *expects* – in due course to take his father's position as caretaker at Knigh, sharing the house with his parents until their death. Whatever else, Pat is a hard worker. But like Tom, he's taken to staying out at night. At first Kate thinks maybe he's just leaning up against a fence somewhere in the dark, smoking. A couple of times Agnes hears her mother go hallooing in the fields and along the wood's edge. She hears the cows answer. But the public house in Puckaun is only twenty minutes' walk away – though longer on the way back – and the mother, finally, reluctantly, accepts that that's where he goes.

With the failure of Mary Rose's marriage, Mrs Kavanagh pinned her hopes on the next two. Bridie and Josie, however, are not only ambitious and hard-working but desperate to get away from home. Showing no inclination for marriage, they've taken work in Dublin, apprenticed to a seamstress. Dressmaking has a degree of refinement to it, but apprentices are worked every hour God sends and paid a pittance. Both Agnes and Cathleen have had the benefit of a convent education and much good it's done them. Cathleen has turned down an offer as school monitor, complaining that just the very idea of waffling through the days teaching filthy brats to speak Irish is enough to make her throw herself in the lough. As for Agnes, helping out at the Brophys' is all very well but it contributes very little to the family income. Worse, the shop is separated from the bar by only a flimsy curtain.

It wasn't supposed to be this way. In the Free State there was to be work and opportunity for everyone. There is not. Five years into Ireland's celebrated independence and all around them the economy stagnates. Industrialization and growth have been written off by the powers that be, both government and Church. The economic war with Britain – ruinous to Irish exports – that had followed the years of violence now elides seamlessly into the Depression of the '30s. Ireland's one reliable export continues to be her own people. And perhaps a mother expects to lose her sons. But Kate fears that, without knowing it, the education she encouraged her daughters to have has only prepared them the better to leave her. Either that, or they'll have to fall back into a life no better than her own.

On the nights of the dance class, Kate sleeps badly and if the wind is blowing in the right direction then, faintly, she can hear the girls singing as they walk home, reminding Kate of her own youth and inducing in her a sense of relentless repetition. The dances at Carney attract boys like the Kavanaghs – boys like Jim Cooney. Decent enough lads but lads with nothing, reincarnations of what John had been when Kate first met him, an innocent young man with bones too big for his skin and no prospects.

Sometimes, Josie and Bridie come home for the weekend. Before they do so they write, like strangers, and the gravel in front of the house is raked over a hundred times to be worthy of receiving them. The girls arrive with Dublin written all over them, carrying umbrellas, for pity's sake, and with diamanté pins in their shampoo-scented hair, like pictures in a fashion catalogue. Bridie in particular is remembered for appearing one summer afternoon, tall and resplendent in a yellow sheath dress wearing a golden hat the size of a bicycle wheel. When news gets out that all five daughters are at home the Garda come up there in droves. Over seventy years later, Annie still remembered the men 'up there like tomcats after the Kavanagh girls'. Tom is furious beyond reason that his parents would even consider a policeman for a son-in-law but Kate, knowing the realities of life, welcomes them in. The boy Sean likes to sit on the stairs eavesdropping and sometimes a stranger is heard to ask, 'Who's the little fella?'

On moonlit summer nights Agnes walks with Jim far and wide but always out in the open, making great circles around the house, going slowly arm in arm, and from under their feet the fresh scent of crushed earth and grass rises up. They halt, every time at the same spot, where Jim picks a spray of something – dog rose or honeysuckle – and presents it to Agnes. They never go into the wood. When my mother remembered this time, innocence and happiness are inseparable.

At Christmas, Agnes helps the Brophys to pack and hand out the charity boxes they give to their poorer customers. The boxes aren't identical but filled with carefully chosen goods: tea, corned beef and tinned peaches for one, biscuits, cocoa and condensed milk for another. Everyone knows who needs the boxes and no one is insulted by the gift. In fact, it's all very jolly, with a lot of banter, some of it clean and some of it not so clean, between those giving and those receiving. Hardship doesn't appear to dull anyone's wits. The second Christmas, Agnes asks Nancy to join them in the shop, but the girl is busy with her own affairs and says no, all ingenuous surprise that she should even be asked to put herself out. The mother's only comment is that Nancy is at least paid for what she does. Agnes is offended. Her disgust is fuelled by the old feeling that her mother prefers Nancy, favouring her, even when she's blatantly misbehaving – or when she's being selfish and cheap. Like now.

Some kind of gulf – involuntary, silent – has opened up between the sisters.

The Kavanagh children flew the nest in pairs. Tom and Dan were the first to take the boat to England, and when Tom was settled he sent for Cathleen to bring little Sean to live with him. Mrs Kavanagh suspected – correctly – that Josie and Bridie wouldn't be long after. Dublin was bad enough, but England was a place especially associated with low moral standards. How can you keep to the right ways when you're far from home, living amongst people who neither know nor care and a priest who's seen it all before, who sees you as just another example of human frailty and not as a youngster brought up to be clean and decent? If the Kavanagh parents couldn't even imagine the places where their sons and daughters now walked and ate and slept, how could those places know their children? And if you're unknown, you are lost.

This must be why, in the summer of 1930, my grandmother formed the intention of visiting Dublin. It's the first I've heard of it, but Annie's quite certain. Mrs Kavanagh bought a new blouse in Nenagh, and Josie, home for the weekend, gave her a fashionable felt hat decorated with artificial flowers. Annie remembers Mrs Kavanagh talking of little else. But nothing came of it. Somehow it turned out that it was Nancy, not their mother, who went up to join her sisters.

I'm surprised. Nancy? The youngest, and her mother's favourite daughter. Annie says something else that surprises me: around that same time, Agnes stopped dancing. Then, as Annie recalls it, some time later that same year, Agnes went away from Knigh, too.

'It was about that time,' offers Jim, 'the priest started to go up there to Knigh.'

'Why was that?' I ask, recalling Kate's intense dislike of a priest in her house.

'Because Mrs Kavanagh stopped going out,' says Annie. 'When those girls were all gone, Mrs Kavanagh stopped even going to church. So it was the priest went up there to Knigh.'

Well yes, children grow up and fly the nest. But what could have happened, I wonder, that reconciled my grandmother to the priest with his sweat-stained prayer book coming into her own kitchen, kneeling down on her clean floor, bringing with him like dust in the folds of his black robes whatever it was that she was so averse to. I feel a chill run through my grandmother's paradise.

'It was good of him,' Annie is saying. 'But then, wasn't Father O'Meara a walking saint?'

'Will you talk sense!' puts in Jim. 'Father O'Meara didn't walk anywhere.'

'She might have done better to go below to the Graces,' Annie concedes. 'Or come here, why not, to talk over her troubles. Mother would have listened. It was a woman she needed to talk to.'

'Maybe she didn't want to talk?' I suggest. 'It was you, Annie, who said my grandmother didn't blab. You said she spoke "quietly and to the point".'

''Tis true. Excepting Nancy, none of the Kavanaghs were great talkers.'

Then Jim remarks, to no one in particular, 'Mrs Kavanagh did still go out. She used to walk out alone over the hill.' He turns to me: 'She used to go out at twilight to

231

look at the hares, and there was a grand number in them days.' He laughs. 'There was a belief then that there were women who turned themselves into hares.'

A censorious look passes from Annie to her brother. I gather up my things and prepare to leave. I kiss Annie on both cheeks. I shake Jim's hand. I don't want to talk about my family any more. I'm tired. 'Stupid with tiredness,' as my mother used to say. And something more: cold. As if the chill that entered my grandmother's paradise has got into my bones. Annie's door opens and I step out into the starlit dark.

The night is mild. Quietly I cross the hillside hoping that I, too, might see a hare. Hares have a double meaning. Nocturnal creatures whose large, almost human eyes gaze at the moon, they are associated with black magic and shape-changing. But because they are believed to sleep with their eyes open, they also symbolise Christian vigilance.

As I walk I brood on what I've been told. 'None of the Kavanaghs were great talkers.' I think of my mother. When she was old, speech tired her, projecting her voice became a huge effort. But even as a woman with all her strength, a woman who liked to please and entertain, I saw her sometimes flounder under the need to make conversation. Perhaps it was just conversation English-style that inhibited her, making her stiffer than the English themselves, listening, as if anxious she might mistake her cue. By the time I knew her she'd almost completely lost her Irish accent and along with it some of the mischievous, dancing quality that I associate with Irish conversation. Nancy had it in spades. Even in the years when illness was slowly killing her and her voice was gravelly from smoking, Nancy's eyes and her voice still danced, and when the sisters were together, sometimes when we were laughing together as a family, my mother's did, too.

Then there's my aunt Bridie. When Bridie was in the mood, *she talked*. By the time I got to know her – after the other sisters were dead and my mother had revived some kind of relationship with her – my aunt Bridie was old, a big powerful woman with a warning glitter in her eye. With me, her sister's snooty English daughter, she kept her guard. The sound of my voice got up her nose. But my husband could charm her – as she could charm him – and I came to realise that Bridie was a great teller of jokes. Smart, sharp jokes. But for all her talk not *a word about Ireland*. I recall Gerry Adams's description of the Irish as 'gregarious garrulous and tongue-tied' – Annie, for instance, may famously be a talker, yet she's discretion itself. Telling and not telling in the same breath. And Agnes certainly thought her sister was economic with the truth. 'You can't believe a word Bridie says,' she would say, and maybe at some time in their past Bridie's 'economy' had mattered. But all I knew of it seemed harmless enough. Still, I know what my mother meant. Bridie was both watchful and opaque. In a different life, she might well have been a shaman. My mother was made of altogether lighter stuff. And Kate? Jim telling me how my grandmother used to go out to watch the hares, or even – wasn't this his sly suggestion – to *become* one, had sent a shiver of superstitious fear through me.

There was something Annie didn't want me told – and obviously I didn't want to hear, since I'd got up and left. My own guess is that it was illness that prevented my grandmother from visiting her neighbours, an illness she wouldn't have wanted to talk about but which would have benefited from fresh air: TB. She may even have thought she was dying. In fact, she had eleven more years to live, but if she already had death on her mind, might that not explain why she was prepared at last to talk to a priest? To admit him up here into her house, to walk in her garden. On a warm evening, the scent of Kate's flowers must have been intoxicating. I understand their intense significance to my grandmother.

Standing very still on the dark track I fancy I can smell them now. But there are no flowers and – though I've been quiet as a shadow – no hares.

I'm coming to suspect that my mother, in narrating the story of this period in her life, may have been a good deal more troubled and unhappy than she'd been prepared to tell me. That she may have been desperate to get away, to be fully independent. She certainly had ambitions. But for Agnes, aged nineteen, this didn't mean England, or even Dublin – how else to explain the surprising fact that Nancy had gone away without her?

Agnes had, in fact, been keeping an eye on the notice-board in the Ladies' Club in Nenagh for some months. Local jobs were advertised there, services were offered – a thirty-four-year-old 'lady's companion' had been suggesting herself for the best part of a year with no success – and small items named for sale: a Singer sewing machine, and a pair of fawn-coloured high-heeled shoes, size five, 'as new'. Then, in October 1930, a new notice was pinned up. Agnes's attention was taken first by the large, beautiful handwriting in royal blue ink. Then by the address, the names: 'Busherstown' and 'Moneygall'. Busherstown.

Now there was a place my mother had talked about, not when I was a child, but on those Monday evenings we had together during her last years.

3

As she walks up the long curved driveway, Busher's Castle
– enclosed deep in a circle of ancient trees – is gradually
revealed to her in all its faintly eccentric glory. It's not, in
fact, a castle but a large, imposing house set in parkland
and orchards, with turreted towers at each corner. Agnes
doesn't quail. Only when she comes in sight of the huge
drawing-room windows, so clean she can't believe there's
glass in them – so clean that were she a bird she'd stun
herself on them – does her heart start thumping. Inside,
there are no dim corners. The room is swathed in pale
yellow brocade and rose-coloured velvet. It's like a garden.

Then, as Agnes turns to follow a path around to the back
the angle changes, the glass in the window flashes, fills
with swirling reflections of grass and trees and in amongst
the branches she sees a young woman approaching. It's
not that she doesn't recognise herself, but she doesn't quite
identify yet with the image she's created. Her black hair
shines, her navy-blue costume is immaculate, her shoes
are polished like new conkers. Her walk is confident but
decent – there's no swing to her hips – her back is straight,
her white hands are clean as new paper. She's honest,
hard-working and keen to learn. What more could Mrs
Minchin, the lady of the house, want?

The answer is, nothing. The Minchins are Anglo-Irish
gentry, yet Agnes and Mrs Minchin are the perfect match.

Mrs Minchin is a big woman with white hair and one glass eye. Her real eye is brown and her glass eye is blue – 'Who wouldn't have blue eyes if they had a choice?' she says, by way of explanation – which underscores her resemblance to a well-fed Persian cat. She has surprisingly delicate hands, encrusted with rings, like a child playing at being adult. Her voice is unlike anything Agnes has ever heard before, a mellow voice, yet the vowels are clipped between almost lost, lyrical consonants. Agnes, entranced, occasionally misses the meaning but has the sensation of watching the sentences being written out calmly on the sunlit air between them. It's immediately taken for granted that Agnes will take the position that falls vacant on the first Friday before Advent, the position of trainee cook.

The word 'trainee' had caught Agnes's eye as much as the words Moneygall and Busherstown. Seeing it she realised it was what she'd been waiting for. She would be trained. Qualified. As a cook she would 'command a fee' – the phrase Mrs Brophy had used. She would have a room of her own. She would be prepared. 'No experience required but good references essential.' Agnes has her good references ready in her pocket, one from the Mother Superior of the convent, and one from her father's employers, the Crosses, who are known to the Minchins, though not quite of their social circle. But Mrs Minchin hasn't asked to see them. She leads Agnes into the kitchen, a long, high-ceilinged room with an iron range and huge cupboards painted cream. It smells of clean dishcloths and, faintly, of mice. But for a large plain calendar and an amusing advertisement for OXO, the walls are bare. Agnes shows no surprise at any of this. But when she's told she'll have a kitchen maid and a parlourmaid working under her she gives Mrs Minchin a quick look to see if she's having her leg pulled. It seems not. It occurs to Agnes the lady may have mistaken her for someone else, some other applicant for the job. She wonders if she should volunteer the references tightly folded inside her pocket, but decides against it. Mrs Minchin is obviously prepared to believe the evidence of her own eyes and ears rather than the testimony of others.

Agnes learns that, during the week, she will be catering for three – the lady herself, her younger son, Geoffrey, and an elderly uncle – plus five staff (Agnes included); for seven or eight members of the family most weekends; and for the occasional house party that may go up to twenty. The guests will sometimes include three children under five, Mrs Minchin's grandchildren, the children of her daughters. Her elder son, William, a captain in the British Army, is sometimes home from England and likes to bring friends with him – there may sometimes be up to a dozen young gentlemen in the house, hunting and attending balls, and this requires the cook to be on duty into the small hours in order to provide them with breakfast. Dancing is hungry work. Agnes knows this from personal experience, but even her brothers, even Dan, is perfectly capable of cutting himself some bread and cheese when he's walked home from the dance in Carney.

Agnes wonders how she'll get on with the present cook whose job it will presumably be to train her before leaving. She's dumbstruck to learn that it's Mrs Minchin who'll be her teacher. Indeed, the 'present' cook is already gone.

In the following months Mrs Minchin will come into the kitchen as the stable-yard clock strikes ten, every morning except Sunday, when she walks on Geoffrey's arm to the Church of Saint John at Loughan. She will take off her rings – all nine of them – and place them in a little china dish, shaped like a rose, on the windowsill. Then, rolling up her sleeves, she will proceed to teach Agnes the difference between frying and sautéing, roasting and baking.

All the confidence Agnes had when applying for the job evaporates: her hands shake, she drops things, she seems unable to take in her instructions. During the second week she breaks a dish and hides it, a deceit she could most probably have got away with. But, having not slept, she goes to Mrs Minchin and confesses. After that, everything flows naturally and easily. Agnes opens up. She softens, as if regaining her innocence under Mrs Minchin's benign influence.

Mrs Minchin isn't a snob. She's interested to hear what Agnes has learned about cooking at home and at the convent, and Agnes is proud to show off her skill with boxty and colcannon and tripe. Mrs Minchin is familiar with these things but she's always keen to learn new tricks. She doesn't treat her girls as inferior at all – which goes some way to make up for the fact that she doesn't pay them either. That's to say, the job is 'all found', with a small amount of cash – twelve and sixpence in Agnes's case – provided monthly for personal items like clothes and sweets.

Agnes is quick to notice that money isn't wasted, either in the kitchen or on Mrs Minchin's person. Mr Minchin is never mentioned though he's referred to in the long, ambiguous glance Mrs Minchin gives his portrait which hangs on the dining- room wall and would be more than enough to put Agnes off her food. Agnes, of course, does not eat in the dining room. Like Mr Minchin, the previous cook isn't mentioned. But Agnes learns from the housemaid that she suffered a heart attack whilst lifting a muslin-wrapped boiled pudding from the saucepan. She fell to the floor clutching the pudding like a dead baby to her breast.

'Did she die of it?' Agnes asks.

'No, she did not!' replies the housemaid. 'But she was a changed woman.'

'How was she changed?' asks Agnes, anxiously.

'Well in the first place, didn't she have a terrible pudding-shaped burn on her breast and her showing it to anyone she thought might like a look? And in the second, she took to cursing something terrible,' says Violet, with a little squawk. 'Pardon me, but morning, noon and night it was "feck this" and "Jeysus that". She had to go. Even the mistress thought so and she loved that woman. By which I mean to say she loved the food she made, as didn't we all. But her cursing was enough to curdle the milk.'

A little flight of steps mounts out of the kitchen into a bed-sitting room which is Agnes's exclusive territory. The rug, the curtains and the bed with its white cotton sheets are all her own. The room's only window looks down into the kitchen itself, but a second door opens on to a landing which links with the servants' quarters and there's a window here overlooking the stable yard. A pleasant smell of hay and horse droppings is wafted in. On a little tower standing directly opposite there's a two-faced clock with only one face working. Every time it strikes the hour a fan of white doves unfurls from the stable roof. When Mrs Minchin first showed Agnes her room she pointed out that she'd be able to lock both doors if she wished. She said this with no particular emphasis, but it served to remind Agnes there were men sleeping in this house who were neither her father nor her brothers.

The back of the house is a labyrinth of dark corridors and damp, pokey little rooms. These are the servants' quarters, and the sculleries and the cloakrooms where generations of Minchin boots and galoshes have been stashed away on wooden racks, and riding crops and waterproofs are hung on rusty hooks on the whitewashed walls. In winter, the whole house – except for those areas immediately around the big fireplaces – is damp. The mirrors and glassed paintings on the walls fog over, and ferns of ice grow across the inside of the windows. In spring, all the carpets are taken out and laid face down on the lawn to have the chalky mould brushed from their undersides. In the servants' quarters, the bare stone floors are ice-cold and, even at noon, waist-deep in shadow. This is because the windows in these rooms are set halfway up the walls and when Agnes asks why, she's told 'So the gentry won't be disturbed by the sight of us working our bollocks off.'

Violet tut-tuts. 'It's so you won't gawp at the gentry going about their business,' she says.

Seamus, the butler laughs. 'Business! Is that what you're calling it? Keep your eyes peeled, Aggie, and you'll learn a thing or two.'

Agnes is a surprise to the staff at Busherstown. They are struck by her seriousness and self-possession. Their first instinct is to tease, their second to be circumspect, and in the pause they discover she has both a temper and a sense of humour. Or, if not a sense of humour, exactly, a sense of fun. If one of the men tries to get away with a coarse remark she turns very chilly. No, she has to be the one to see something rude implied in an innocent look or gesture. Seamus is quick to manipulate this little conceit in her. It tickles him to set the bait – it might be an arrangement of chicken giblets on the board, or the stage-managed sounds made as he pulls his wet galoshes off at the door – then to watch the secret, knowing grin that makes her bunch her mouth up to one side until the laughter is squeezed up into her eyes and Seamus, with a quick wink at the others, gets the chance to say, oh, very surprised and indignant, 'What's the big joke, Aggie?'

Not that Agnes spends much time with the others. She might join them for a cup of tea in the staff sitting room if she feels like it, only she rarely does. She prefers her own little kingdom of kitchen, pantry and bedroom. The pantry is cold and the bedroom dark, but the kitchen has large windows which face west so it's always bright and warm – too warm, at times. She's no sooner arrived than she sets about reforming her predecessor's slack habits: outdoor boots off before anyone steps into the scullery, every utensil used for milk or butter to be scalded before and after use, hands to be scrubbed before handling any of the food, raw or cooked. She's her mother's daughter, with new scope for her perfectionism. She prepares the work surfaces in her kitchen as if getting ready for surgery, and scrubs them down afterwards in the same spirit.

All this naturally affords the rest of the staff much amusement, especially if something goes wrong and she loses her temper. If mayonnaise or soufflé is on the menu, Violet learns not to go near for fear of a tongue-lashing. But as far as the others are concerned, it's pure comedy. And even Agnes isn't all sound and fury. The new cook – she's quickly given this title and sometimes, ironically, 'Madam' – is also known for her habit in quieter moments of sitting on the step at the open door with her feet planted square, her skirt dropped between her knees and arms akimbo, cooling off. Beside the door there's a rosemary bush planted on a box of sand. Agnes takes the leaves and rolls them between her fingers, dreaming and sniffing the lovely, unfamiliar scent.

This is what fills her few moments of relaxation. In these vaguer, looser moods her eyes cloud over and her inner world fills with majestic, slow-moving forms and

241

shadows, and great shimmering plains of light towards which she is moving without ever quite arriving, but with her own self, suffused in warmth, somehow being the centre and the meaning of it all. Sometimes she lifts her hand up to the sun and sees the bones outlined in rose-coloured blood. Her abiding memory of this place will be the scent of rosemary and the light. It will be recalled to her one spring day sitting on a hillside in Cyprus above the Mediterranean. She'll make the same gesture, crushing wild rosemary between her fingers and sniffing the scent.

In a lobby between the dining room and the pantry is a mahogany dresser. Here, in two wide, shallow drawers, the Minchin silver is kept. It's laid with all reverence inside protective layers of green felt. Silver. The only person allowed to touch it is Seamus. It's no part of Agnes's job to lay the table but there's nothing to prevent her watching the thrice-daily ritual of laying the table and the twice-daily ritual of laying the tea trays. Seamus has been performing these routines for the past thirty-five years. His dark, blotched hands with prominent veins and long, sensitive fingers seem to act blind, like feelers.

In the dining room where the windows go from floor to ceiling Agnes hovers at Seamus's elbow, discreet enough for him to forget she's there watching his every move as he takes the knives, forks and spoons out of the felt, eyeing each piece as it flashes light before being laid meekly in place. Seamus lays the table in total silence. There's no clashing of knives, no tinkle of spoons. Silence and a single flash of light, like a man preparing for a duel. Agnes notices everything – the tiny bone-handled knives for bread and butter, and soup spoons as big as ladles – she picks up on everything: watching, listening, learning. Sometimes she doesn't even know she's doing it.

It's not just the preparation of food, the laying of the

242

table, but Mrs Minchin's person: her lace cuffs, her custom of making herself presentable for tea and changing for dinner, her manner with the servants, her quiet voice, her quiet footsteps and gentle gestures, her scent, fresh and delicate always, as is her breath and her skin, even when, heads touching, she and Agnes lean close in the creation of a sauce or a pudding. And Agnes knows, because Violet has told her, that even Mrs Minchin's underwear – shabby though it may be – is ironed, including the straps of her camisole and the silk gusset of her knickers. This information gets stored away in Agnes's mind along with the correct way to wear jewellery: if the clasp of your pearls is diamond then it's permissible to wear it turned round to the front of your throat, and: never wear gold and silver together. More than anything else, however, it's Mrs Minchin's way of speaking that fascinates Agnes: soft as dewfall, with the authority of iron.

Mrs Minchin's younger son, Geoffrey, is what the staff call 'a bit queer'. It's one of their great entertainments to watch him wander through the garden with his hair smarmed down, chewing on the corner of a lavender-scented handkerchief, followed by his mother's black pug, Oscar. As he walks Geoffrey talks to himself, or to the dog, and it does no good to remind Seamus and Violet that Saint Francis talked to the birds. Oscar is not a bird. The dog takes a fancy to Agnes, though God knows why since she can't bear him snorting and wheezing as he waddles after her down into the orchard. There he's content and noses peacefully around amongst the scratching chicken whilst Agnes picks over the windfalls. The gardener says of Oscar, 'That dog hasn't even the manners to cover his arse.'

This same gardener, middle-aged and boney, with the restless eyes and body of a much younger man, describes his employer and Agnes as 'book cooks', squeezing so much contempt into those two short words Agnes can't believe Mrs Minchin allows it. But apparently it amuses her.

'It would do you no harm, Michael,' she says, 'to have your nose in a book once in a while instead of in the muck-heap.'

This remark has a double meaning because Michael is a famous gossip. Every morning Michael comes to the back door with a basket of vegetables for the table.

'What the heck is that?' Agnes asks when presented with a bunch of fat, anaemic-looking stems.

'Look it up in one of your books!' the man, retorts, giving her a furtive once-over as he steps away, adding, with a snort, 'It'll make your piss smell like poison.'

Agnes takes down a grease-splattered Mrs Beeton from the shelf and hefts it over to the kitchen table. She leafs through the illustrations until she finds it: asparagus, for which there is no better recipe than 'boiled and dressed with butter'.

The village of Moneygall is an odd, glowering sort of place with one straight-as-a-die, windy main street and a grim atmosphere. There's hardly ever anyone about. Years later, Agnes was to liken it to those one-horse places in Westerns where everybody's hiding behind shutters before the outlaws hit town. On the rare occasions their paths cross Agnes doesn't go unnoticed by the young men of Moneygall but, not only are they slow on the draw, they put her down as unapproachable. They're right.

Twice a week Seamus puts on his chauffeur's cap and drives Mrs Minchin and Agnes to Moneygall to the butcher's shop where Agnes is shown the various cuts and taught how to judge a good piece of beef. The butcher offers up slabs of meat for their inspection. Agnes attributes his not quite genial decorum to Mrs Minchin's presence, but it's just as likely her own manner. Partly because she always wears her navy-blue costume for these outings she holds her body fastidiously away from the blood and sawdust on the counter, jutting her face forward. A little crease of concentration appears between her eyebrows. As the butcher pats and prods at the raw red flesh with thick meaty fingers the usual little comedy of suggestiveness and po-faced denial is played out. When they get back into the car, Mrs Minchin pats the back of Agnes's hand and with a smile murmurs, 'Good girl.'

Agnes isn't quite sure why. It makes her feel halfway between one of her employer's daughters and her dog. But Mrs Minchin never asks her anything about herself, not one thing, so maybe she's closer to dog than daughter. In fact, something in this young woman prohibits intimacy. Had Agnes actually been one of her daughters, she would have asked, 'Darling, is something troubling you?' But Agnes isn't her daughter. They speak of other things, and the names of Tom and Nancy and the others, the beauty of her mother's garden and the death of their dear old donkey, all these are sealed up inside Agnes's head like dreams. Sometimes she stays on in town to buy cheap ready-made dresses and Pond's face cream. Then she walks back to Busher's Castle alone.

Mrs Minchin comes into the kitchen one day to turn everything upside down and back to front. The only eye in her head is the brown one and she keeps clapping her hands together to underline her points. The butter is to have more salt in it, there are to be lightly scrambled eggs and grilled bacon (streaky but not smoked) for breakfast – which will now be served any time between seven and ten o'clock – and there are to be no onions or other root vegetables with dinner. Mrs Minchin's elder son, William, is coming home. For an indefinite period. It's always an 'indefinite period' with William who complains that, as a soldier he must submit to rules every minute of his waking life and he's damned if he's going to do the same when he's at home.

'Now just you wait!' says Violet, nudging Agnes in the ribs, and her laugh turns to a gasp.

William is a captain in the British Army, stationed in Gloucestershire where, fortunately – the kind of fortune William takes as his due – a distant cousin is master to an excellent hunt. Hunting forms the basis of all William's friendships and, since he's coming home with three other young gentlemen, the horses must immediately be brought up to par. As Agnes stirs the fruit for the barmbrack she hears the sound of horses' hooves crossing the yard. Some minutes later comes the hollow drumming of their feet across the pasture, fading away as they are ridden up towards the open moorland.

William is blonde, a term Agnes associates with women, but nothing else will do. His hair slicks down over one cheek and his mouth is held tight against his teeth in a childish show of determination. But he's older than Agnes expected – thirty at least – and treats his mother with distant amusement, polite, but without affection. Mrs Minchin does her best to interest William in what's been happening on the demesne. She wants him to take a look at 'the books'. She refers to this in a cheerful tone of voice Agnes recognises as false – as no doubt her son does, too. He groans, but follows her into the library and the door closes after them. It's an open secret amongst the staff that what Mrs Minchin conveys to William during their brief closeting in the library is not good news. Indeed, as the 'hungry thirties' progress, the news goes from bad to worse.

246

Agnes had once overheard a brief exchange between Mrs Minchin and her younger daughter, the one living in England:

'Wouldn't it be better to have British staff?' the young woman had asked. 'They're vastly superior and you've none of that Catholic nonsense to deal with.'

'No one could be better than Agnes,' Mrs Minchin replied. 'Besides, all that is in the past.' Adding in a very bitter tone, 'Isn't it the British government we're at war with now?'

When Agnes, somewhat alarmed, asked Seamus what the heck this meant, Seamus replied, 'Sure, the Brits can't even look after their own. But then, aren't these poor critters the black sheep of the family due to their Irish half being English and their English half being Irish?'

Sometimes William falls into an irritable-looking dream, standing with one hand cupping his elbow and the other loosely curled around a cigarette that has an unfamiliar, sweet scent. The scent lingers in the hall and dining room. Agnes finds one of the cigarette's coloured paper and gold tips ground out on the path to the kitchen garden. She observes the young men as she goes about her chores and they, of course, observe her. William is heard to remark that she's a huge improvement on his mother's previous cook – a remark he makes before having eaten any of her food. But only one of the young men takes Agnes's eye, not because he's good-looking so much as because he's the least arrogant of his companions, his voice is the quietest, and when his eyes rest on Agnes they do so with interest but no obvious sense of superiority. She learns he's an Englishman, on his first visit to Ireland. So! she thinks, they're not all like the soldiers in Puckaun. The men with sour breath, men she'd heard called 'the scum of the earth'.

There have to be oysters, apparently, oysters from Galway. Agnes is incredulous that anyone can eat the things. And cold beef. And trifle. Trifle with raspberry jam – no other will do. The fact is, there's to be a ball, and Mrs Minchin is determined to make it the occasion of the decade. If the thirties is a time of anxiety and deprivation, her party will be remembered as a triumph over difficult circumstances. Everything and everyone is pulled into the gravitational field of her passion. Every lily, every rose, every branch of lilac in the garden is used to decorate the house: the ballroom, the dining room, the stairs, and the blue bedroom, which is to be put aside for the young women to use for their coats and to rearrange their hair. Outside, Chinese lanterns are hung in the trees and cushions placed on the stone benches. To Agnes, it's fairyland. Far from feeling nervous about her own essential role in the proceedings, not a bit of it. She is protected by magic. Busherstown is under a spell. As twilight falls, the musicians arrive to stand in the glass porch that adjoins the ballroom to play the traditional reels and dances, many of which Agnes knows.

In this lyrical setting, the behaviour of the young people is almost comically stiff. In an hour or so it thaws to positively liquid. Halfway through dinner the place erupts into a wet-napkin battle, set off by William hurling a champagne-sodden napkin at his favourite girl. In the garden, amongst the palely flowering hydrangeas, couples embrace, invisible in the darkness but for the men's white shirtfronts – and, in one case, a soft white thigh and a man's white buttocks. The young man's companions – loudly condemning him for having forgot himself – rush at him and beat him across the backside with knotted napkins. The young women are as bad as the men. In the early hours they're bundled away by their parents or chauffeurs, drunk and bedraggled.

The pungent scent of exotic cigarettes drifts into the kitchen and seeps in under Agnes's locked door to where she lies sleepless and rigid with disapproval. Footsteps softly approach her room, softly the door handle turns, but no one speaks. Soon comes the sound of footsteps stealing away again with a thud and a muttered curse as the man misses the last step down into the kitchen.

William stays on just long enough to play at least two of his young women guests off against one another – inducing mild hysterics in their mothers. One day in the lull after lunch, the young Englishman with the quiet voice follows Agnes into the orchard. In his hand he has a box of those foreign cigarettes which he offers, opening the lid and saying, 'Would you care for a cigarette?'

'Not one of those, thank you,' she says.

She spoke quickly, softly, but the implication of what she said must have been clear because after a moment, he nods politely and goes away. Then a few days later he and the other young gentlemen leave. The staff have seen it all before. Agnes understands that her first impression of Busherstown – that in this house there were no shadows – was of course wrong. There's not only the long-dead husband and the 'queer' younger son, but William is a womaniser. Not just that. Her brother Tom is, maybe, a 'womaniser', but William is heartless. As perhaps his father was, too? This understanding now lives side by side with the comfort Agnes herself takes from Busherstown and its owner.

Shortly after William's departure, Mrs Minchin goes away as well. It's her custom to be away for a few days after William's visits. Each time she thinks she won't, but without him the house is intolerable. She becomes uncharacteristically short-tempered. Even Agnes gets the sharp side of her tongue for overcooking the beef. Vexed with herself, Mrs Minchin has Violet pack up in a hurry and dashes off in the motor to the railway station at Thurles, vanishing abruptly from the demesne in a cloud of dust and irritability, both of which take some time to settle. On these occasions she always, and with every sign of distaste, goes to stay with her sister in Dublin. Where Oscar is very much *not* welcome.

When his mistress is away Oscar cries, real tears of grief, like a human. The gardener takes the creature by his black jowls and looking into his face says solemnly, 'She's gone away, your mistress has, and she's not coming back.' Oscar listens with his head on one side while fat, slow tears spill out of his black, wet-plum eyes and roll down his cheeks. He refuses food and by the second or third day his digestion is upset. He sits by the French windows sighing and farting, looking for his mistress, refusing to walk out even with Geoffrey, who has to tuck him under his arm and carry him into the orchard to do his business. The staff are beside themselves with laughter at the sight of Oscar squatting in the grass, his watery eyes turned up to his master who leans over him murmuring encouragement in vain until finally his patience runs out and, with a flap of his handkerchief, he walks away back to the house. In an uncharacteristic burst of alacrity, Oscar bombs after him. But too late. The French windows are closed on his sad little monkey-face.

Mrs Minchin comes home with biscuits and chocolate for Oscar, and a new cookbook for herself and Agnes. Together they experiment with poached turkey served with celery sauce and duck with gooseberries. But Agnes knows her employer's mind is elsewhere. Her own mother could at least count on Patrick, her first and favourite son, to stay and take care of the place and his parents. To keep going what they'd started. But William isn't a man to count on. Agnes's abiding image will always be that of her employer sitting in her chair in the drawing room turned towards the long south-facing windows, bathed in light like a TB patient. Yes, like a convalescent taking the sun for her medicine, her book face-down on her lap and Oscar asleep at her feet, waiting.

Agnes is taken ill with excruciating stomach pains. Thinking it's just especially bad period cramps, she prepares the evening meal as usual – duck, as it happens, with all the trimmings, followed by jelly with whipped cream as a treat for the elderly uncle – then she takes to her bed with a hot-water bottle. She suffers stoically through a sleepless night, enduring the extra discomfort of coughing in her smoke-filled room. But in the morning she's unable to get out of bed. Violet runs to Mrs Minchin, and Mrs Minchin comes in to see her. She sits on the bed patting Agnes's hand and murmuring, 'Good girl, good girl. Now don't fret, my dear. We'll look after you.'

The Minchin family doctor is sent for.

Realising, presumably, that it's not a family member he's been summoned to see, Doctor Hough takes his time arriving. Agnes is awed to hear Mrs Minchin reprimanding him in a low voice outside her door. As the man unceremoniously draws back the bedclothes, Agnes closes her eyes. It occurs to her that he may have suspected she was 'in trouble'. But within seconds it appears that her case is urgent. The doctor's diagnosis is appendicitis with the complication of severe peritonitis. Agnes is wrapped in blankets and laid on the back seat of Doctor Hough's car to be taken immediately to the hospital in Nenagh. Although the pain almost makes her pass out she doesn't moan once. Violet begs to be allowed to accompany her, but Mrs Minchin refuses. The interior of the car smells of leather. It's raining. As they drive, the slow windscreen

251

wipers squeak and branches of overhanging trees scribble on the windows. In Nenagh Hospital, a nurse injects Agnes with morphine and the surgeon informs her they don't have the necessary equipment to operate. So, it's into Dublin by ambulance, with a trainee nurse in uniform sitting beside her as they race through the darkening countryside. When the ambulance lurches from side to side, Agnes groans and the nurse taps crossly on the glass, but the driver ignores her signal. Perhaps he's right. Agnes's condition is potentially fatal and by the time they arrive in Dublin she's unconscious.

4

Agnes is there in the Dublin hospital for five weeks – though whether this is in the winter of 1930 or at some other time I'm not certain, as I'm not certain of other things during this period when my mother was nineteen and my aunt Nancy would have been eighteen in the November.

Agnes is in the smaller of two women's wards and, during her weeks here, four women give birth, two die, and one has a visitation from the Holy Virgin which makes her sing, slightly flat, for twenty-four hours without stopping. Or perhaps Agnes in her delirium only imagines it. Throughout the five weeks she's kept sitting up so as to drain the abscess in her abdomen. Until this has been done, and her temperature has returned to normal, the appendix can't be removed. There's a wooden bar across the bed to stop her slipping down. For the first week she's on nothing but water, for the second, nothing but milk and fish. Her first cup of tea is ambrosia. It's three weeks before she swings her legs over the side of the bed and shoves her feet into her slippers. Her shins are sharp as knives where the flesh has wasted away, her feet white as the feet of a corpse.

A nun, scarcely more than a child, offers her a banana and has to show her how to open it. She tells Agnes her father is a sailor. The notes on the foot of Agnes's bed describe her as 'RC'.

'What the heck does that mean?' she asks.

The child-nun laughs.

'Why it's for Roman Catholic, of course!'

Agnes is indignant.

'I'm not Roman,' she tells the nun. 'I'm from Tipperary.'

'My dear, we're all Roman,' says the nun.

One afternoon, Nancy comes to visit her. She looks different. She's wearing a navy coat too big for her and she complains that Dublin is cold and unfriendly. 'Fair city my backside!' says Nancy and Agnes tells her not to make her laugh whatever she does or she'll be in agony.

'Is it splitting your sides you're worried about?' asks Nancy, and that does it, they're off again.

On Matron's radio in the hospital they hear John McCormack singing 'Panis Angelicus' at the Pontifical High Mass in Phoenix Park, Dublin, to an estimated one million people at the beginning of the Eucharistic Congress. The sound of the Pope's voice reduces half the patients and the nurses to tears. The sound of McCormack's voice reduces all of them, even Matron, to tears. So my mother recalled it, though, looking up the date of this congress I see it was, in fact, in the summer of 1932, so perhaps my mother was confusing this occasion with some other Dublin visit?

The nurses have slung a banner out of the hospital windows which reads 'God Bless Christ the King' and the woman in the bed next to Agnes remarks, 'If it rains now, won't He have brought it on Himself.' Nancy visits Agnes every day but this doesn't always cheer Agnes up as much as it might. Sometimes they just sit on the bed, hand in hand, in silence.

At the end of the five weeks, Agnes's aunt and uncle Buckley fetch her to stay with them in the city until she's strong enough to travel home again. Aunt and Uncle Buckley have two boys and two girls and they live in north Dublin in a little brick house in a row of identical brick houses on Grenville Street, respectable but poor, its back turned, literally, on the warren of streets that lie behind it, between the Rotunda Hospital and the docks. Uncle Buckley does something on the railways – a job he'll be lucky enough to keep until the Emergency – and leaves the house every morning wearing a grey uniform and cap which he and Aunt Buckley spend a lot of time getting just so at the mirror in the hall. Under his arm is a lunch box made of green plastic, the first time Agnes has seen the nasty stuff and she can't imagine it will catch on. The bedroom window looks out on to the back of an orphanage – so called, but Agnes understands from her aunt's expression that these children are born out of wedlock rather than orphaned, and in the mornings she sees the babies, like grubs in their wrappings, set out in rows on the porch in all weathers to take the air.

On her first walk out, Agnes accompanies her aunt to the shops. Not to the grocer's or the butcher's, but along O'Connell Street and over the River Liffey to the fancy shops on Grafton Street. Her aunt doesn't mean to buy anything, of course, only to indulge her greatest pleasure: window-shopping. Behind shimmering sheets of glass brilliantly lit treasures are piled high. The reflections of the two women graze amongst jewellery, cosmetics, hats, silver. Aunt Buckley's wonder at these sights never fades, but Agnes tires easily after her operation. As they walk home they go along a crescent of massive old houses with black iron railings and steps up to front doors so huge they seem made for giants. Inside the houses, lamps have been lit but the curtains aren't yet drawn. A woman stands under a chandelier as she works a pair of white gloves on to her hands, tamping them down between stiff fingers. On the floor of a bright nursery, a boy and two

255

little girls in smocked dresses are doing a jigsaw puzzle. Briefly, aunt and niece duck inside the Church of Saint Audoen and Agnes, having nothing else, puts one of her gloves on her head as a token of respect.

My own first memories of Dublin are of the canal at Ballsbridge in the winter of 1961. I associate it with the song 'Moon River' which was so popular that year you couldn't get away from it, neither in London, nor Paris, nor Dublin. My boyfriend had a room in a boarding house that looked out on to the canal where swans came down on to the black water. I remember the icy-cold streets and the ice-cold, not entirely clean sheets on the bed. There were two sooty windows with thin curtains across them. In the room next door was a young man from Ballymena, in Northern Ireland, called Dermot. He tore shelves from the walls of his room to burn in order to keep warm. Like my mother on her first visit to Dublin, I was nineteen. Whilst waiting to go to university I was earning my keep – just – modelling, enough to buy a cut-price fur coat that had the barefoot street kids running after me.

This was the first time I'd visited Ireland and I was there not because of my maternal connection to the place, not at all, but because my English boyfriend was an undergraduate at Trinity College, Dublin's 'Protestant' university, founded by Elizabeth I in 1592. Catholics were told they were in danger of mortal sin if they attended Trinity. The year I was there, students at the Catholic University College still stood in prayer at the sound of the Angelus bell.

Unlike my mother and her aunt, we didn't window-shop on Grafton Street, and although I stayed for ten days I made little effort to explore the city or learn its history. I was beginning at that time to build a romance of Ireland, to relate to it as to another woman, always feminine, an outsider, outside 'the establishment', a country that had suffered contempt, domination and exploitation by England, possessed of a nature that was poetic, mythical and austere. Wild. The place my mother came from almost as mythically as Aphrodite had risen from the waves. That was the fanciful and only half-conscious picture I was building. I breathed in the atmosphere of the place but was happy to remain shockingly ignorant of what lay outside my own narrow sphere. Much of my time was spent in the college theatre, the Trinity Players, where my boyfriend was in a production of a play by John Mortimer. Either there or at the cinema, watching black-and-white movies of the nouvelle vague – those allowed past the Irish censors – *Les Cousins*, and *Lift to the Scaffold* – in which we found exquisitely moody and frankly amoral role models for our sexual and intellectual liberation. In the afternoons we made love in the damp bedroom, and at night we lay wreathed in Arabic music from Radio Cairo played by an Egyptian student in the room above.

Like a whole lot of other people in our generation – in every generation, perhaps – we thought we'd both invented and copyrighted sex, and the evidence that everyone else was at it like knives made no impression on us whatever – or at least not on me. We were the first and only and there was nothing in the least casual about it. It was the Garden of Eden. We were refusing to inherit our parents' sense of shame. But, though we didn't acknowledge it, we were still their children.

Forty years later when – en route to Tipperary – I'm back in Dublin and, recalling my first visit to the city, I tell my friends there were two pieces of good news during that time: John heard that he'd won a scholarship to RADA, and I heard I'd finally passed my Latin examination,

257

which meant I was going to be able to take up my place at University College, London, to read Philosophy. In that cold, glittery city, pockmarked with poverty, we celebrated. What I didn't tell my friends was that, during that icy long-ago winter in Dublin, I also discovered I was pregnant.

5

The first night she's home from the hospital, Agnes is woken by the sound of the fox barking. She thinks of the cold hillside and the animal's body tensed in the dark. But when the bark comes again she realises it's her mother's cough, not coming from the other side of the bedroom wall but outside, in the garden, or on the lane. With a thumping heart, she goes to the window. She sees her mother walking up towards the cairn. Then a shadow moves out of the house immediately below. John is going quietly after his wife with her shawl over his arm.

Inside the house everything's exactly as it was but nothing's quite as Agnes remembers it. Or maybe it's *not* exactly as it was. Immaculately clean as ever, but the old sense of effortless good order has gone. Kate doesn't bake her own bread any more and with so little sewing to do, sometimes in the evenings she sits by the fire with idle hands. On these occasions her eyes often come to rest on her husband with an odd expression, benign but curious, as if she's never seen him before. With Pat and Agnes the only children left at home the place, like Busherstown, is full of silences and shadows. When they kneel for the telling of the Rosary, where there were eleven of them, now there's only four – that is to say, there are four when Pat obliges them with his presence – like the survivors of some catastrophe.

Mrs Kavanagh complains of the cold. She has become,

as Jim O'Brien described her, 'thin, thin as a heron'. Her skin has a grey clammy look to it, though Agnes doesn't confirm this by touch. She does not touch her mother. Her mother is curious to know about Mrs Minchin. She goes quiet when Agnes talks about her, and from time to time gives a cynical little laugh. Especially the rose-coloured velvet and the devilled kidneys for breakfast – these especially make her snort.

Agnes is bringing in peat one morning when a flash of light off something on the lane takes her eye. A newly painted sidecar is coming up the hill. It stops at the gate and a priest climbs down. He is carrying the box that contains the sacred Host. Mrs Kavanagh comes to the door to welcome him and something in her manner suggests that this has happened before, but it's the first Agnes has known of it. It isn't Father O'Connor but a younger man, a priest Agnes has reason to dislike. Rather than encounter him, she puts the peat down by the door and quietly walks away. Later, her mother comments on Agnes's lack of respect.

Agnes has walked into a trap. She had thought herself free. She'd meant to come back only to convalesce, but once here she's slipped into the position of the youngest daughter, the one who's expected to stay at home. Kate *needs* a daughter. Every day she makes her need plainer. Agnes has begun to notice odd lapses in her mother's memory and concentration. Kate can't disguise the fact that she would have preferred Nancy, but since she can't have her, she'll make do with Agnes. But will Agnes stay? Anxiety makes Kate critical and snappy. John appeals to his daughter's understanding. Agnes the child, yearning for her mother's approval, does battle with Agnes the woman who has been gifted with a young adult's indifference.

Luckily for me, my grandmother overplays her hand: when Agnes has been home no more than a couple of weeks, and despite the bitter weather Kate, in a temper over something, orders Agnes outside on to the ice-cold hillside to feed the geese. So here it comes, the favourite of my childhood myths: my young mother stands in a twilit field – a very green field, for isn't this the Emerald Isle? – surrounded by a litter of geese as dead, as white as pillows. They are dead because my mother has poisoned them, and this, I had always believed, was the reason why she had to leave Ireland.

But the fact is, as an account of why my mother had to leave, it won't quite do.

The material I have doesn't seem to fill the years between school and her going to England. And didn't she tell me it was from the *Brophys'* she had to rush to Dublin? Maybe I have the chronology wrong? No, there's something missing. That much is obvious. Something to do with the time she spent in Dublin, in hospital, having her appendix removed – or so she told me.

The Kavanaghs' new donkey is a right little terror. Agnes dislikes it and as often as the donkey tries to kick her she kicks back. Still, once she has the animal in the traces and they are out on the road, it's pleasant enough rattling along under the trees towards Moneygall. She finds Mrs Minchin in the library seated at her desk over the accounts. Winter light has robbed her face of colour. She confesses to worry and dissatisfaction with her absent son, William. Agnes offers the information that her mother feels much the same with regard to her own son, Pat. 'And why is that?' enquires Mrs Minchin, with real interest. There are, in fact, several reasons why Pat is making his mother's life a misery. But, having offered a confidence, Agnes retreats. 'Perhaps all first sons are the same?' she

261

suggests. 'And all mothers,' adds Mrs Minchin, folding her hands around their glittering burden of rings.

But Agnes must harden her heart. When she says that she is going to England, Mrs Minchin immediately asks, 'To join your sister, Nancy?' and Agnes is touched that she remembers the name. 'Yes,' she says. 'Nancy.' Mrs Minchin studies her a moment. 'Then I can't persuade you to come back?' Agnes shakes her head, and looks away at the long sad sweep of the garden. 'My dear,' says Mrs Minchin, 'I'm extremely sorry to lose you.' 'Thank you, madam,' is all Agnes can manage. 'Thank you.'

On the platform at Nenagh Station, John Kavanagh takes the last of his daughters in his arms and kisses her. Agnes believes it's for the first time. Well, maybe he kissed her when she was a baby. At her baptism, for instance – she's seen fathers do that in the church in Puckaun, stooping awkwardly to kiss the baby's forehead. But on no occasion that she remembers has Agnes's father kissed her, though she has never, not for one moment, ever doubted that he loves her. His feeling for her has been the yardstick against which she's measured what she takes as her mother's lack of feeling. Now he pulls her close and through his old coat and his thin ribcage she feels the pounding of his heart. His clothes, his hair, the rough skin of his face all smell of turf and pipe smoke and probably it's this that brings tears to Agnes's eyes. She feels her chest heave. She experiences a moment of panic. She can't go. She mustn't go. He's too old to leave, but this doesn't stop her picking up her hatbox and turning away. Light flashes off the metal step. She puts her foot there. She feels the cold come up through the thin sole of her shoe. This is only the second time she's ever boarded a train.

If Pat or my grandmother had been standing on Knigh Hill and the day was clear, they would have seen the trail of smoke go up from the engine as it left the station. Agnes was gone. This goodbye to her father is the point at which my mother's storytelling broke off.

PART SIX
STAYING

1

'Such a heart! Should he leave, how I'd miss him. Jewel, acorn, youth. Kiss him!'
  —Anonymous, trans. from the Irish by Brendan Kennelly

My uncle Pat died in the county home, the Hospital of the Assumption, in Thurles. In his pocket they found a hand-written copy of the inscription on Saint Patrick's breast-plate. On his death certificate his name is given as Patrick Kavanagh and his home address as Knigh, Puckane (spelt in the modern way), Nenagh. He's described as a widower and his age is given, correctly, as seventy-eight. He died a week or so short of his seventy-ninth birthday. Under rank or profession it says he was a retired farm labourer and old-age pensioner. The certified cause of death is given as (a) coronary occlusion (blockage) – three days, (b) atherosclerosis (arteries narrowed by fatty deposits) and (c) hypertension.

Billy Foley, the keeper of the Knigh graveyard, lives up a narrow road on the east side of Knigh Hill. His business is as a car mechanic and in the yard opposite his bungalow car corpses and car body parts spill out into the fields on either side and even out into the road. I found him cooking potatoes in the kitchen whilst his twelve-year-old daughter was idling over her homework in the corner of the living room. Billy told me he'd be happy to show me where my grandparents and my uncle are buried and wouldn't he take me to the very spot once he'd got the potatoes on. This took only a moment as, having scrubbed them, he placed them whole and unpeeled in the pot – my aunt Bridie's favourite way with a potato. Billy then gracefully offered me tea but I asked for water, which his daughter sprang up to fetch me. There was an atmosphere of remarkable tenderness between father and daughter. A few years younger than I am, Billy remembers my grandparents by reputation only.

'Lovely people they were, gentlefolk, much respected. My parents always spoke well of them. They were missed, Maggie, I know that.' Then he adds with totally unexpected vehemence, 'But their son Paddy was a MONSTER!'

I reel at the violence and baldness of this claim.

'Paddy married a Griffin, from Nenagh. They lived up there in the house—' Billy jerked his head towards Knigh Hill which that afternoon was bathed in the serenity of May sunshine '—and he was violent to his wife, a real bastard. The children used to come down here to us crying and one night they were taken into Nenagh to be looked after by one of the aunties.'

Billy's daughter remains sweetly expressionless, milk-white and blue-eyed. She gets into her daddy's car to come with us to the graveyard, enclosed by a low stone wall, in the middle of the field which today has Joan Cleary's cows grazing in it and one – can it be? – yes, dead, lying under the cemetery wall humming with flies. As we enter via the stone stile, Billy indicates one of the new marble headstones on which is recorded the death of his son, aged twenty, in a motorbike accident in America and, below that, the death of his wife a year or two later. Reeling from this, too, I stumble after the stocky figure of Billy and his palely drifting daughter to a spot in the centre of the graveyard which he identifies as the place of my grandparents' burial.

The grass licks our ankles. Billy suggests I should try to remember the location by lining it up with a feature on the chapel to one side, and the black marble edge on one of the graves to the other. This spot isn't at all the one I had in mind as the right place. But Billy Foley is the keeper of the graveyard plans and, like everyone else I've approached, remarkably generous with his time and his memories.

'And how the feck would Billy Foley know where your grandparents are buried?' demanded Mick Grace when I met him the following day. 'Billy Foley wasn't even *born* when they were buried so he went and put Paddy in the wrong fecking place, so he did. I was *there* the day your grandfather was buried, and your grandmother, too.'

Mick Grace, Danny Grace's uncle, is a small, crooked-toothed man with sticky-out ears and a mischievous expression, like a dark little leprechaun, eighty-seven years old and living alone in a tiny terraced house in Nenagh. Taking my hand in his – which was dry and cold – he looked into my face and, with deep emotion, he said, 'Your family and mine were neighbours' – giving that word 'neighbours' an almost sacred inflexion – 'at Knigh long ago.'

He showed us into his front room which was about the width of a railway carriage. There he perched on his single bed that was covered with a grey blanket, and Danny and I sat opposite on a sofa side by side, slightly lower than Mick, our knees and his almost touching, whilst a steady stream of traffic passed by just the other side of the small, net-curtained window. Mick is a little dark pip of a man, dry as biltong, so chewy, so fibrous, it's hard to imagine that, like the rest of us, he must have emerged from the blood and mucous of a woman's body, or that he has ever engaged in the messy business of animal congress himself, but he did, and he has.

Mick had a piece of lined paper torn from an exercise book folded over in his hand. But his sense of mischief meant that first he had to give me some of his anecdotes about my uncle Pat: the Daw did this and the Daw did that.

'I remember one time the Daw was coming down the lane in the cart when it crashed into the ditch below with the donkey caught in the shafts – well both he and the donkey hollered fit to be moithered and it took a team of us neighbours to pull them out. Didn't I put my own ten-year-old pennyworth into the pulling? And himself laughing so much he made no effort to help, not at all, and with a cut over one eye and bruises from head to foot. Anyhow, wasn't it a Monday morning and Doctor Courtney there at the surgery – twice a week he came there to our house to give out the physics – and he was willing to help your uncle Paddy out with getting medical insurance. But as they was waiting to get assessed in the office in Nenagh, Paddy, with the arm they were after saying was broken, he was stood there looking at the girls grinning and twisting the baccy into his pipe with his right hand, until Doctor Courtney saw and slapped it down!' Mick cackles with laughter. 'But he got it, he got what he wanted. "I didn't come down in the last shower!" he crowed. And with that money he said he'd buy a dacent suit to be married in, only he didn't. Buy the suit, that is.' There is a pause. Mick shakes his head. Then he's convulsed with laughter again as he remembers: 'After he was married he used to say, I've had enough of this ould place, I'm going to

London to join Tom, and after that I'll take the boat to England.'

So Pat was laughed at for his ignorance. (It brings to mind the middle-class rural couple in Jane Austen's *Emma* who don't know where Paris is.) But was he actually considered stupid, I wondered? As if reading my mind, Mick goes on:

'Your uncle Paddy was clever.' Mick taps his nose. 'He used to cut scallops in Knigh Wood—'

'Hazel sticks,' offers Danny.

'—and he'd sell them for thatching. He was known for that. There were people would come there to the Cross and ask for Paddy.'

Another story has a friend of my grandpa's arriving above at the house to find it all closed up and Grandpa calling out to him through the keyhole: 'I can't let you in and I can't get out. Pat's locked me in and taken the key in his pocket.' To my ears the story has a disturbing ring. And in other anecdotes, well, my uncle Pat comes over to me as a cod Irishman, a parody of the stupid, amoral, pitiably small-minded peasant. His being called 'Paddy' doesn't help me but 'the Daw' – whilst suggesting all those characteristics – at least has the virtue of surprise, of novelty.

Still I'm at sea. I've no idea how to take him, how to weigh him. Was he a 'monster', or just a leprechaun on drink? I'm back around the family dining table as a child. 'Did you hear the one about the Paddy who said he was going to fly a rocket to the sun? His colleague said, "You'll get burned up, mate," and Paddy replied, "I've thought of that – we'll go at night."' Boom-boom! I think of an English friend of mine being maddened by her Irish son-in-law's 'fawning respect' – her phrase – for 'a small-town lawyer in Wicklow'. Scratch an English person and you often find a degree of condescension or scorn for the Irish, very different from their feelings for the Welsh or the Scots. Mick now unfolds the piece of paper he has in his hand and shows me what he's written:

> Your grandfather, as far as I know he came from Borrisokane
> John Cavangh Knigh
> His wife né Buckley
> Sons, Tom, Dan, Paddy
> Daughers Nan, Agnes, Cathlein, Mary Rose, Brigid, Josie
> John worked at Crosses Norwood about 6 miles from his Home
> He lived in a house of the Crosses
> Buried in Knigh and his wife and son Paddy
> Your grand Uncle Jim Buckley was gateman in the Nenagh work house
> His sister Mary was going the roads of Ireland
> They had a grandson John (Sean) Gavin
> He was Mary Rose's son he went to England
> All went to England except Paddy he married a Griffin from St Jessop Park

Apart from Pat, the one he remembers best is Tom. He describes him as 'a bit of a swank' who used to drive the threshers and wore two watches. Mick remembers when Tom went away to work on the 'electrification of the Shannon'. It was a German firm, Siemens, working the contract and the scheme was expected to solve the electricity needs of the west of Ireland. To the boy Mick it had seemed a thrilling adventure, and he envied Tom being picked up in a lorry and waving from the back, grinning, with a cigarette between his teeth, as he set off into the unknown.

Later, Mick learned conditions at the site at Ardnacrusha were bad, and that when men were killed on the works they were just thrown aside and work continued. Two fourteen-year-old boys were sent to one of Ireland's soon-to-be notorious 'industrial schools' for destroying just £2 worth of insulators at the Shannon Electricity Scheme. Tom and Dan both came home safely from Ardnacrusha, but this was the hungry thirties and soon they were away again, this time to England, disgusted by the only work Ireland had to offer them: breaking stones, work for which the men were paid by the yard.

My eye, meanwhile, has been taken by a name on Mick's list, a family member I've not heard of before: my great-aunt Mary, nickname 'the Maid of Arra'. The Arra Mountains are within sight of Burgess, where my grandmother Kate and her siblings were born. Mary was my grandmother's older sister and for whatever reasons, choice, or having fallen on hard times, or the sheer difficulty of her personality, she was, I'm now told, 'going the roads of Ireland'. I'm mesmerised by this information: Kate Buckley, who had 'notions' and whose kitchen floor you could eat your dinner off, had a sister who 'went the roads of Ireland'. Mick recalls she had an old sack in which she'd collect dropped potatoes, blackberries, mushrooms, hoping to sell them at someone's door, and often she did, or at least she exchanged them for bread, milk, a lump of cheese. She had a habit, too, of collecting stones, little stones that took her fancy, and when they weighed heavy in her pocket, she'd sit down and make an arrangement of them at the side of the road. A shape. A pattern. A sign. Having done so to her satisfaction, the irritation, or rather, the agitation she exhibited during the arrangement of her stones would be replaced by a cosmic calm. Not everyone was good to Mary, there were some who'd make her run, but Mick remembers a widow bringing up seven children on her own and she always shared bread and tea with Mary when she called. Then, whether she began to make a nuisance of herself, or perhaps she turned funny in the head, Mick doesn't remember, but, 'One day they got the horse and cart to take her to Thurles to the workhouse.'

'Who's they?' I ask.

'Your grandmother. And as they loaded her into that cart, ould Mary bit your grandmother's hand.'

Danny throws me a slightly anxious look, but Mick, who's clearly judged me to be made of sterner stuff, goes on:

'She didn't last long in that place and it was back here they brought her to be buried. The priests were busy on the day of her funeral and Tom had to bring a bucket of clay to them to have it blessed. They couldn't dig deep enough because of the stones and after an hour's huffing and puffing the Daw said, "Will you give it a rest? She won't be coming back up out of there anyways."'

When Mick's merriment has quietened down, Danny indicates that it's time to go. In the doorway, Mick squinnies up at me:

'Isn't it Irish everyone wants to be now, Danny?' he says. Danny laughs.

'And not just Irish, God help us, but descended from an Irish cattle thief into the bargain.'

'Is that so?' says Mick.

'Or better still, from some criminal who was politically motivated, that's what they're after now.' He gives me a little nudge. 'Be honest, Maggie, wouldn't you like to have found a Kavanagh forebear who was hanged for shooting an English landlord? Or skinning a Black and Tan? What novelist worth her salt wouldn't?'

274

'Looks like I'm out of luck,' I say. 'I'll have to make do with my uncle Pat.'

'Your uncle married into a rough ould crowd,' observes Mick, waggling his head. 'Pat's wife was trouble. Everyone could see that.'

I decide it's time to visit the registrar's office again to summons a copy of the certificate of this wedding. The first thing that strikes me is the bride's glorious name: Anastasia Griffin. And then, with a sinking heart, her age, recorded merely as 'underage', meaning under eighteen. The legal age for marriage in Ireland in the '30s was fifteen. My uncle was thirty-one. Annie O'Brien believes Pat's wife was pregnant when they married and when the marriage finally broke down she heard the children were taken away into care in Nenagh. I ask Danny about this and he recalls being told that when the older boy came out to visit his father, Pat pushed him away, not wanting to know, until eventually he was talked around and had the boy on his knee. 'I knew Pat when I was still a child,' says Danny. 'And a lot of the old people then didn't tolerate children – it wasn't just a case of 'children should be seen but not heard', sure they didn't want to *see* them either. We kids used to thieve from Knigh Wood, and Pat must have known. So long as we kept well out of his way he never bothered. But if you came within reach you'd get a thump from his stick just for being there.'

'But the neighbours thought well enough of him. Everyone says Pat was a wonderful worker.'

'Oh he was,' Danny agrees, adding, 'Do you want my considered opinion? I'd say Pat was as contrary as a bag of cats.'

But Pat wasn't just the subject of stories; he told them,

too. A man who could be silent for days on end, he would then, one hand raised to remark the fact that he was about to speak, tell stories that rivalled old Scholl's in their poetry and strangeness. And one of the stories Mick remembers him telling began like this:

'It was from Mayo my grandfather Patrick came riding on his da's shoulders, and that was in the Bad Times which no one speaks of but will never be forgotten.'

Pat liked to claim his grandfather told these stories to no one but his younger son, Daniel who, being deaf and dumb, neither heard nor told. It was characteristic of Pat to enjoy seeing a look of puzzlement come on to his listeners' faces and the notion of a deaf and dumb child being the only link with the past certainly appealed to him. But of course he himself had heard these stories from his daddy, sitting beside him on the seat of the donkey cart as they travelled from the high bogland down to Clashnevin. And naturally enough it was stories concerning his namesake, Patrick, that appealed to him most.

'The boy had never seen a tree in his life before and wasn't the voice frightened out of his body by the very sight of them, shaking their fists at him in the night...?'

In this way the stories of Pat's – and my – forebears came to be told and remembered. Stories from the days of his own life, too, and those of his brothers and sisters. The other side of the picture, the side my mother never gave me, but which has found a place here in this book.

Recently, I came across an old photo, one I didn't know existed: my father in the open doorway of the house at Knigh and at his shoulder, in the half-dark, my uncle Pat. This is the summer of '38, when Agnes came back to Tipperary, briefly, with her English fellow. To receive her parents' blessing. And Pat is like a man of a different generation – though only twelve years older than my mother – a different century. Different world. In his rough workingman's suit and hat, the faint shape of a grin, almost saturnine, on his shadowy face, he embodies the life my mother was escaping, whilst my father, little more than a boy, sunlight catching the fair gleam on his ginger curls, the crease in his grey slacks, glows with a history that still conferred an easy confidence on its young men. English to the core. The future. They stayed a week, and then they were gone.

'Health and life to you, a child every year to you, and death in Ireland.' – Old Irish saying

My grandmother's death came late one March, when her spirits might have been rising with the spring. But of course she'd seen it all before. This was in 1944, during the Second World War, known here in Ireland as the Emergency. Mick Grace remembers how during that time my grandparents often borrowed a little tea from his family, then returned it when their rations came through. During the war an estimated £12 million was sent back to Ireland from emigrants in Britain alone. No doubt the Kavanagh siblings contributed in some small way to this incredible sum (Agnes did on at least one occasion) although, apart from rationing on such items as tea and sugar, my grandparents were little affected in the matter of supplies – less than their children in London – being self-sufficient in most things. But loneliness, old age and distress, these were other matters.

On my grandmother's death certificate her name is given as Kate Cavanagh (spelt with a 'C'). She's described as sixty-six years old (she was in fact sixty-nine), her condition as married, her occupation as housekeeper and the cause of her death as anaemia and bronchitis. The informant of her death was Josie McGrath (that same Josie McGrath who, as a young woman, tore the mask off the face of the policeman on the night the Clearys' farm-house was raided). On my grandmother's death certificate Josie is described as a nurse, 'present at death'. Doctor Tony Courtney registered the death but was presumably not present.

The details of my grandfather's death certificate are much the same. He died only ten months later, in February '45. His condition was widower, his age, seventy years (actually seventy-six), his occupation, herd, and the cause of his death was bronchitis. Josie McGrath was again 'present at death' and this time is described as 'Red Cross nurse', which means her attendance was free. Bronchitis. Anaemia. I think about this. Can you die from bronchitis? And anaemia? It sounds to me like the sort of death you might expect from poverty and bad housing. But these weren't my grandparents' circumstances.

TB notoriously leaves its victims tired and thin. There was, of course, a definite stigma attached to TB and perhaps a doctor was no more likely to write 'TB' on a death certificate than he was to write 'alcohol'. My grand-mother may, indeed, have had TB and been cured – my mother once referred to her being away at a sanatorium in Wicklow – only to then neglect herself, especially with no daughter left at home to nag her into eating. And then, after her death, my grandfather would not have done much in the way of cooking.

'What'll I do, what'll I do? She's gone,' he said piteously and repeatedly, to the neighbour who used to come up to shave him.

'Sure, you could join the navy, why don't you?'

The day of Grandpa's funeral there was a foot of snow on the ground and the earth was hard as stone. Thank God Pat had Tom with him, home from England – under special dispensation in spite of the war – for the second funeral within a year. It was Tom who made the arrangements, paid for the coffin, hosted the wake. Mick Grace remembers they all nearly froze solid and fell into the grave alongside the corpse. Blind Lane was an ice-slide. Pat suggested they just let his father's body slide down to the bottom, why didn't they? – but they managed it, hoisting the coffin into the back of the cart and then, slipping and sliding and cursing, two at the donkey's head, two at the back of the cart to stop it capsizing over, they manoeuvred their way slowly down the lane, taking it on the diagonal, from side to side with much creaking of the wheels, down towards the Cross where the priest and the serving boy waited, pinched blue at their extremities. Mick recalls the men had to fetch kettles of boiling water from the Clearys' kitchen to soften up the frozen earth, Pat groaning as it yielded at last, and there was the lid of the other coffin, the cheap wood already rotting, cracking audibly as it received the weight of the second which swung from the ropes and clumsily dropped the last few inches.

Pat, as the first son, then crouched down and shoved back into the piled earth the little wooden cross on which Tom had written, 'Here lies Katherine Kavanagh nee Buckley, d. 1944, and John Kavanagh, her loving husband, d. 1945. Sleep in God's Peace.' This cross would have lasted ten years or so before it, too, became part of the earth, like my grandparents' bodies, part of this land over which there have been so many bitter disputes.

Knigh farmhouse and its accompanying glebe had been home for generations to a family named Harty: tenant farmers there from at least 1820, in 1876 they purchased the land for £500. On the eve of the First World War, Rody Cleary married Kate Harty and, there being no Harrty sons, over the years, it was Rody who consolidated the existing farm and, in 1920, he headed the poll for Sinn Fein in Borrisokane in the local elections. In the hungry thirties' Rody went on to buy land on the outskirts of Nenagh, driving a hard bargain in what would now be described as a buyers' market, when many were selling both cattle and land for a song. Finally, in the 1940s – indeed. whilst the Kavanaghs still lived there – it was Rody Cleary who bought Knigh Hill from the Crosses. Both the old house my family lived in and the land they farmed still belong to the Clearys. That is to say, to Rody's daughter-in-law, Joan Cleary.

Learning this I'm not just surprised but shocked, though why I should be I'm not quite clear. My grandparents had been dead for almost a decade. Besides, I know perfectly well my family could never have afforded such a thing. I *suppose* I know that, though, naturally, I wish they could have done. Is it that I feel, in not having had this revealed to me before, I've been somehow *fooled*? Things – and my companions – having not been as transparent as I'd imagined? Both fooled, and caught out in being foolish enough unconsciously to have patronised Rody Cleary's daughter-in-law, Joan, for a simple countrywoman who had missed out on the rampant prosperity of the new Ireland? Taken in by Joan wringing her hands and moaning: 'And dear Lord, isn't everything so expensive! And the government not allowing you to do this or that or anything else to get the benefit of what you have!'

'Sure,' says Annie, with relish but no malice, 'she owns enough to buy half the Vatican.'

And indeed, in 2012, Joan Cleary is said to have sold land and property near Nenagh for two million euros.

I've just come across a photo of Rody Cleary in Danny's book – that smile! The watch chain, the easy posture, the

281

tilt of the hat. Charm and confidence radiate from him. During a decade or more of Troubles, Rody was brave, committed, and canny. He had risked his life. He had spoken out. He had proved himself to be intelligent and capable. He had taken part in the building of an infrastructure that would be independent of English jurisdiction. Did he not deserve his reward? I recall Mick Grace saying of the Kavanaghs, 'Politics? They had *none*.' As if I'd asked did they go horse racing or collect watercolours. 'And nor did we. What difference did it make to the likes us?' No politics, and no land, neither.

Pat wasn't able to benefit from the sale of the woods where he'd been caretaker for so many years, nor from the sale of his old family home. He was, however, able to auction the contents. There was a trivet, a gridiron, a toasting fork and iron-stand, a meat mincer, a wooden rolling pin; there were skillets, iron cooking pots, the gallon bucket that had been used to collect the pig's blood in – 'the little gentilman' as the O'Briens had called it – his father's leather strop used for sharpening his razor, a box iron, a little iron for collars and cuffs, a keeler for cream, a small butter churn, a set of wooden butter pats – including one with the initial 'A' on it. There was a Jones's hand sewing machine, a squat iron machine with a griffin holding arrows embossed on its side, a chest of drawers and one large wooden box containing a stack of 'linen' made from flour sacks, very fine, soft and much worn. There were the rush-seated sugan chairs and the settle, a game with Bible pictures that Pat remembered the girls playing with, and a damp-smelling pile of Tom's old Westerns. There were wooden and tin eating implements, ten china plates, eight cups and seven saucers, including a cup from Manchester, and a big green dish Agnes had brought home from Busherstown. By the open door stood the magnificent mirror and reflected in it my grandmother's precious collection of eighty-two jam jars. Not sparkling any more. Upstairs there were two double beds on one of which Pat laid out a blue dress of his mother's.

By midday it was all gone, to neighbours, to people come out from Nenagh. But no one remembers who bought the brass lamp that had made such a pretty tinkling sound when my grandmother pulled it down on its chain.

So Paddy the Daw 'gave up the key' and left the house on Knigh Hill. After my grandparents' hard-won triumph, and with the prosperity of Ireland putting out green shoots all about him, Pat was firmly set on the road that would take him down, down. A road begun years, generations, before but with a very different destination in mind. I'm told he was in and out of the hospital at Thurles during the decade or so before he died. Sometimes it seemed he might manage all right in the outside world. He might be out for a year or more at time, but he always spent his pitiful allowance on drink and he always had to return.

But Pat didn't vanish from Knigh. He kept coming back, as a tramp, as 'little more than a common tinker' as Annie said – like a ghost, haunting the magical place where he no longer had a home, relying on the extraordinary generosity of the Graces who fed him and allowed him to sleep in their shed which was dry and warm, and he slept there curled up on the hay like a stray dog. Like his grandfather, Patrick, when he came to Tipperary from Mayo, a traumatised child in the time of the Great Famine. In my imagination I've followed Pat there, sneaking in on him when I supposed him to be asleep only to become aware of two dark eyes – his grandfather Patrick's famously black eyes – glittering at me. He wasn't a sad, quiet, dignified old drunk; he was still lively, malicious, and crafty.

As I talked these things over with Annie a pained look came on her face.

'How could Paddy let himself sink so low?' she asked. 'Sometimes, Maggie, he was sleeping on a bench in Nenagh where the women would bring out food to him.'

It was from that bench, or perhaps from the roadside closer to home, in the early hours of a bitter night in December 1981, that Pat was taken back to Thurles, to the Hospital of the Assumption. It was there in the hospital he died, in the middle of trying to take his boots off, saying it would never do, not at all, to come into the kitchen with his boots on. And raising himself up to express his indignation, he demanded: Who did they think he was?

PART SEVEN
INNOCENCE AND EXPERIENCE

1

'Every generation is born innocent, and if that is bad for history it is nevertheless necessary for life.'
– *The Talmud and the Internet,* by Jonathan Rosen

When my father, David, was a small boy the two most important things in life were maths and cricket. The wonderful thing about maths was that there was only one correct answer and, once you'd got the hang of it, it wasn't difficult to work out what that was. Cricket was another matter: cricket was poetry. By the time he started school, aged four, following the others across the road to the little schoolhouse, my father knew his twelve times table and could bat a tolerable ball so long as it didn't matter too much where it ended up. In both these skills he was self-taught. His father was an invalid and of his three elder siblings, one was a girl – my aunt Dorothy – interested in neither maths nor cricket, one was a boy whom his mother had dressed as a girl until he was five, and the eldest was a serious boy too preoccupied with his looming role as head of the family to give time to his baby brother. The baby of the family, and perhaps his mother's favourite, David was self-reliant, inclined by nature to go to sleep when it was bedtime, to wake up when it was morning, and to enjoy school – all of which put him in the way of much teasing from his older siblings. In every other way he described his upbringing as one of 'healthy neglect'.

After cricket my father's great pleasure was reading 'Rupert Bear' in the *Daily Express*. He never tired of examining the pictures, trying to work out what was going to happen next before the few rhyming lines told him. Rupert Bear was his friend. He understood and approved of everything Rupert said and did. It was in the spirit of Rupert that he escaped on to the village green as soon as it was light on a Sunday morning, taking his cricket bat, which his mother had got for him by saving Oxo coupons. My father was always first out on to the green but before long two or three other boys joined him. David didn't mind much who it was so long as there was a willing arm to throw the ball and no one chattered too much. My father himself was a chatterer but only in class, or when getting under his mother's feet, not out on the green with a cricket bat in his hand. On summer evenings and at weekends, whenever an adult match was being played, he would be there poised somewhere on the edge of the pitch, imitating the strokes, learning the vocabulary: leg glide, drive, square cut, stonewalling – he prayed he would never be guilty of that – hook, block, snick and sweep. And from the bowler: spin, flipper, daisy-cutter, donkey-dropper, Chinaman, a maiden over or a hat-trick. On the field there was the leg side, the gully, the first, second and third slips, there was silly point, mid-on and silly mid-on. There was the crease, the popping crease and the bowling crease.

The boy gave a lot of thought to which cricketer he liked and why. Even as a child he admired a player with style more than a mechanically successful scorer of runs. He liked a man who was casual and cheerful, who showed no pride when he did well and no petulance when he was run out. The sight of the players in their white ducks and pads was accompanied by equally delightful sounds: the

288

cluck of the ball on willow 'a noise like a trout taking a fly' – deep male voices offering throwaway words of appreciation – the patter of applause from prettily coloured heaps of dresses which were the girls and women reclining on the grass or in deckchairs around the edge of the pitch.

My father was born in Slinfold, a small village in Sussex, in August 1918, shortly before the end of the Great War. On his birthday the following year, a peace pageant was held in the rectory gardens and the little boy, a lace-encrusted guest in his mother's arms, never quite threw off the happy belief that the flags, the cheers, the songs and the cakes were all in his honour. David was the youngest son of the local wheelwright, and their blacksmith, Ted, carried the flag for the victory celebrations. Electricity came to the village when new cottages were built in 1928. Water came from wells, many of which were contaminated with medicinal salts, but the Wadeys' own well was a source of good, sweet water and was supplied to the house by a rotary pump over the sink. Their house was big enough to host the Saturday cricket lunches, and it did so. The Wadeys' business, though not thriving – few were – was respectable. They saw themselves as a family with a 'position to keep up', and my grandmother, Ella, was proud to do so.

This life – the village and the layout of its amenities – might have been designed with a small boy in mind. And not any small boy, this one in particular, as if his mind and character were not formed by the place but vice versa, as if he had dreamed it into existence to his own very precise specifications. I think of the exceptionally neat and exact architectural drawings he made as an adult, one of these being the drawings for a small house his uncle built on the outskirts of Slinfold in 1947. The name 'Slinfold' means

'Fold in the Slope' and this suggests its gently protected character, palmed in a shallow dip in the Weald. There was the forge with a deep pool full of goldfish close by; an old tannery; a small slaughterhouse beside the butcher's; and next door, a neighbour who made sweets and sold them to the schoolchildren in their dinner hour. There was a railway station and a timber yard. Anything that didn't fit his design – the Baptist chapel (into which his black-bonneted grandmother disappeared every Sunday and emerged even more sour-tempered than when she went in), the pub, the mobile library – these the boy ignored.

This was a knack he maintained for the rest of his life so that, far from becoming over-adapted to the life in which he was born – and correspondingly unfitted for any other – my father took his world with him: he perfected his natural inclination to see what he wanted to see, to eliminate from his field of vision what didn't interest him and therefore cheerfully to fit in almost anywhere. But probably nothing ever compared with the thrill of cutting a fastball through the slips, or a straight drive all the way to the boundary.

From when David was seven or eight years old, his father was bedridden. This had its advantages. The boy was left remarkably free. At the same time, the only paternal example he remembers is one of invalidism and failure. He was the fourth child and, so he believed later in life, 'a mistake', born when his father's health was already giving cause for concern. For the most part the little boy was ignored – 'healthy neglect' as he describes it now. But he received two important moral injunctions from his parents, injunctions he never forgot. In his workshop, his father had a verse up on the wall: 'Right is right, and wrong is wrong, and no man's wrong is another man's right.' From his mother, David had a story: 'Two little boys are fighting in a lane and in the process they knock over a tramp. One of the boys helps the old man to his feet and the other says to him, "What are you bothering with him for? Who's he?" To which the first boy replies, "It doesn't matter who he is – the point is who I am."'

Scarcity of money runs through my father's childhood like veins through marble. Not something that crops up in my mother's memories at all. But however much David was aware of it, it doesn't appear to have distressed him. It was just one more problem to be solved, no more to be fretted over than the 'from-we-takes', as his mathematically challenged older brother called subtraction. My father's presumption that the world makes sense and that practical problems can be solved is a characteristic that I inherited – not one you'd expect to stand the test of time but is in fact remarkably, idiotically resilient – another instance of the triumph of expectation over experience.

By the time my father was born, my grandfather, Charles, had become incapable of the physical work in the forge. Bright's disease, or nephritis, is an autoimmune disease, rare now due to improved living and working conditions. Long after there were younger, stronger men to call on, Charles – the only qualified wheelwright in the business – insisted on doing his part of the physical labour, making the wooden wheel and then, all four men working together, manoeuvring the heavy, red-hot iron tyre. Once in place, the tyre was doused in water until it shrank into a tight fit, producing copious noxious steam in the process. An attack of acute tonsillitis turned Charles into an invalid. Aged only thirty-nine – and with Ella in charge of the bookkeeping – he had to be content with a general supervisory role. Sometimes he would fall down in a fit.

Salty food, which he loved, especially brought on fits, which could be quite violent. He would crash to the floor and tear all the buttons off his pyjamas. Ella used to get Dorothy to go racing out for help and then they'd all sit on him. My father remembers none of this.

So Dorothy has a different story to tell. Or rather, she has an extra story, her own, that of the only daughter in a household where the mother made no pretence that girls were as good as boys. From when she was eight years old it was Dorothy's responsibility to cook the Sunday breakfast. One morning, the frying pan handle caught in the lace on her vest, sending sausages all over the floor and hot fat down her legs. She fled crying to her mother, sobbing that she had spoiled their breakfast, to which Ella said, 'There you go thinking of your stomach again.' And Dorothy recalls either her mother or herself – never one of the boys – forever toiling up and down the stairs with the chamber pot her father filled with dark urine. The smell of urine, unpleasant because it was associated with the illness, pervaded the upper floor of the house. Charles, who had been scrupulous about taking care of his workmen, was less so in making provision for his family in case of his early death. Even after he'd become bedridden, when Ella begged him to make a will, he only replied, 'Then all I have to do is die, isn't it.'

He died anyway, in 1928, when he was forty-six, leaving Ella with four children under fourteen – David was only nine – and nothing to keep them on but his unpaid doctor's bills. Chas's doctor's bills were unpaid because so many of the bills sent out to his customers were unpaid. The business was bankrupt. There was no pension and soon there was no home. My English grandfather had been a spectacularly bad businessman; too soft-hearted to collect debts from customers he knew were in difficulties.

For a brief while after her husband's death – and still a sweet, pretty little thing of forty – Ella had hopes of a good-looking riding master, an Irishman, as it happens. In fact, it was understood that they were engaged to be married but, returning from a visit to his mother in Ireland, he jilted her shortly before the wedding. By the sound of it, Ella had a narrow escape. The riding master appears to have had a brutal, even sadistic streak. Still, when the prospect of marriage to the horse master failed, Ella became bitterly unhappy. Her independence, her status, had gone. Nothing mattered any more except survival. In this depressed frame of mind, in the summer of 1932, she accepted a position as housekeeper. Going into service was a painful humiliation for Ella, made worse by the fact that her two older sons, having left school at fourteen, initially had no prospects either. The family was finally broken up.

Yet in many ways my father's life was unchanged. He was thirteen and his school days weren't yet over. Although he went to live with his aunt, he continued at Collyer's Grammar School for boys in Horsham. David's education was now his mother's priority. He became a prefect, and was made head of house. On Saturday and Sunday he played cricket. If asked, my father always says he had a happy childhood.

One spring day in 1935, my father travelled alone by train to London. He walked from Victoria Station to the Aldwych, following his street map and not needing to ask anyone for help. He was sixteen years old and on his way to an examination at the Vocational Guidance Department of the National Institute of Industrial Psychology – strange-seeming words to be placed side by side – and I have their report here in front of me now, kept all these

293

years by my father and volunteered to me recently whilst talking over these times.

In the intelligence test, my father scored 'considerably above the average for boys of his age and type of education'. Of his temperament it was noted: 'He is a rather quiet, retiring boy who does not find it easy to take the initiative in making fresh social contacts. [Speaking of my father now, aged ninety-five, my husband remarks, "You could have fooled me!"] We feel, however, that he is of a fundamentally social disposition... During the examination he was very willing and co-operative. He is perhaps a trifle lacking in forcefulness. It is not that he is wanting in firmness; should the occasion arise we feel he would not easily be over-persuaded. We would not, however, expect him to develop permanent leadership characteristics...' The conclusions of the institute were that my father had a 'general level of intellectual ability very considerably above the average. We feel his work should be predominantly mathematical, with a practical bias, if possible. We feel he should aim at an occupation which will afford him a reasonable degree of security.'

There's an almost eerie sense of accuracy about these observations, as if the examiners, in their brief encounter with this sixteen-year-old boy, had X-rayed their subject, seen, indeed, into his very soul. Of course, my father was, apart from his shyness, a very open character – both in the sense that honesty was characteristic of him and that he was 'an open book', easier to read than many. This examination may have amounted to the most concentrated attention he had received in all his short life. How much, I wonder, are we affected by reading such 'objective' descriptions of ourselves? Suggestibility is a deep, hidden response. The very accuracy of the report in some areas might incline us to accept other of its observations that are less certain. Is it possible that in defining a young person so clearly, setting out in black and white his limits, a report like this could act as a self-fulfilling prophecy?

My father stayed overnight in London with his cousin. Mary Remington was ten years older but unmarried, a forceful, attractive woman who was an artist and already a Royal Academician. It was the kind of encounter that could have had some profound effect, that might even have been life-changing. But it wasn't. If my father thought Mary was selfish and a snob, he wasn't alone, and he was sufficiently self-assured to know that her febrile world of social ambition and aesthetic values was of no interest to him. Five months later, having received a printed and bound copy of his psychological tests, my father was articled to the borough surveyor at Lewes, a pretty, ancient town famous for its anarchic and militantly anti-Catholic celebration of Guy Fawkes Day – the guy burned on the mountainous fire is usually an effigy of the Pope. Twenty-four years later, I was to have my first job in Lewes, too, in the public library, earning £4 10s a week and desperate to find a way out of the boredom – desperate, in fact, for a world more like Mary Remington's, but as yet having found no way into it.

In 1935 – indeed, for the first two years of his being articled – my father had to get by on an allowance of £1 a week. For his midday meal he bought milk, and bread with a scoop of yeast on it from the brewer's. Hardly enough to keep even a very modest body and soul together. But, his position being without pay, he was fortunate to have so much. My father had a mentor. Mr Henderson, a master at Collyer's, had been prepared to give David his

295

small weekly allowance and to provide the £100 premium due to the surveyor. Without this support he would have been unable to take the opportunity. My grandmother had to pay two subsequent sums of £25 to the surveyor. In this she was helped by Dorothy, who contributed two and sixpence a week from her tiny wage as a nanny to help support her brother through his training and on up the professional and social ladder to better things. His mother's and Henderson's generosity my father remembers with deep gratitude, but he doesn't remember – he quite possibly wasn't told at the time – that Dorothy contributed quite as much as she did.

My father's aunt Ruth, with whom he now lived, had meanwhile moved house. Aunt Ruth was fat but her husband, Bert, was a lean, sinewy man like something carved from dark wood, known as Tigger Garton for his fearsome reputation as a fighter. Bert had taken the post of gardener at a 'big house' in Lindfield, east of Haywards Heath. There they lived in a tied cottage – just as my Irish grandparents lived in the house on Knigh Hill – and my father lived with them. He paid Aunt Ruth 12s 6d for board and lodging. Ruth was a good cook and they ate fresh produce from the garden. Her first and only child, Joan, was a little girl of three or four who adored my father even though he teased her mercilessly. A shrew lived under the stairs, and in the woods giant puffball mushrooms grew as bald and white as stellar observatories. In the evenings they often sat in the firelight singing songs accompanied by Ruth on a pretty, upright piano which, until very recently, stood in my own spare room. Ruth's voice was alto, Bert's tenor, and David's a very sweet baritone.

It was Bertie who said one day to my father, 'Are you going to the New Year's Eve dance then, boy?'

My father had heard there was to be a dance in the village hall but, as his uncle perfectly well knew, he'd not thought of going, and said so.

'Well,' said Bertie, 'there's a girl at the house who's looking for someone to take her. She's the new cook, and she's very nice. I think you should ask her.'

My father decided a look would be a good thing before committing himself. The effect of this look almost made him lose his nerve. On the cook's day off, he waited by his aunt's gate until the new girl came cycling down the driveway, holding her skirt down with one hand, a lit cigarette between her fingers. David was eighteen, handsome, with a natural wave to his hair and a graceful way of standing. He wasn't unaware of these things but at the same time he didn't expect this young woman with her proud, pale profile to even glance in his direction. Then at the last moment, a light flitted over her face and, almost invisibly, Agnes gave him her reticent country-girl's smile.

2

'*During most decades since the 1880s more women than men have emigrated from Ireland. The vast majority of these women were single, younger than their male counterparts and travelled alone.*'

– *Irish Women in England*, by Clare Barrington

There is a series of paintings by de Chirico of Ariadne in exile, motionless and melancholy. Two things about Ariadne most define her: she provided the thread – in the case of the ancient story she provided a literal, physical thread to lead Theseus out of the labyrinth, but also a metaphorical thread, as in the thread of a story; secondly, she went into exile where she was alone until rescued by a lover who took her up to Heaven – is this an early instance of the later Romantic convention in which love and death are conflated? Or is it more a case of love being an earthly paradise? In any case, Ariadne spent a long time alone on a rock, abandoned, and that's how de Chirico pictures her, lost in a state of deep contemplation. If there'd been someone there on the rock with her, would she have told her story, or maintained an enigmatic silence?

When my mother left Tipperary, she took very little with her. But what she had was beyond price: her chaste white body, her skills, and her inspiring 'notions'. She also had a hatbox. It was Mrs Minchin who had given it to her. Old, but in good condition, it was in dark blue leather with a striped silk lining (I still have it). On one side there's a little ruched pocket, on the other, a buttoned-down pocket in which Agnes found a new £5 note and – what she had most needed – an excellent reference as to her character and her professional ability. Yet when I asked if she'd been excited setting out for a new life, she had replied, 'I wasn't excited. I was terrified.' Along with everyone else, at Dublin she would have had to go through a humiliating 'delousing' procedure because the English authorities were still afraid of disease coming in from Ireland.

In north-west London, Agnes had four Kavanagh siblings already established in marriages and in work. Church was all-important. But on Saturday nights they could, if they wished, socialise at one of the clubs and dance halls that were just beginning to be part of the emigrant Irish life. These were men and women having a good time, a touch defiantly asserting their exiled Irish identity here in the heart of London. But Agnes bypassed London altogether. It was no part of her intention to declare herself one with a minority, to 'wear the shamrock', or go to Mass as if her mother was still there looking over her shoulder. No, my mother took the train to a village in Sussex where she joined Nancy.

Why Nancy, the baby of the Kavanagh family, should have come to Sussex, I don't know. It's not explained by the fact that she had recently married an Englishman, since Bill was himself a Londoner and, at the time of my mother's first meeting him, he wasn't employed locally – or anywhere else. Bill was not to my mother's liking. He doesn't seem to have been much to anyone's liking. It turned Agnes's stomach to see Nancy curled on his lap in the mornings, drinking his kisses. And she was distressed by the conditions in which Nancy was living: happy, poor as the proverbial church mouse, and, by now, pregnant. Her knowingly raffish young husband had no sooner married than he was out of work. Nancy had never had a spare ounce of flesh on her small frame. Now, employed as a laundress, she was owed a few ounces, and her pregnancy showed as a tight little bulge she kept cupping with her red, chapped hands. When the buttons dropped off her cheap flowered shifts, Agnes was the one to find them, where they'd rolled away into the dust, and sew them back on.

Nancy had married William Tanner at the Catholic church in Haywards Heath in the autumn of 1934. The bride's father was described as a 'farm labourer', the groom's father as a 'police constable (retired)' and Bill himself was described as working for the county council as a road labourer. Neither of the witnesses was a Kavanagh. The London Kavanaghs certainly disapproved of their sister's marriage and had done their best to dissuade her. Dan told her she'd spend the rest of her life scraping the pennies together and Josie said a woman could tell, just looking at Bill, though what she could tell she didn't say. Anyway, according to my mother, it was always Nancy and not her they used to get on at for marrying an Englishman. All of which might, I suppose explain, the young couple moving away to Sussex. But, when the war came, Tom found Bill work as a nightwatchman in Southall, and the family moved there.

In Southall Nancy lived on a long, treeless road of small grey-coloured houses. By that time – in the '40s and '50s – enough Indian immigrants had begun to arrive for people to remark on it. It never occurred to me to think that my mother and her sister were immigrants, too. My aunt Nancy – 'Nancy with the laughing eyes' – was still so pretty, with her black hair and blue eyes, her voice gravelly from smoking. She was careless and outspoken, unlike my mother in everything – or so it seemed to me – except that she, too, had married an Englishman. If the sisters ever reminisced about 'the old days', they never did so in my presence. They talked about their children – Nancy had three – about their husband's jobs; they laughed about their sisters and speculated about the cat's nightlife. My mother always gave Nancy the sweets and the clothing coupons from her ration book since very little of Bill's earnings found their way to his wife.

We were grateful for the fact that since Bill worked nights he was usually asleep when we visited. But sometimes, as we sat on the pockmarked grass in the back garden, Bill's grey, spoon-shaped face appeared at the bedroom window, casting silence on us like a spell. I intuited from my mother's tone of voice whenever she spoke of her that Nancy was unhappy. Then, as the years went by, it became obvious that she was also unwell. There was always this very particular, deep sadness in my mother over her sister. Illness destroyed Nancy's prettiness. The drugs used to combat the illness killed her. She was fifty-two when she died, the last of the Kavanagh children to be born, the second to go, and hers was one of the funerals we went to.

Within weeks of her arrival in England, Agnes found a live-in post as cook in a 'big house', bright and white with glittering windows, like those she'd seen from the train. Big houses were plentiful in this claustrophobically rich countryside of overpainted, swanky villages with their stands of ancient trees and dull, taciturn natives. No doubt Agnes could have found a post in several of these houses, but she chose Copse Hill because it was little more than a ten-minute bike ride from her sister.

301

Relief to be away from Nancy's cheerfully shambolic rooms was tempered by the bone-chilling fact of her solitude. She unpacked her few belongings from the hatbox and distributed them about the room as she was supposed to: coat in the wardrobe (on a wooden hanger printed with the name of the Hotel Linden, Berlin), hairbrush on the dressing table, nightdress under the pillow, wondering at her own obedience, seeing herself as an animal trained to do what it has been told. Her heart froze. In God's name what had she done to herself? Only now did she know how far she was from home. It was an amputation: sudden, irreversible. In this place she was without substance. No one looking at her here would know she had her mother's beautiful eyes. The hard little armchair had oil from another woman's hair on the headrest, and grease from another woman's hands on the arms. It faced the fireplace, directing each inhabitant of this room how to sit, facing the fire, looking into the flames, feet up on a pretty little hassock embroidered with a bird of no particular kind. If you keep a rabbit, Agnes thought, you give it hay. And to a canary you give seed, to make it sing. You give a woman a footstool, and a pretty little bin for her sanitary towels.

On her day off she cycled into the village but no one spoke to her. She couldn't for the life of her work out what was wrong with the miserable devils. So she cycled back to the house and, unsure if she was allowed to sit in the over-manicured garden (she wasn't, at least not in sight of the house, which only left a small area behind a yew hedge which was used for the compost heap), she sat on her bed and watched sunlight unfold like a pale fan across the slate roof.

'Tipperary?' the housekeeper had said when they were introduced. 'That's a long way to go.'

She laughed at her own wit. After that, Agnes didn't mention the word 'Tipperary' again. She didn't want to see that smirk – 'Irish, are you?' – as if to answer 'Yes' was to admit to something comical or shameful. She was dismayed to find that Busherstown had not prepared her for the English. Her pride baulked at having to explain herself to cold, ignorant people who were fixed like oysters in their superiority. Silence had been one of the first lessons she learned at school. Now she was learning what to hear and what not to. She became adept at having, apparently, not picked up either news or gossip. It was now that, speaking only when necessary, almost unconsciously Agnes began to lose her Irish brogue.

There's a question mark over exactly which year this was. As early as 1934, or as late as 1936? My father always believed Lindfield was my mother's first position in England and that the Whittingtons, whom she liked, were her first English employers. But she spoke to me of being first in this other household, where she had not been happy, with people she described as being 'vulgar', and 'having no idea how to treat servants'. My mother had sniffed out 'new money'. Another word she used was 'abrupt'. But everything – the lady of the house, the menus, the silver as well as the manner of speaking – everything was compared unfavourably with Busherstown where she'd learned not only skill but refinement of an especially Irish, inclusive kind.

On one of our evenings together, sensing she was in a relaxed mood, I asked if she'd found England – and the English in general – difficult when she first came over here.

'I did,' she said. 'It was horrid. So unfriendly.' A laugh, and then she added, 'I don't know, I think perhaps they're afraid of us. But very unfriendly. When I think what it was like back there at home…'

303

Joe Hogan wrote in the *Irish Post*, 'The past and memory, the immigrant's curse, especially the Irish. The Irish pushed out of Ireland were left with one thing and that was their memory, their own hidden Ireland. Of course they handed it on to their children. What else did they have?'

But in this, as in so many ways, my mother was not typical. The last thing she wanted to hand on to her child was her memory of Ireland. Hidden is what it remained. She went forward, she forgot, she cast off. She took up every little clue thrown her way and pieced together plans for her future. She was young. She was strong. Maybe there's murder at the heart of emigration as often as there's preservation, as much forgetting as there is memory. She did not, however, forget her parents. She wrote to let them know she had settled, and she enclosed a money order to cover the purchase of a pair of fine breeding geese. The following year she took up her position as cook at Lindfield, and life took a turn for the better.

She once said of being 'in service' that it gave you everything you needed. Except freedom. 'But then,' my mother said. 'I never minded that.' By which I think she meant the lack of sexual freedom didn't worry her. The freedom that mattered to her flourished inside that other, apparent lack of freedom: she was her own mistress, free to reinvent herself and, by the time she met my father she resembled – in appearance and style – no one so much as Mrs Simpson, the king's consort. But my mother didn't like the comparison and when it was first made, she had her hair cut short. However, like Mrs Simpson, she never cast off that air of being different, of being an outsider, an enigma.

After my mother's death, I asked my father for something in her handwriting. My father found a recipe for queen's pudding: gelatin, caster sugar, egg whites, angelica. She had a pretty, rather unusual hand, neat and feminine without being at all flowery. I tried the recipe one day, following the instructions exactly – not my usual way with a recipe – and, predictably, it worked perfectly. Some months later, I was sorting through my mother's books. A photograph of Bruce Chatwin cut from a newspaper article fell out of his novel, *The Viceroy of Ouidah*, and a folded sheet of yellowing paper out of a book I'd given her: Lady Gregory's *Selected Writings*. Like a sheet torn from an old exercise book but, disappointingly, there was nothing on it.

Then I realised it was being used to mark a page on which the title of the poem had been underlined: 'May'. Not just the title, but some of the phrases were underlined: 'the sad restless sea is asleep', 'the girl in her comely power', 'the cold has caught the wings of the birds.' I'd never known my mother do this before. I believe I blushed at the sense I had of glimpsing her private world. Usually she didn't even turn down the corner of a page. To annotate would be unthinkable. This book, another I'd given my mother but not read myself, now became my constant companion – a cliché, but, in the months following her death, that's exactly how it felt. I was sure that this was a poem she had first read at school when she began to study Gaelic literature.

When David came to the kitchen door that evening, the first thing Agnes noticed was his youth. He was scarcely more than a boy. A strikingly handsome boy, true, but it was not – so she would have us believe – his good looks that made her accept his offer to accompany her to the dance. It was the fact that, within minutes, she'd decided she could trust him. That's how she put it to me all those years later: 'I felt I could trust your father.' And she was right. David was, and still is, kind, reliable, trustworthy. I always had the impression that from my mother's point of view his trustworthiness had something to do with his being English – and a great deal to do with his not being Irish.

But, as I was about to discover, there was one secret she never did entrust him with.

3

'uisce fe talamh' – an old Irish saying, literally: *water under the ground*

I have an unexpected call from Joan Cleary, inviting me to tea. When I put my head round the kitchen door she gives me her most deeply knowing smile.

'There's someone I want you to meet,' she says. 'Will I wet the tea?'

She does so, then disappears into the depths of the house and I hear the low murmur of voices. I stand looking at the Sacred Heart on the kitchen wall and at the same time, by a curiously Renaissance-like painterly trick of propinquity, through a little window just to one side of it, at a square of green sloping field where a cow grazes in the afternoon sunshine. I imagine one of the purposes of doing this in Renaissance paintings was not just to show off the artist's skills but also to suggest how life continues outside the narrow focus of the picture – in this case, Christ's suffering – to suggest other places, other times. Indeed, to 'put things into perspective'.

A few minutes later, Joan and I carry a tray through to the sitting room, passing as we do so the front door, the door Kate Cleary opened that night to the soldiers of the North Hants Regiment – the soldiers who 'politely' took away two young men sleeping in the house, and murdered them. The panels of the door are filled with pretty ornamental glass and, arriving at the house earlier, I had noticed pots of geraniums on the doorstep. My eye had also been taken by an expensive-looking silvery car on the driveway. The sitting room is a pleasant shadowy room I've never been in before. A woman I would guess is in her early seventies rises from the chair, with that slight hesitation I recognise as accommodating the pain of arthritis. She's tall, with blue eyes set in a face that has something indefinably familiar about it. Joan introduces us – 'Catherine is an old family friend,' she tells me, 'here for the blessing of the graves'; I have time to wonder idly who Catherine might have to remember here in the Knigh graveyard – and then, rather to my surprise, she leaves us alone. I am in an atmosphere of intense, unexplained emotion. There is a pause. Catherine's mouth opens to speak.

'I'm your aunt Nancy's daughter,' she says. 'Born the wrong side of the blanket.'

Catherine was brought up by a foster mother, Mrs Hogan, in County Kildare. Mrs Hogan was an elderly widow who had no children of her own and only now – for both money and company – thought to foster a child from the Catholic Protection and Rescue Society in Dublin. Catherine had always known that 'Mammy' was not her natural mother. She recalled being told how, when she was handed over there'd been an older woman with the girl, and the older woman had to say several times over, 'Come on Nan,' to urge the mother to give away her seven-month-old baby. This was in August 1931. A week later, Mrs Hogan wrote to the fostering agency:

This is just a note to tell you that the baby is getting on grand and quiet at home. Never made a bit strange and out every day in pram. I got one in Dublin that day and bottle. The pram is chair and bed. Cost 9 shillings but what matter when it suited the baby and it does eat bread and milk and Neaves food. I got oil for it also and powder. It is doing splendid so far and quiet. Everybody is delighted with it.

By 'everybody', Mrs Hogan must have meant neighbours, as she lived alone and had neither relations nor friends. The following summer, Catherine was diagnosed with bronchial pneumonia and spent two weeks in hospital. When she was safely home again Mrs Hogan wrote,

'My darling baby is better thank God but has got awful weak and very thin. You would not hardly know her as she was so fat. She will take a lot of care and nourishment. I did give her Bovril, New Milk and a little Whiskey. I do have her out again in the pram for her good. It was very lonely while she was away.'

The secretary of the agency replied saying she was glad Catherine was home again and informing Mrs Hogan that she had, of course, to deduct from her maintenance cheque the two weeks and five days that the little one had spent in hospital – a burden on the State rather than on Mrs Hogan.

Mrs Hogan appears to have been genuinely fond of the child. She was never unkind. But the fact is she was almost entirely unfit to play the role of mother. There was little natural affection expressed. Catherine says that Mrs Hogan was a bit – she searches for the word – well, there was a 'streak' in the family. At first, Catherine was treated more like a pet bird than a baby. Later, 'Mammy' frequently forgot to buy or prepare food, and just as often,

Catherine would come home from school to find no one there. She would sit on the doorstep until dark, when Mammy would drift home, having gone off to gather firewood and forgotten about the girl, literally forgotten she existed, so that she would start at the sight of her. Yet she taught the little girl to read and write before she went to school, and when the mood was on her she sang old songs from her own childhood though she could never remember the words.

Mrs Hogan was a retired bookkeeper at the family draper's in Monasterevin in County Kildare. She lived just outside the town in a tiny cottage on the canal. The child Catherine was imprinted with such dire warnings about the dangers of the canal she grew up terrified of water. Mrs Hogan received £1 10s per month from the Society. The Society was, of course, a Catholic institution, but when Mammy was annoyed with Catherine she used to throw it at her that she'd come from 'the Birds' Nest' (nickname for Protestant 'Homes'). Why she should have come from a Protestant Home, the child had no idea, but it was an accusation that made her into an alien. She describes herself as growing like a mushroom, popping up overnight without roots, come from nowhere. Or worse.

As a girl, Catherine did not have robust health but she turned out to be very bright. 'Always being very brilliant,' as her school principal described her, 'and able to say her prayers both in Irish and in English.' But there was never a spare penny; not for clothes, not for schoolbooks, and certainly not – in spite of Catherine's studying hard and being very anxious to get on – a chance of her staying on beyond the minimum school-leaving age of fourteen. And Catherine admits that, bright as she was, she was also troublesome. Mammy wrote to the Society complaining that Catherine was not going to school, that she was smoking and *staying out late at night*. The sort of behaviour that is a hundred times more significant in the illegitimate child of an unknown mother. Catherine's opportunities seemed to be narrowing down into the familiar pattern: service at the big house and early marriage. Then fate stepped in: a free place was offered with the Sisters of Mercy in Athy to any bright girl wishing to start her training as a nurse. Catherine jumped at the chance.

It turned out a mixed blessing. The 'training' didn't amount to much and Catherine was worked so hard she became ill with glandular fever. As soon as she had recovered, she took her savings and travelled to England, to Liverpool. There the newly founded NHS embraced her. She was given the opportunity to qualify as a nurse, though one unexpected problem cropped up: having done so much of her schoolwork in Gaelic, Catherine needed evening classes in English in order to cope with the written medical examinations. At first she was homesick and exhausted, but after two years she had her SEN badge – not the full SRN qualification, and a green uniform rather than the blue one she craved, but still an achievement. Then, Catherine fell pregnant to a young Irish ambulance driver, Seamus. History looked set to repeat itself. Only it didn't. Their feeling for one another was real. Catherine adored him. They married and five months later their son arrived, legitimate but premature and weighing only four pounds. It was thought he might not survive. But Catherine was determined nothing would take her baby from her. He flourished.

Seamus still pined for his home county, Cork, for his family, and for the old life. In '52, moving against the tide, the couple returned to Ireland. Seamus had ambitions. Within ten years, he had established his own taxi company, and Catherine had given birth to two more healthy children. For a while during the last years of her life Mrs Hogan lived with them. She taught Catherine's daughter to walk.

Aged thirty-five, Catherine returned to Dublin and took the first step in a search to find her real mother. At the Four Courts she obtained a copy of her birth certificate. On it were just two pieces of information: her mother's name, Annie (as Nancy had been baptised) Kavanagh, of Nenagh, Tipperary, and Catherine's date and place of birth: March 1931, at 18 Capel Street, Dublin. 18 Capel Street was a Protestant Bethany Home for unmarried women and their children. So this is the 'Bird's Nest' she'd come from. But why? And who was her father?

It was many years before Catherine – against her husband's advice – found the courage to trace her mother to Knigh and to learn that she, Nancy, was the youngest daughter of John and Kate Kavanagh. It became her habit once a year to come here to where she had been told her grandparents – our grandparents – were buried. She came to be known locally by her smart expensive cars, a new one every couple of years or so. It was on one of these visits she had met and, in due course, been befriended by Joan Cleary. Soon she learned that when Nancy was fourteen she'd gone to work as housemaid for the Protestant minister, Reverend Burroughs, at his home near Puckaun. This was the job my mother so disapproved of her doing. Catherine became convinced that this man was her father. Certainly it was then, whilst working in the Burroughs' household, that Nancy became pregnant.

This is the sum of Catherine's information on the

circumstances of her conception and birth. But this is about to change. On a recent trip to Dublin she visited the Catholic Society . They have undertaken to forward copies of the records of Catherine's birth and fostering to her here, at Knigh.

Before we part I give Catherine an edited version of what I know about Nancy's life.

I tell her that Nancy married an Englishman in 1935, had three children, and died some time in the '60s. I'm ashamed not to remember the exact date because I had known and loved Nancy, but at that time I was in the full spate of my own young life. When I tell Catherine that Nancy had suffered badly from arthritis, that it was, indeed, the drugs for arthritis that finally killed her, Catherine confirms that she, too, suffers from arthritis. When I mention that our grandmother had agoraphobia, Catherine exclaims that she, too, for a period when the children had grown up and left home, had suffered from agoraphobia. This *does* surprise me. Catherine has a strong presence, a good mind and a quick sense of humour. Agoraphobia suggests hidden conflict, but clearly there are good reasons why I shouldn't be surprised by that.

Whilst Catherine has been speaking I've tried to fit these new pieces of information into the pattern of dates and events as I know them. The burning question for me is, *Did my mother know*? Did she know *at the time*? She must have done. She was still here in Ireland in 1931, and weren't she and Nancy 'like that'?

As Catherine tells me her story, as she tilts her head back to rest it on the back of the chair, I can't take my eyes off her face which seems to metamorphose under my gaze, manipulated by memory and apprehension: I see no likeness to Nancy, except the blue eyes and, of course,

313

the arthritis. But I *can* see some kind of 'family resemblances' emerging like the build-up of an identikit image on a plasma screen, and they are all to Aunt Bridie. Or to my mother. Mouth. Gestures. Something in those long limbs, the width at the cheekbones, the emphatic, dark hairline. The longer I look, the stronger the resemblance to my mother becomes. So the question I'm really asking myself is this: was 'Annie' in fact *Agnes* Kavanagh? Is the woman I've just met my half-sister? It would explain several features of my mother's own story: the slightly odd chronology I've already puzzled over, the somehow unsatisfactory explanation for her flight to England. Her silences.

Yes, there are baby-shaped gaps in the account I've put together, and the 'appendix operation' could have been a cover – as it often was – for a quite different reason necessitating a visit to Dublin.

A digression – if that's what it is: a couple of years before my mother died she was rushed into Kingston Hospital with stomach pain. This resulted in her having her appendix removed at the age of eighty-five. This was how I came to discover that she had not, in fact, had her appendix removed as a young woman in Dublin. My father, naturally, thought it was all 'very Irish' but there was a perfectly good medical explanation for her scar and her long hospitalization: peritonitis requires a long draining of the poison before an operation is considered safe, and the doctors in Dublin may well have felt it remained unsafe, or even unnecessary, to proceed.

Eventually, the papers Catherine has been expecting arrive. They include her 'long' birth certificate, and a dozen or so letters. First amongst the letters we devour is one written to our grandmother in August 1931, from the Catholic Protection and Rescue Agency in Dublin:

Dear Mrs Kavanagh,
I am writing to you about your daughter Annie. She was brought to this office on Saturday by one of the officials from Bethany where she has been since her child was born. The little child, who is five months old, was baptised this morning and your daughter is waiting to hear from you and wants you to send her fare.

Your daughter informs me that her own sister (Joanna) [my aunt Josie's baptismal name] put her into the Home and I am very surprised to hear that you left your daughter there and risked losing her soul and the soul of her little child. I certainly think it was you or your people's duty to have come to Dublin and taken her out immediately. I want the address of your daughter who is responsible for doing this dreadful act.

It was Agnes who, by return of post, replied to this terrible letter. She must have been trembling, because the wobble is clear in the first few lines, her hand immature yet shockingly familiar:

...your letter to hand this morning. I am Annie's sister and as my mother is very delicate I could not let her see your letter as dear mother is such a good mother to us. I have to keep any bad news from her as she is in bed very ill. As regards to the Protestant Home where my sister's baby was born I knew it was a Protestant Home but I did not tell my dear mother as she is so easily worried. Father nor brothers know anything about it at all. None of them knows about her. It is hard to tell a lie but it had to be. If my father knew about Annie we would all be killed. At the time poor Annie went away we were so worried and it is

315

*keep a secret that we did not know what to do. I cannot
sleep or work only worrying but I trust in God to save her.*

This letter established beyond doubt who Catherine's
mother was.

It surely can't have been later than August or September
of the previous year that Agnes came to know her sister
was pregnant. Perhaps she saw her from far off. Maybe
she saw Nancy come dawdling up the hill from work,
saw the outline of her sister's body and knew, she just
KNEW, there was a baby in there. I can imagine Nancy
denying it at first. Stormy-faced. Denying the possibility
of it. Denial was the only plan she'd come up with so far
and if she denied it for long enough, maybe it would go
away? Agnes's first question must have been, 'Who is the
father? WHO IS he? He must be made to marry you! Is he
willing? *How could you think so little of yourself?*'

Quite what occurred next, and why, I don't know, only
that there was no wedding. And Agnes gave up any ideas
she'd had of moving on. Across the years I can feel my
mother's shame, her fear and her fury. Pity only came later,
much later, when she felt she could afford it. Now she had
to act. But what? How? Agnes had never been to Dublin,
never made a telephone call, never addressed an envelope
or bought stamps. She only knew Nancy must be got away
before the men realised what had happened. So the sisters
wrote to Josie in Dublin. Or did they ask, face to face, that
time when Josie and Bridie were home for a visit with Dublin
written all over them, carrying umbrellas, and Bridie wearing
a golden hat the size of a bicycle wheel? This would be the
time my grandmother's eagerly planned trip to Dublin did
not take place and my mother stopped dancing.

4

The fashionable dressmaker for whom Josie and Bridie worked drew her clients from the Protestant gentry. Amongst them was a philanthropic lady, a lay evangelist and a member of the managing committee of the Bethany. It was Josie, the more driven of the sisters, who finally plucked up the nerve to ask this lady, Would the Bethany take a respectable Catholic girl who found herself in trouble? It seemed it would. The obvious advantage to the sisters of such an arrangement was that, in removing Nancy from the Catholic network, they hid her away as if she'd never been. There would be no communication with the Kavanaghs' family priest back in Puckaun. Who knew if a priest could be relied on not to inform the girl's father? The Reverend Burroughs appears to have played no part in any of this. In due course, a letter came back from Josie to say a refuge had been found for Nancy – no doubt adding that Nancy should thank God first and her sisters second for scouring the charities of Dublin and humiliating and shaming themselves in the process and who would ever believe they were decent girls from a decent family. And so on.

It was most likely Agnes who went shopping for Nancy. She was the one who would have been able to draw her raincoat belt tight round her slim waist and look the shopkeeper in the eye as she chose a nightdress and a pair of slippers. Handing over the money she caught a brief, inquisitive glint in the draper's eye which he extinguished with the wipe of a nicotine-stained hand over his brow. I see her roll the nightdress around two pairs of clean knickers and a new flesh-coloured brassiere and put them into a bag for Nancy who sits on the bed behind her, chewing the ends of her hair. 'And for the love of God,' Agnes says bitterly, without turning, 'will you remember to darn your stockings and keep yourself clean.'

The men and women who made up the managing committee of the Bethany were obliged to sign a 'doctrinal pledge' proclaiming amongst other things 'the utter depravity of human nature...and the eternal punishment of the wicked'. The nurses hired were explicitly enlisted as evangelical and 'missionary-minded'. Internally, the Home was known as 'the Mission'. The Protestant Church of Ireland, it turns out, was as zealous as the Catholic in getting and keeping possession of its own. In its passion to save souls the Bethany appears to have neglected the health of mothers and babies in its care. In Mount Jerome Cemetery are several unmarked common graves for the many children who died there. They died of convulsions, heart failure, wasting disease, pneumonia, meningitis. When the State (the newly independent Catholic state of Ireland) intervened, it too showed itself more concerned with the religious issues than with the physical welfare of mothers and babies.

In November, more than six months pregnant, Nancy travelled, alone, by train from Nenagh to Dublin. There she hung about in the cold, looking in the shop windows on Grafton Street until it was dark before walking to number 24 Marlborough Street, where Josie and Bridie lodged. Josie gave her a cup of tea, then the two of them cut across O'Connell Street and walked along the river,

318

past the smart south-facing houses and the Four Courts, a long walk to a poorer part of town, to the Bethany, Protestant home for fallen women, which took her in.

For over two months there was silence. Josie and Bridie were already gone away to Canada, chasing the man Josie would eventually marry, abandoning Nancy and her baby to their fate. In Nenagh, Agnes was stacking shelves in the Brophys' grocery when Pat appeared at the door. He had a letter come for her from Nancy. He took a drink at the bar then threw his leg over his old bike and left. Agnes ran out to the back and opened a letter that put the responsibility for everything on to her powerless nineteen-year-old shoulders: secrecy, her mother's health, her sister's salvation, and the baby's future. I think this must be the time Agnes recalled having to rush from the Brophys' to Dublin.

Nancy wrote that during her labour, and in terror of death, she had been denied the Catholic rites. She had been told she must have the baby baptised in the Protestant faith or the Home would not undertake to have it fostered and, in six months, she'd be put back out on the street. If nowhere could be found for her, wouldn't she just turn up on the Home doorstep with the baby in her arms? Only she didn't have the fare. Only by then, she and the baby would most likely be dead.

In fact, 1931 was a 'lucky' year at the Bethany. In 1936 twenty-nine babies died, but in 1931 it was fewer than five. Agnes found her sister easily enough in the stinking little dormitory because she could never mistake Nancy's eyes for anyone else's. With no source of heating other than the bodies it contained, the room was cold and damp. On all sides, babies lay in dirty nappies, screaming, and their mothers either screamed back or sat sunk in a stupor. Some attempted to air damp clothes against their own bodies. There appeared to be no one in charge, no one to offer care or relief. Agnes, with the shilling she'd put aside for lunch, went out and bought zinc ointment for the baby's head.

Only now – so it emerges from the later three-way correspondence between the sisters and the Rescue Society – with the prospect of being turfed out looming over her, did Nancy confess: the father of her baby was Jim Casey, the young surveyor who'd come there last summer surveying the roads for the county council, come like a bird and gone away again, the one Nancy had pretended not to care for, the one whom their mother had marked down for Agnes, the nice one with the brown eyes. Jim knew and had promised to pay for all, only Nancy had thought to get by without him.

Before leaving the Bethany, Agnes spoke to a large pale-eyed woman called Miss Lettie Cullen who stared the way one small child stares at another and told Agnes that her 'only aim in life was to bring sinners back to Christ'. Matron didn't have time to say anything at all as she was 'busy attending the sick babies', though Agnes had seen no sign of her.

Agnes stood a moment trembling on the doorstep. Then she ran to the nearest Catholic church and there in the transept she found the address of a Catholic agency called Saint Patrick's Guild. Returning home, she told her mother only that Nancy was perfectly well. In secret she then wrote to the matron of the Bethany, asking her to discharge Nancy into the care of Saint Patrick's Guild. She wrote to the secretary of the guild, asking them to rescue Nancy. These were the first real letters Agnes had ever written to anyone other than her sisters, though she had, of course, been taught at the convent the correct way to go about it: Dear Sir/Madam, writing the address on the right, date on the left, and signing Yours faithfully with her full name. She received no reply. Nor did her letter to the surveyor, care of his company in Limerick, provoke a response.

Agnes prayed to Mary Mother of God to save Nancy and her baby. Images of her sister's shrunken face and of the baby with its red weeping eyes haunted her nights and took away her sleep. She remained convinced that if her father and brother got to know what had happened, they would all be killed. In a family who weren't great talkers perhaps secrecy was easier, but the physical symptoms of intense anxiety are difficult to hide. Sometimes on her nightlong vigils Agnes saw her father go outside to block the foxholes for the hunt – because of course she'd known for a long time that that was what he was doing. Even under these circumstances, and terrified in case Nancy did something foolish – she recalled stories of desperate girls throwing both their babies and themselves into the river – still it was a couple of weeks before Agnes was ready to go to a priest.

In the presbytery of the Church of Saint Mary of the Rosary, in Nenagh, Agnes went down on her knees before Father O'Donnel, a priest previously unknown to her. She asked politely, in a voice so low as to be almost inaudible, for the church's help in this, her sister's hour of need. Father O'Donnel was experienced in these matters. He knew all the deceptions, denials and panics of young – and not so young – women caught in these circumstances. Rather than admit their own shame, their most common manoeuvre was to name a friend, or sister, as the one in trouble. Having listened patiently to the supplicant, it was Father O'Donnell's habit to pinch the girl's chin between finger and thumb and turn her blank face up to his. 'Why would I be helping a young woman who is not only wicked but a liar, too? Eh? Tell me that.' In the face of such injustice, every nerve in my mother's body dictated silence. Yet, as the silence was prolonged, her heart must have flooded with terrible self-knowledge: she'd rather die than be found guilty of the same filthy crime as her beloved sister. Father O'Donnel proceeded in his usual manner: shoving her head down, he demanded she bow to the Lord God and pray that through the merciful intercession of the Virgin Mary she might be forgiven her sins, whether of commission or of omission, that is to say, if nothing else, for what she, the elder, had *failed* to do: to be the guide and shield of Nancy's innocence. The word 'innocence' would have been too much. Where speech would not come, tears did, hot and wet, the mark of her submission, the price of the priest's mercy.

Only then did he say, in an almost tender voice, that the woman had done the right thing in coming to him. Stepping back from her he told her he'd decided what best to do: he would refer the whole distasteful business to the higher authority of Monsignor Quinn of Drumcondra, Dublin. And so he did.

One summer morning, I see my mother, as thin and pale as a flayed bone, slip out of the house and away towards an anonymous letter box in Nenagh with two letters in her hand. One is to Nancy, explaining what she has done, and giving her the address of the Catholic Protection and Rescue Society in Dublin. One – the result of hours of writing and rewriting – is a letter to Monsignor Quinn thanking him in the most abject terms for his kind intervention – he had indeed been both kind and prompt – putting pressure on the Protestant Bethany Home and then, crucially, writing to the Catholic Society itself, standing witness to the decency of the Kavanagh family and to

Nancy's lifelong Catholic devotion. The CPRS wrote its terrible letter to Mrs Kavanagh, my mother replied, and the Society declared itself 'ready to take charge of the little child', adding, 'but of course it will have to be paid for'.

Soon Jim Casey received the following letter from a worker at the Society:

Annie Kavanagh has informed me that you are the father of her child and the girl's sister has written to the same effect. My committee wishes to state that you will have to pay for the maintenance of the said child that would be 30 shillings per month while the child is being nursed out by the society. The committee do not wish to report the matter to your superiors unless you refuse to admit your responsibility and then they shall have to take a very serious view of the matter.

Jim Casey replied a few days later, saying, '*I will meet responsibilities as they become due. Thanking you for any trouble you now have taken in the matter.*'

He enclosed the first thirty shillings. Within just a couple of days, the Society had Catherine settled with Mrs Hogan in Monasterevin and Nancy, having been sent her fare by Agnes, was on her way home. The Kavanagh women had achieved what they wanted: a Catholic home for the child and not a whisper of the matter having reached their menfolk.

Catherine had always believed her mother couldn't possibly have gone home. But she did. There is a letter she wrote to the Society from Knigh in December:

'*...to enquire for little Catherine. Please God I hope to see her after Christmas. I expect she is a very big girl now and a bold girl. Of course in the country people are always* *busy and then mother not being well all this time [Kate had been in and out of hospital all through this unhappy year] and I am attending the doctor myself nearly since I came home [not surprising that eight months in the Bethany had undermined Nancy's health too] I am sending her a little frock and cap and little overalls. I thought to get her a little pair of shoes but I don't know really what size would fit her as I am sure she has a big foot now. Sending my best love to my own little pet.'*

The following spring, the Society informed Nancy that Catherine's father had stopped sending the agreed thirty shillings. Nancy replied that she would try to contact him herself but that she wanted 'to give him a chance and find out his reason for failing to pay'[4]. I feel that Nancy's protective concern for her one-time lover needs an explanation, but I don't have one unless it was just the sweetness of her own nature. And I doubt if she ever did get to see her baby who was a world away in County Kildare and, coming to the point, what useful purpose could it serve but to open painful wounds? I'm sure that time in the Bethany was the only time my mother ever set eyes on her little niece. And now it occurs to me that the occasion when the sisters sat side by side on a hospital bed, in silence mostly, hand in hand, was there in the Bethany, and not – as my mother had recalled – when she was rushed to Dublin to have her appendix out. No wonder seeing Nancy hadn't cheered my mother up much. 'Why was that?' I had asked. 'Oh, I don't know.' Her shrug. 'Seeing one another like that. So far from home.'

---

4. *In all, Catherine's father did pay towards her maintenance for two years. After that he failed to do so, citing his father's death and consequently his own responsibility for his mother and younger siblings.*

Abandoned children is a recurrent theme in the Kavanagh story. Mary Rose's son, Sean. Nancy's daughter, Catherine. Pat's children 'taken into care' in Nenagh. Even Katherine, my aunt Cathleen's only child, was abandoned when Cathleen died of self-neglect following her husband's death at sea in World War Two.

Even as Nancy had gone running out to meet her lover on those sweet May evenings, the Carrigan Committee was gathering information to report on immorality in the Free State.

By immorality the committee overwhelmingly meant illegitimacy (though by European standards, the rate in Ireland was low) and prostitution. Violence, abuse, the mistreatment of children and the old were apparently lesser matters. In the mind of the committee, both unlicensed dance halls and the car were seen as great facilitators of moral decline – which no doubt they were. The Carrigan Committee

Report might at least have provoked an airing of these social problems. Instead, the report was suppressed. 'Any chance that, for example, child abuse or contraception (the sale and importation of contraceptives was banned in Eire in 1935[5]) would be debated in Ireland was buried with the censoring of that report.'

The spread of VD – in so far as the committee could bring itself to recognise it as a public health issue at all – was, of course, largely blamed on women, though a distinction was made between those 'relatively unchaste' and those considered 'irredeemable', meaning professional prostitutes *and women born out of wedlock*. 'Irredeemable'. In

---

5 *And remained so until 1985.*

1985 it was still possible for a journalist in the magazine *Magill* to observe that 'the unmarried mother is still a pariah and her child is still a bastard, because there is only one sin in Ireland and only women can commit it'.

The treatment endured by women and children in the Magdalene Laundries, the industrial schools – and, as I now know, in the Protestant homes, too – is something I hardly need enumerate. Starvation, neglect and abuse were common. Children born outside marriage were five times more likely to die prematurely. Nancy, however, wrote of the kindness *'shown to myself and little Catherine by Nurse Farrell'* at the Society's nursing home. And Catherine herself says that though her mother would have been made to work in the Catholic Home – hard, punishing work at that – 'Who but the Church would have taken us in?'

Ireland has traditionally been depicted as a woman – romantic, irrational, vanquished. But the men of Ireland must themselves take some responsibility for the mass emigration of their young women who, the nation's newly won freedom notwithstanding, continued to leave, alone, and in greater numbers than ever – the six Kavanagh sisters amongst them. Speaking in the senate on censorship in 1928, the writer Oliver St John Gogarty said, 'It is high time that the people of this country find some other way of loving God than by hating women.'

When Agnes went to Busherstown, the young men of Moneygall knew better than to approach her. They reckoned she must have had some kind of bad experience, and Mrs Minchin sensed Agnes was troubled but would resist the comfort of intimacy. I never knew my aunt Nancy well enough to imagine, retrospectively, what it all did to her. I believe hers was the more resilient nature. Wasn't Nancy the one who had no common sense, the one inclined to bend with the moment? Wasn't Nancy forgetful and trusting? Careless. Where our perception of character is concerned, I'm less resistant to the idea: 'It all depends.' Even, especially, our most intimate understanding of ourselves may have to bow to the judgement of others. We have a sense of ourselves, but others have a sense of us, too, often very much at odds with our own estimation and, to make matters worse, each person's view may be at odds with another's.

My mother had an expression: 'I speak as I find.' I, of course, can't 'find'. I never met my mother or Nancy when they were girls. I decide to visit someone who did: Annie O'Brien.

Finding her alone, I'm able to ask her frankly if she ever heard of Nancy having a baby when she was still very young and she immediately says, Yes, she had. It was in the winter of 1930.

'I was only twelve,' she tells me. 'What did I know? Except that Nancy had gone to Dublin too early for her mother's liking.'

When she was a little older, however, Annie understood what had really happened. Indeed, she had to confess that Nancy was held up as an example to be at all costs avoided. Not that anyone would dare to admit that to Mrs Kavanagh's face! Can you *imagine* it? Someone did once make some kind of sly reference to Nancy being the youngest 'and isn't it the youngest give you the most to worry about?' My grandmother had turned on him like a viper. 'I'll thank you to keep a civil tongue in your head!' she hissed. As to the father? It was the Reverend Burroughs. How did she hear *that*? I ask.

'Sure, 'twas well known.'

I am at least able now, so many years later, to set the record straight on that particular issue.

'But you didn't tell me any of this before,' I point out.

Annie raises both hands in a suggestive gesture. Then she adds another memory of her own: in the winter of 1930, when she was twelve years old, Annie was sent up to the Kavanaghs' for an old coat of Nancy's which my grandmother had offered to cut down for her. This was the time, she recalled, that my grandmother had given up on the idea of going to Dublin in her new hat. Annie took with her a bag of sweet-smelling cherrywood kindling. They stood in the in the kitchen, very quiet and easy, and the neat, spacious house was empty around them. There was a clock ticking, a beautiful old grandmother clock that had come from Mary Dunne. Mrs Kavanagh was pleased with the results of her sewing. She told Annie the blue coat suited her fair hair. She never made the child feel in any way looked down on, not even when she came to collect milk or butter – Annie stresses this fact – there was no superiority in my grandmother's way of giving. But on that day, the child noticed that Mrs Kavanagh seemed troubled and, when she went down on her knees to pin the hem, Annie thought she heard her murmur through heavy sighs, 'Poor Annie, poor Annie!' which was strange and disturbing, even though she d Mrs Kavanagh must be referring to her own daughter. 'I was only twelve,' says Annie, 'what did I know? Except that Nancy had left school too early for her mother's liking. We all knew Mrs Kavanagh was a great believer in education, for her girls as much as the boys. "Stay at school" she told me. "It'll be the crowning of you."' Annie laughs. 'Well I stayed, and it wasn't. But without it I'd never have had the confidence to go to America. No one else ever said anything like that to me.'

It was maybe a year or so later, after Nancy had been away for some time – 'working in Dublin' as her mother said – Annie remembers her coming there to the O'Briens' gate on her bicycle, and stopping to have a chat with Annie's mother. Annie remembers her mother seemed a little – what would she say – not distant with the girl, no, not one bit, but shy, a little awkward, and Nancy was just her old self, laughing, with a cigarette in her hand. Just the same except for her hair, which was red.

Ah yes! I have a photo of Nancy sitting in a garden somewhere – it could well be here, at Knigh – with a melodeon on her lap and her thick hair is coloured in red. Why had she done that, I wonder? Was it an act of defiance? Red hair being associated with a wild, dangerous nature. With sex. Perhaps it was part of a process of recreating herself. Two years later she was gone to a new life.

By September 1935, Nancy was in England and married to an Englishman. The chronology I've puzzled over is beginning to fall into place. When I check the date of Pat's shotgun wedding I see that it was in August 1933, which means that when my mother went home to convalesce, Pat must already have been living there with his eighteen-year-old wife, Anastasia, and their first child. And things had already gone badly wrong. Pat was drinking, there were outbursts of domestic violence and constant squabbling between Kate and her slovenly daughter-in-law. Sometimes, as Billy Foley related, Anastasia ran down the hill to take refuge with the Foleys. One day my grandmother locked them into their room to prevent them shaming her in such a way. Occasionally, Pat, Anastasia and the baby took off back to her family in Nenagh where Pat's behaviour deteriorated even further until he crawled back home again.

329

Anastasia is remembered for saying, 'Paddy's mother thinks the sun shines out of his arse, well, if she knew him as *I* know him, she'd have many a dark day.'

So, home during this period would have been Agnes's idea of hell on earth. Pity for her mother would have been mixed with a good deal of impatience, yet surely a powerful sense of responsibility, too? Who knows which way the scales might have tipped but for one thing. As I'm leaving, Annie comes to the door with me. She remarks on the fact it was hardly surprising if, by now, even Mrs Kavanagh had the priest come up to the house to see her.

'Do you remember that?' she asks. I say I do. She hesitates. 'It was Jim reminded me last night: there were fireworks up there at Knigh over the priest's visits.'

'How do you mean, "fireworks"?'

'Agnes didn't like it. You see, it wasn't Father O'Meara, I was wrong there. It was Father O'Donnel, and your mother had taken against him.'

Here it is, then, the last missing piece, dropped light as a feather into my hand.

The priest who climbed down from his newly painted sidecar that bitter morning at Knigh was the man who had humiliated my mother when she appealed to him in her sister's cause. Monsignor Quinn, having interceded on Nancy's behalf, had then extended the hand of the Church to Mrs Kavanagh in the form of Father O'Donnel. When Agnes saw him, she dropped the armful of peat she was about to carry into the house and flitted away out of sight. That her mother should be reconciled to any priest nauseated her, but that it should be *this* priest, *this* man whose hand her mother kissed, before whom she knelt to confess her sins and ask forgiveness, sent a whirlwind of pain and anger through her. Later, when she came in

330

chilled to the bone, her mother said lightly, 'Shame on you! Father O'Donnel knew you were there.'

And Agnes cried out, 'How could you let that man into the house?' Her mother turned towards her and her face was suddenly very white. 'A man who treated your own daughter like she was something he'd brought in on his shoes!'

'Who are you to speak of a man of God in that tone?'

Mrs Kavanagh brought one of her pans down on the stove with such ferocity it struck sparks. 'Is there no decency left in you?'

The air between them was solid with anger. Kate reeled slightly. Then, as if stepping back from a blaze, she held up both hands, turned away, and said in a quiet voice, 'It comforts me to have him here. Isn't it the only comfort I have?'

'It is now!' Agnes cried bitterly.

As she pulled open the door a cold blast came into the kitchen. Kate's maternal authority was shocked back into action. In a steely voice she commanded Agnes to get outside and feed the geese, a job which properly fell to Pat. Scarcely aware of what she was doing, Agnes took the feed from the bin in the outhouse and, ignoring the mould all over it, she heated it up, then lugged the steaming bucket out on to the icy hillside. A few hours later the geese lay scattered across the twilit field, as white, as dead as pillows.

In the morning Agnes went to Busherstown to say goodbye to Mrs Minchin, and the following day her father took her in the pony trap to Nenagh Station. She was gone.

When my parents and I visited Ireland together in 1994, our tour ended in Dublin. Sitting across the lounge in the Shelbourne Hotel that afternoon was a table of black-frocked priests. Like us, they were taking tea. My mother watched them – to be honest, she stared – and several times she nodded towards them with a little grin. Then, somewhat wistfully, she said, 'It must be a wonderful thing to believe. To have faith.'

She emphasised the word 'faith' both with her voice and with a strong, meaningful glance at my father. There then followed one of those conversations I remembered so well from my childhood. My father agreed that religion wasn't a bad thing, indeed it was necessary for civilization – 'Or rather,' he corrected himself 'for the civilizing of mankind' – it was just something civilization should grow out of. My mother's eyes glazed over. 'Spirituality' wasn't a word she ever used but, if she had expressed herself here, I think she would have argued that what my father was recommending was the very *worst* aspect of religion: its dogma and repression, its rules, its HYPOCRISY. Buttering some scones energetically as he spoke, my father went on to suggest that, just as toys are necessary to children, so religion is necessary to growing minds. Two red spots appeared high on my mother's cheeks.

'*Are* toys necessary?' she demanded furiously and, in terms of the logic of my father's argument, apparently beside the point. 'Most children have to get by without toys.'

The priests finished their tea and the maître d'hôtel graciously accompanied them to the door.

It was the following day, on the ferry boat coming back to England, that I asked my mother how she had felt all those years ago, as a young woman leaving Ireland.

'My feelings about leaving Ireland were mixed.' She had shot me a look. 'You know what mixed feelings are, don't you?'

*

I have the photograph in front of me now, my mother as a grown woman on the arm of a handsome young man, a *younger* man as is obvious even in this full-length snapshot of them standing in an English garden facing the camera – I don't know whose – which has somehow, even in this still image of a still moment, captured movement, the movement of affection and desire, showing them already confident and familiar enough to touch, shoulder to hip. I like to think I'm there, part of the laughter, even though I've still got a few years to wait. My parents are too absorbed in one another to be more than glancingly self-conscious. Maybe she has an Irish look about her, maybe she hasn't. Yes, with that glossy black hair and white skin I imagine you might guess she's Irish, and probably her voice would still give her away but, though she will speak of home and family if asked, she doesn't volunteer such information. She is as newly minted as Venus risen from the waves. She has arrived. She is her own woman. To judge from my mother's hairstyle, I guess it's the late 1930s. Yes, it must be the autumn of '39, shortly before their wedding. Here in the first photo I have of her, my mother looks disconcertingly mature. Not matronly, she's too slender and fine-featured for that, but certainly a good deal more mature than the young man whose arm she holds and who's only just had his twenty-first birthday. My father who – did I say? – is wearing the uniform of a private in the British Army, and is about to have six of his best young years consumed by the war.

333

5

When David asked to see Agnes again after their first date she said, 'Yes, so long as we don't go to another dance.'

When he asked her to marry him she said 'No'. She admitted to being some years older than he, a fact David insisted was of no interest to him. But my mother had already had the best part of ten years out in the world, and she was actively looking for 'a better life', something I imagine she hadn't defined all that clearly but felt she'd recognise when she saw it. On the face of it, David may not have looked all that promising. My father was only just setting out on life and, professionally, he was still in the foothills. The fact that he was living on the £1 a week allowance Henderson paid him can hardly have been in his favour. When my parents began courting, all David could afford to buy his sweetheart was a weekly packet of ten Craven 'A', price 6d. Anyway, Agnes refused even engagement for one whole year.

So that's how it was: on New Year's Eve 1938, exactly a year after they had first met, they became engaged. By this time, not only had my father's income risen to the enviable sum of two pounds a week – paid by the council – but it was clear that, when he completed his Articles, he had the prospect of a secure and successful professional career. My mother was certainly not materialistic, but nor was she a romantic fool. Prospects were important. My father had a future. Just as importantly, he had no past. And – *no small matter this* – he wasn't checked or weighted with religion. You can't get much fainter on the religious spectrum than lapsed Church of England.

Agnes often said the reason she married David was because she could trust him – she who had never trusted anything in trousers. Except, that is, for Jim Cooney. But of course there was more to it than that. Perhaps, in spite of his youth and penniless condition, she recognised in this decent and handsome young man a willing and worthy collaborator in her not-quite-imagined but expansive future. In Sussex they went on the motorbike together along green lanes to Glyndebourne where they heard Mozart for the first time – the beginning of a lifelong love of opera. Their tickets were 10s each and admitted them to the dress rehearsal, for which no evening dress – which, naturally, they didn't possess – was required. In the interval they sat on my father's raincoat on the lawn eating watercress sandwiches amongst the toffs, laughing secretly at the braying voices and fancy clothes. And on her night off, David would always be there waiting to meet Agnes on the lane from the big house. She had no light on her bike but he could see her coming in the dark by the pulsing red glow of her cigarette, hear the swish of her skirt, the hum of her wheels. It was a romance. Each was the other's adventure.

Enclosed in a box of memorabilia for these years are some notes of Dorothy's. They end with the following paragraph:

> *For a couple of years, Mother was with a family named Whittington, supposedly descended from the famous Dick. From there she heard about the job as cook at Collyer's School. She was there for nearly twenty years*

335

and that's where you come in, Margaret, and I'm sure
that you remember those school years and why we were
all thrown together. I came home during the war, as you
know, because my marriage had gone and I had Elizabeth
to rear on my own and no one would rent a house to
me without me producing a man! David had meanwhile
met Agnes – she had taken mother's position with the
Whittingtons – and he was afraid that with the war she
would be sent back to Ireland.[6] So the school was the
answer for us all.

At the door to the register office in Chichester there
were posted two signs: 'All illegitimate children must be
registered' and 'No spitting – fine five pounds.' Marriage,
of course, required my mother's papers, a birth certificate
at the very least. None was forthcoming. It was at this
point my mother claimed that her birth certificate had
been destroyed in a fire in Dublin.[7] The problem was
solved by the acquisition of a temporary passport. My
father's old mentor, the Collyer's School teacher, Mr
Henderson, verified that a photograph was indeed a true
likeness of Agnes Kavanagh and obligingly fibbed about
the length of time he'd known her. My mother travelled
with Dorothy and David's older brother, Charles, on the
train from Horsham to Chichester where my father – in
the first wave of men to be called up – was stationed.
She sat all the way on her handbag in order to protect
her pale coat. She wore a lilac-coloured hat of fine
straw and matching lilac gloves. She turned and turned

6. *Rumours that Ireland – neutral in WWII – was sheltering German*
U-boats led England to threaten taking the Irish ports. This would
have involved invasion of the country and mass repatriation of Irish
nationals.
7. *Certainly it was the case that, during the Irish civil war, the public*
records office in Dublin was destroyed in a blaze.

the engagement ring on her finger and only relaxed, as abruptly as if she'd inhaled Valium, when she saw David was there on the platform, waiting for her, and his warm hand took hers, shaking a little, but strong.

It is September 23rd 1939, just a few weeks after an IRA bombing in Coventry that killed five people. My mother is making her own statement of loyalty by marrying an English soldier. My father is wearing the uniform of a private in the 4th Battalion of the Royal Sussex.

They'd intended to buy the wedding ring there, in town, at one of the classy jewellers, but it was a Wednesday afternoon, early closing, and all the shops were closed. They walked a while through the sun-filled, oddly deserted streets. From an open window came the sound of someone's wireless playing American jazz. Then, at three o'clock, they were married – using my father's signet ring – by a man with such a pronounced stutter it was difficult to understand him and therefore difficult to know when to respond. They laughed afterwards saying God only knew what they'd let themselves in for since they might have been saying 'I will' to anything and what a poor show, wasn't it? to have such an unsuitable man for the job. Agnes said she didn't care – she would have been happy to be married by a donkey so long as it was all legal and above board. They parted from the others and shyly walked away alone, hand in hand, towards their hotel.

I have, naturally, seen a copy of my parents' marriage certificate. On it, my mother maintains her lie about her age – such a little lie, shaving just a couple of years off her age – and describes her father as a farmer. But most interesting is the fact that my mother's marriage was not Catholic. It was an English register office wedding. Agnes

337

Wadey was, it seems, perfectly happy to have her soul look after itself.

My parents had just the one night together, then my father was back to barracks. For a few months these were at Chichester Racecourse, then in Dorset, at Long Burton. The men were on active war training until the battalion went to France in February 1940. In that time he had just three two-day leaves. My father, made desperate by this particularly torturous form of separation from his bride, took seriously to cards. He played pontoon and solo whist. After the war he progressed to bridge, at which he turned out to have some skill. He played for money, hour after hour, with a fag at the corner of his mouth, his right foot tap-tapping under the table. Harder to imagine is my mother being a camp follower, but on a couple of occasions that's what she had to be, walking the gauntlet of the envious grins and whistles of the other soldiers before she could close the door on privacy with her man.

As Dorothy said, the war years had thrown her and my mother and my English grandmother together. This family tie was never broken. On the sixth anniversary of my mother's death, Aunt Dorothy wrote me the following letter:

> *I still see her by David's side when he comes to Horsham and I go to New Malden, my dear companion of those dreary war years, which had to be lived without our 'men' and how after the war, when we moved to Farthings and on the day of the move she came to the cottage and pushed Anne[8] in her pram to my new 'home' with Bob's mother and the tongue lashing she gave me on my pitiful future*

8 Anne was Dorothy's fourth child by her second husband whom she had married after the conception of their son – something she made no secret of.

with another baby and no permanent roof over my head!!
Well – I had many other scathing remarks from others
too – but I was young and it didn't seem insurmountable
and really wasn't!

But I knew that sort of life wasn't for her, I was in a
different league, but admired her muchly all her life and
if it wasn't for it being in black and white I find it hard to
believe it has been all of six years today. Thinking of you.
The weather is surely against a trip to Shere. However – it
doesn't stop, the thinking about her I mean.

Much, much love Dorothy.

More than her mixed feelings for my mother, Dorothy's letter reveals the essentials of her character: her remarkable generosity, her capacity (especially in old age) for veiled spite, her undeserved self-deprecation. The letter is, in fact, a good example of her style: her memories, her most casual remarks, were frequently spiked, laced with a dash or two of arsenic, odourless, tasteless until you felt its effects in your bloodstream. My mother's style was very different – plainer, both less composed and much less communicative. She either exercised rigid censorship – like her parents, she rarely spoke ill of anyone – or she told alarming, blistering truths. Poison or the stiletto might have been Dorothy's murder weapons. My mother's would have been a gun.

But weapons were never drawn. My mother had a sense of her own worth. Dorothy never really did. My mother, more confident and more ambitious, took control of her own life. My aunt never moved more than thirty miles from the village where she was born and she never fulfilled her obvious potential. After her death, a stash of her own poems was found in the drawers of her dresser. But these two women, so very different, never did less than

339

support and co-operate with one another. They were the strongly contrasting guardian spirits who presided over my childhood.

On at least a couple of occasions during the war my mother took me to stay with her sister Nancy in Hanwell. I was in her arms, about to be laid between pillows at the foot of her bed, when a passing doodlebug fell silent and drifted past the window to cause murder and mayhem half a mile away. On a later visit, I remember my mother's white-lipped fury at Dan coming there and showing off a great wad of notes and not giving a penny to Nancy who was kept on such tight money by her husband, as Dan well knew. As Dan had foreseen, and was certainly not above saying so. I don't remember any of the other Kavanagh sisters being there, though Nancy always remained in touch with them. There may have been bad feeling between my mother and Bridie and Josie. It may have been returned: my mother, after all, had not just married an Englishman, she had left the Church and the Irish community, which Nancy most certainly had not.

At this stage, in the late 'forties, Nancy was still a healthy young woman, with three children. The two women were still very close and, in a childish way, I was very aware of it. The comforting, seductive intimacy of their voices in the kitchen whilst the children and I played in the garden, the blind ease of their body language. Something quite different in my mother from when she was around the Wadeys. I was aware, too, of that very particular sadness in my mother's feelings for Nancy, a sadness which increased through the years of Nancy's troubled marriage and illness.

I only recall this being made explicit once. We were in the kitchen one day, laughing at Nancy's two-year-old son's comic attempts to stand, all of which ended with him plumping down on his bottom. Suddenly Nancy said,

'There's something wrong with him.' There was. Soon the child was diagnosed with a genetically inherited disease, inherited only through the male line. Nancy was told her son would become progressively more crippled. Telling my father this, my mother broke down.

But did they really talk of nothing but husbands and children, of how to beat post-war austerity or deal with their mothers-in-law? Did they, in fact, talk of any of that? Mostly I remember Nancy's laughter, and wreathing conspiratorially around their dark heads, clouds of cigarette smoke out of which Nancy's hot blue eyes flashed their unquenchable mischief. Still. In spite of everything. So, did my mother and her sister ever look at one another and ask, Where is she now?

On April 5th, 1947, the sixteen-year-old Catherine Kavanagh sat down at Monasterevin and wrote the following letter to the Catholic Rescue Society in Dublin:

> *...it is so long since I wrote you will be forgetting me. I hope not. I was in Athy with the Sisters to get my training as a nurse. Everyone was very kind but the work was hard and I fell ill with glandular fever. As soon as I am better I plan to go over to England to finish my training properly.*

But in the second half of her letter, begging forgiveness for her *'impertinence'*, Catherine asked to be told where she had been born. Sometimes she was asked, for the census, or by the doctors, and she could only tell them *'Dublin'*. Also, she wanted to know her mother's name, and, *'Do I have a father? Please don't think I am taking a liberty. There is no one else I can ask and it is only my natural curiosity makes me ask. I remain, Catherine Kavanagh.'*

341

The agency replied to say they were glad Catherine was hoping to finish her training and enclosing a pound towards her expenses. They wrote, '...but we do not know anything about your mother as we have never seen her since she handed you over to the society. I don't think you need worry about that.' Shortly after receiving this letter, Catherine left for Liverpool.

She had asked for her parents' names. They did not give her her father's. Her mother's took several forms, only the first of which Catherine knew. On her birth certificate she is a simple Anne Kavanagh; on her marriage certificate she is Nancy Teresa Kavanagh, and on her death certificate she is Nancy Mary Tanner. Nancy's death certificate makes unhappy reading. The first cause of death is clearly stated: acute renal failure. In the family it was always said that Nancy's kidneys were destroyed by the drugs she was given to cope with arthritis. But the death certificate tells a more complicated story than that. The second cause of death given is systemic lupus erythematosus. Lupus is an autoimmune disease which can be difficult to diagnose and can lead to both arthritis and kidney failure. It would also explain the sad change in Nancy's appearance in her later years – she died aged fifty-two – when her face was puffy and covered in red patches. The disease is still incurable and, apart from a possible genetic factor, its causes are uncertain. Stress, smoking and sunlight play some part. Ninety per cent of cases are women. It was side by side on a hospital bed the sisters last saw one another.

There's one last footnote to my mother's relationship with Nancy. Bill lived on until 1983 and it was my parents who nursed him through his final illness and death. To do so, they stayed several nights a week in his little flat, which meant sleeping on a mattress on the floor, exhausting themselves – my mother was over seventy. The whole episode infuriated me. Knowing what I did about Nancy's marriage, and knowing that my parents knew, I couldn't bear the idea of them giving her husband their blessing – as it seemed to me. My view was, he'd been unkind to Nancy, who had loved him. Let him rot.

It was my husband who said they wanted precisely to do it *for* Nancy. My father has reminded me that Nancy's son was still living at home and could not possibly have looked after his father: it was for him, too, for Nancy's care of him, that they were there. Perhaps there's an echo in their kindness of the Graces' kindness to my uncle Pat? Still, I wasn't entirely convinced. Not quite. But then I'm part of the 'me' generation, the generation whose idealism quickly turned to self-centred individualism, a creed that knows no community, nor austerity, nor self-sacrifice. I remember dropping my parents once at Heathrow to take a flight to Italy for their summer holidays. There was some kind of delay. Looking back from the exit I was touched to see them waiting hand in hand, looking up at the departures board, patient and cheerful.

Three years after the war was over we were living in a timber-built 'hut' near the gasworks in Spalding, Lincolnshire. This took us far away from the family, just us three and our cat Tibbles, who went ahead with my father in the sidecar of his motorbike. The hut which was to be a temporary arrangement, was quite well fitted out, but it can hardly have been part of my mother's dreams for our post-war life. My father's welcome home from the war had been a drop in income. Still articled to the council, he was obliged to fulfil a six-month contract or risk being called back into the army. When the six months were up he had immediately applied for work as an architectural assistant in Spalding and here, with some misgivings, we were. Not surprisingly, my father's temper suffered. I was bumptious, confident, curious. I didn't mind battling my way back across the estate to defend my position as the only kid whose school uniform included a panama hat. But my mother wept as she swept the floors of our prefab and I got the occasional 'clip around the ear'. Within six months, however, we'd been moved into the house we had been promised, a newly completed house on a council estate.

In springtime the nearby fields were gaudy with ranks of tulips that marched out to the horizon, their stiff foliage squeaking in the wind. My father owned a motorbike and sidecar and when he set off for work on dark mornings the dogs on the estate chased after him, barking, an annoyance he dealt with by dealing out hefty kicks to the muzzle. At night he studied to sit the exams he had missed to go soldiering. My mother was a full-time housewife and mother, and had no ambitions to be anything else. It was a post-war dream, and, for the time being at least – David was thirty-one – it had to be good enough for my father. A much-repeated family story tells how, when lucky enough to be in charge of a stone quarry in Italy for the last two years of the war, David never troubled to walk the two miles into Pisa, not even to marvel at the leaning tower, which might have interested the engineer in him. But my father is shameless. Teased, he will only shrug and remark cheerfully, 'I'm a simple chap. It's the way my mother put my hat on.' The family speculation was that David was wary of a foreign town, of the pickpockets and – above all – the prostitutes? On this last score my mother was confident, saying, 'One thing I do know, David would never *pay* for it.'

At this point my father loses patience and stands up to

344

remind his mocking brothers and sister that Pisa was actually seventy-five miles away from where he was stationed and – had they forgotten? – there was a war on. In fact, some twenty years later, when he returned to Italy on holiday with my mother, Pisa and its leaning tower was one of the first places they visited.

The winter of 1950–51 was the snowiest for more than half a century and Lincolnshire, as so often, was scoured with bitter winds. But never mind the climate,

I doubt a council estate in Spalding would have satisfied Agnes for long, and where her daughter was concerned she'd never been content with the school down the road. Recently, Dorothy expressed surprise that it was Agnes, not David, who'd made the decisions about my schools: 'How on earth did she find out about them?' she asked, the implication being, 'I didn't know she had the nous.' But from the beginning my mother chose carefully: Froebel, Montessori, PNEU, exceedingly civilised, even rarified and child-centred educational systems. In Spalding, true to form, she'd found me an excellent – and expensive – preparatory school. Which might explain why my hard-pressed father couldn't afford the cost of new curtains. My mother nevertheless insisted – or so the family story goes – that a life in which we couldn't afford new curtains wasn't worth living.

At that time, every night after supper my father cleared the table and sat down to moonlight, drawing up plans for bathrooms, kitchens, home extensions, anything that needed council approval. He had already tried – and failed – to economise by giving up smoking (I'm not sure my mother joined him in this trial) and he felt pretty sore to see delivery boys on bicycles puffing away as they rode by. What more could she want? My mother was crystal clear. What she wanted was a new order of things. She wanted my father to shoot his bolt, ride his horse, fire that rocket.

It was a spectacular row, the first and only one I ever overheard. I heard my father accuse my mother of imagining she'd been born with a silver spoon in her mouth and he was here to tell her she hadn't. My mother, characteristically, became emotional not gradually but at the flick of a switch. Repeatedly she missed the point my father – with diminishing patience – repeatedly made: they must wait until his examinations were done and he was qualified. It was only reasonable. But he was like a man pissing in the wind. My mother pointed out that, since he claimed to be unable to afford even to go down to London to sit the exams, they might wait forever.

Later in life, when as an adult I ask my father what he was like as a young man he tells me,'Oh, very hot, very quick-tempered. Your mother, too. We had some right old ding-dongs. And those rows took some time to recover from.'

But on this occasion, my father bowed to the inevitable: something had to be done, and he was the one to do it. Without hope, with exaggerated laboriousness – with one of his just-five-a-day fags in his mouth – he sat down and looked through advertisements for positions with the civil service abroad. Work was difficult to find at that time. As it turned out, he was surprised: 'Knock and it shall be opened unto you.' Two applications he made were unanswered, but the War Office quickly offered him a posting in Egypt. It was a triumph. When he asked my mother how she'd feel about living abroad she answered that where he went, she would follow.

So it came about that, just a year later, in 1951, my parents and I walked along an avenue of mimosa to the shore of the Bitter Lakes in Egypt. Some of the best and happiest times of our life together as a family came about because my mother had insisted that life without new curtains wasn't worth living.

I lie awake in the early morning watching a pattern of sugar cane leaves shaken across the whitewashed wall of my bedroom. My earthly paradise has been restored to me – and, I believe, to my parents. I am nine years old, brown as a nut and skinny as a feral cat. From the kitchen comes a quiet murmur of voices: my mother is instructing our young Sudanese servant in the preparation of béchamel sauce. Said's black skin has a copper sheen, his white robes are immaculate, his cummerbund discretely fancy. He is the first black man my mother and I have ever seen. His deep, edible colour is part of what we love about him. The blandness and stodginess of our food amuses him. Sometimes my mother, listening and watching in that sharp-focused way of hers, takes lessons from Said: yoghurt, garlic, eggplant. These strange ingredients enter her sphere for the first time. Said does everything. Cleaning, shopping, gardening. When we have a supper party – as we are doing tonight – he goes secretly next door to borrow extra chairs, and crockery he considers more suitable for the grandeur of the occasion. Our guests may recognise their own plates on our table but no one complains. It's common practice. Besides, a good servant is like gold dust. The English wives would cut out their tongues before they offend a good servant.

If I turn on my side, I can see through the open door into my parents' bedroom where one of my mother's best Horrockses dresses is laid out on the bed. Under the little dressing table is a pair of white, peep-toed high heels. She had chosen her clothes for this posting without any help

347

from anyone – except Dorothy to tell her what they looked like from behind – including her first pair of shorts, from Barkers Ladies' Wear in Horsham. Tonight is my parents first turn as hosts in a formal middle-class milieu. Fayid isn't Cheltenham, it isn't even Port Said. But my mother takes pride in getting things right and if she feels lost then there's always the colonel's wife to observe and emulate. She's aware of passing a test, a large part of which is to 'manage' on whatever resources are available, and to do so graciously. These are the virtues of an army wife and it appears they come naturally to her.

Our house is a two-bedroomed, whitewashed bungalow built of mud bricks, with a flat roof that lets the rain in. It is nevertheless a spacious, airy place with a simple kind of elegance and a veranda groaning under a riot of purple bougainvillea. Set in a shady garden, it's bordered at the back by a sweet-water canal thicketed with sugar cane where little white egrets delicately stab at the water. This evening I'll help Said unlock the water channels around our flower beds, sending up a scent of sweet earth and peppery zinnias, flowers the little red-cheeked goldfinches love, gossiping as they feast. I am instructed to pick a few for the dinner table, a task I'm proud to perform. But actually I rather resent tonight's dinner party because my favourite routine of the day will be cut short: the time when my father returns from work, undoes the buttons of his shirt, gives us each a kiss, and lights up. Then, side by side, the three of us sit under the bamboo awning. We talk and laugh quietly, waiting for the sweet relief of the evening breeze to start up, and for the swift Egyptian twilight to fall.

In the kitchen I hear Said's low laugh and a little snort from my mother. I sigh and stretch luxuriously across my little bed. Tomorrow, Said will be paid, and then he'll disappear for three or even four days. When he returns, his robes and his woolly head will smell of hashish, he will be shamefaced and *exhausted,* with a greyish tinge like a veil of ash drawn over his beautiful skin. My mother will return his graceful lies with her own graceful acceptance. She tells me that Said is a young man in a foreign land, far away from family and friends. She tells me it's hard to keep to the right ways when you're a long way from home, living amongst people who neither know you nor care.

6

Over the last few months I've done this so often, walking up here on Knigh, watching the days slowly lengthen. It's summer, and I should have been long gone. Once, after the first thrill of encountering this place, I felt I was being held at arm's length: what I saw was mesmerizing but unreadable, like the face and body of a man who's not yet your lover, may never be your lover but is close as your held breath, full of things untold. Then, as I came to know it, with a shift of light, a change of perspective, it uncovered the encoded traumas of its past. Still nothing here frightens me. Even at night I've come up here alone and felt only benign spirits.

But, I know that silence and darkness aren't necessarily benign. Sometimes they close in on you, muffling your ears and your eyes, making you inhabit a smaller and smaller space, pushing you deeper inside yourself until you feel you'll go mad. Now, in twilight, I go slowly up the white track behind the house and then, having climbed through the hedge, I go to sit on the circle of stones on the skyline where my mother used to sit as a girl, placing myself at the centre of that imaginary circle she drew around Knigh. The place she knew, mistakenly, that she would never want to leave. This evening, I've come to say goodbye. On the horizon, the ever-present loch mutates from duck-egg blue through ultramarine to silver, swaying above its forgotten, drowned islands.

The last few days have disturbed and exhausted me. I've been avoiding phone calls, failing to visit people. As ever in a crisis, I've gone to ground. During Kate's lonely last years, did her neighbours manage to help and comfort her, I wonder? When guilt was added to disappointment she probably went beyond helping. It was in her nature to turn away, to walk up on to the hillside here above the house, alone, to see the hares. As it's mine, too. 'Dear Lord, and don't you have a look of your grandmother about you!' Annie had exclaimed the first time we met. But I couldn't have lived my grandmother's life, and clearly the grown-up Agnes didn't believe she could, either. In my own case, if by some miracle I'd survived the physical ordeal of nine births, other things would either have died or never have been born in me. Perhaps something died in Kate.

Now I suspect that what Jim's remarks had really been suggesting was madness, or rather, depression. Depression and agoraphobia are both diseases of the mind and heart. But sometimes disease lets in things we otherwise resist, lets us see things we otherwise deny. And who's to say when she came up here alone at dusk my grandmother didn't see other things: stars as well as hares, moonrise, and all the countless little births and deaths that make up the natural world, both material and immaterial. But if she ever did feel the great beyond tug at her skirt, if she found a stinking corpse or a bright swan's feather there was, it seems, no one's doorstep she wanted to lay it on. Whatever she saw, she kept to herself. Unlike me.

And there's the rub. What I find, I tell. The shut-off place my mother went to came, as in Kate's case, with secrecy. *My* shut-off place is associated not with secrecy – not in the long run, that is – but betrayal. Whatever I see there, whatever I find, I feel compelled to lay on her doorstep, on the world's doorstep. What else is this book but both an intimate, secret act of love and loyalty *and* the last act of betrayal in this story – an act my mother is powerless to ward off.

The Ireland I'm about to leave is not, of course, the Ireland my mother left seventy-odd years ago. The Celtic tiger may have died, but it's left its mark. At its height, Ireland was no longer a place to leave but a place to come back to – or indeed to emigrate to. The Liffey ran with champagne and, ironically, young women didn't want to look Irish any more but sexy and glossy, like American movie stars. Having got the land, having got the euros, inevitably there followed the building. A new Ireland rose up, one I'm glad my mother never saw – neither in its sudden triumph nor its abrupt decline. Out there along the mystical coast of Connemara, the vandals got to work scribbling obscenities all over the sad, lovely face of Ireland. The ostentatious display of wealth was apparent everywhere. 'Botox-Ireland', as Tim Robinson has called it in his trilogy *Connemara*, describing that once magnificently remote (and famine-plagued) coast as 'Costa del Bog'. Even Mary Grace, not inclined to hyperbole, remarked that in Donegal the speculators had lost all sense of when to stop: 'They've gone MAD, mad with greed' – an observation made all the more striking for being delivered in Mary's lovely voice.

But no one, no individual and no country, fast-forwards in a vacuum, free of baggage. Unlike the invaders, unlike the institutions of the Church, the past – the dead – never lose their power and their presence. They are there with us, in Galway Bay, in the bars, in the bedrooms of the newly built farmhouse bungalows and in the Taoiseach of the new Ireland, spurring the living on to do what they never did, to have what they never had – and no matter where we run, no matter how far, the voice of the past follows. In such circumstances, new gods come into power: sex, Mammon, and the fantasy of invulnerability to age, poverty and suffering. But the old gods have an unpleasant way of striking back. As indeed they have done. But for a brief spell, like a cork blown from a champagne bottle, the Irish became dizzy with the present and with fantasies of an even better future. They were living the dream: the good life was here, now, ours.

'But history is always waiting in the wings to repeat itself,' said a speaker at the Ormond Historical Society. Adding, 'Don't forget the past. It has something to say to you.'

In the morning, I wake early. I place my packed suitcase and shoulder bag beside the open door. I take my mug of tea to the table with a copy of *Portrait of a Parish*, Danny's book, which he's given me as a goodbye present. I sit and leaf through it, starting from the back, looking forward to the hour or so I'll have on the plane to read it with proper attention. One of the chapters is called 'Teaching and Learning' and it falls open at a photograph. Thirty or forty children, with their teacher – several of the little boys in grubby three-piece suits and the girls with bows in their hair – and not a smile between them, staring at the camera as if it might pounce.

At first I don't recognise her. In fact, when my eyes run along the lines of names and I see 'Agnes Cavanagh, Knigh, and Annie Cavanagh, Knigh', I'm disbelieving. I read the caption: Carney School, 1924. I stare. And then this pale child with black hair to her shoulders transmogrifies into my mother, with a look on her face I know so well that now I can't believe I didn't spot her instantly, a look I've seen on my own face in long-forgotten childhood photos. A brooding look, defensive, shy, apprehensive, even, but at the same time dreamy, suggesting that at this moment when she's first captured for history, her thoughts are elsewhere. And if I'd been her teacher, I think I'd have seen both anxiety and scepticism. She's reserving her judgement, withholding herself. And beside her just as unmistakably now that I look again – is my aunt Nancy, the bonniest girl in the class, but quite without the expected hint of mischief.

This photograph was taken when my mother was thirteen and about to move on out of this tiny world to the convent. When I was thirteen I moved on, too, leaving the convent in Cyprus to go to an English boarding school where I would put on the manners, the accent and the confidence of that tough breed: the young English lady. When my mother told me that in order to go to the convent you had to show you could benefit from it, she added with a dismissive snort, 'But none of us were expected to be *intellectuals*!' Her tone of voice suggested that such a creature was as fantastic as a unicorn. But for me, determined to turn my back on the traditional woman's role, what better than to scale that male-dominated height of academe, a philosophy department? I took the view that there was something faintly, inherently comic in the masculine: pompous and anxious. I'm not sure how much I believed this. But in my view, men already had too many advantages. If I fell into the trap of taking them seriously I was done for. It was shortly before taking up my place at university that I made my first visit to Dublin. Unknowing, uncaring, I brushed up against my mother's Irish past.

When I stood on the towpath of the black canal in Ballsbridge, Dublin, that icy day in January 1962, I did not in fact imagine my mother as a young woman on the other side. I didn't know she'd ever been there. Scarcely aware of my surroundings, I had walked there deep in self-centred reflection, brooding on my future: having finally passed the necessary Latin exam, I knew my place at University College London was secure. Having been independent of my parents for more than three years, I also knew I'd receive a full grant. Having, I believed, wasted my time since leaving school, life now had a sense of purpose. I was my own woman. But I was also a woman with a problem. I had discovered my entire future project was in jeopardy. Like many a pregnant young woman before me, I took the boat to England.

Now, forty years later, I'm about to drive to Shannon Airport to take an aeroplane. I close the book and place it in my shoulder bag. I gather up my papers: passport, ticket, credit card, driving licence and car-hire and insurance papers. When my mother left, she needed only her ticket. No passport, no ID, no record taken of her leaving or of her arrival. I've already said my goodbyes. I place the key under the fifth stone to the left of the front door and drive away.

Embracing me as we said goodbye, Annie O'Brien had asked, 'Why did your mother never look anyone up when she came back? Sure there'd have been many at that time glad to see her. Mick Flynn – he had a fancy to your mother. He married in '47 and, though he's long passed away, there's an eighteen-year-old grandchild, and Mick would have been alive still in '89. He would have been glad to see her.' But how could she? Fifty years away. I think of myself when I first came, lost, asking questions like a stranger, looking for something. I had nothing to lose, but my mother was walking carefully, like Annie with her jug of milk, mindful not to spill her past.

Whatever else I take away from Ireland, amongst my abiding treasures is the generosity shown to me by my family's neighbours, a stranger on their doorsteps, claiming the rambler's rights. Not expecting to *be* claimed. But I was, and now I'm caught in the web of their *v*oices, their memories, the great tree of generations through whose branches they moved with such agility, turning the leaves of life, finding on each leaf a name, a name leading to another name, back through the years until they seemed to touch hands with Adam and Eve only to trip nimbly sideways to reach back to those still living – even to those yet unborn. Now my name's there, too, with Agnes Kavanagh's and those of her great-grandchildren, Tom and Erin Foley. Names on the leaves of life.

At the airport the security guard on the gate indicates I should halt the car. Smiling pleasantly, he leans down to the open window.

'Collecting, is it?' he asks.

'No,' I say. 'Leaving.'

How nice if my book ended here, but it doesn't. The past has one more thing to tell. As Ireland falls away behind me, my story narrows down again to two women, in a scene which could be said to have determined my entire adult life. My own little bit of untold history. Small, personal, secret.

CONSILIENCE

'I will not let thee go, except thou bless me.'
      – Jacob to the Angel, Genesis 32.26

When I came home from Dublin in 1962 I was twelve weeks pregnant. On the way back across the Irish Sea I was sick as a dog. In London I went about acquiring an abortion. Fast. At that time, abortion was illegal and expensive. Through a friend who was a nurse, I was put in touch with a Polish doctor who, for the fee of £100, was prepared to do the operation. I gave neither the safety nor the morality of my decision much thought: actually, to call it a 'decision' feels inaccurate. Whereas getting pregnant had seemed to me an impossibility, the getting of an abortion was necessitated by its possibility. In a sense, I had no choice (by which I certainly don't mean to exonerate myself of responsibility). I was about to take up my place at university and neither motherhood nor marriage played any part in my plans. The doctor, an attractive, world-weary man wearing several gold rings, was sufficiently morally – or maliciously? – engaged to tell me the foetus was a healthy male child. The last abandoned child of this story. I still catch myself occasionally looking at a man in his late 'forties, a handsome man whose hairline is maybe already beginning to recede, and thinking, That could be my son.

Whatever else it may be, abortion is always an act of

violence and usually, even now, of secrecy. Of course it is. And that's a matter of more than hypocrisy or 'delicacy'. In my own little drama of life and death I chose, after all, to destroy an entire and unique script, perhaps denying – for example – a new life to my uncle Tom's blue eyes, or his way with girls and horses. After the operation, I got up and walked out of the surgery. I spent one night with my boyfriend in a friend's flat where I remember hearing a record of the Everly Brothers singing 'God Only Knows'.

Early the following morning in New Malden the telephone went and my mother answered. A man's voice: 'Mrs Wadey? There's something I thought you should know. Your daughter's just had an abortion.' We never knew who made that call. The doctor – perhaps conscience-stricken, or merely anxious? A malicious ex-boyfriend? My mother sat waiting for me to get home.

I closed the front door behind me. My mother turned from the window where she'd been waiting. Her face was white, twisted with pain, and there followed the most bitter scene that ever took place between us. My mother returned to the blistering form I remembered from my childhood when, at the flick of a switch, she could summon a hurricane that threatened to annihilate anything that got caught up in her whirling skirts. My argument that it had happened, it was over, that although I was too young to have a baby my boyfriend and I loved one another and wanted to live together, every link in this argument provoked a volcanic reaction of anger and distress: 'Go then! Go and live together in some filthy hole and see how happy you are! You're intelligent, you've had an education, and you've thrown yourself away on a young man who'll stick at nothing. You'll never keep him! He's too charming for his own good. You've made

360

yourself cheap as dirt, like any common stupid girl with no upbringing and no sense. So STUPID.'

How would it have been if my mother had then broken down and told me the story of Nancy and her baby? If she'd broken her silence and confided frankly in me, woman to woman, that her own most beloved sister had been equally cheap, dirty, and 'STUPID'? How would I have taken it? Would I have been consoled by a sense of continuity, of a shared female fate – or would I have felt labelled, trapped? Surely, surely my mother and I could have spoken heart to heart and been comforted? Did she perhaps feel, even now – thirty years later, but Nancy was still alive at this time – that Nancy's secret was not hers to tell?

The fact is, even under these extreme circumstances I wasn't told, and that day's terrible outburst – and its consequences – remained part of our relationship over the coming years. But none of it was referred to ever again and my father never knew. 'If my father and my brothers knew they'd kill us!' Shame. Sexual shame, a constant it seems in all societies and almost always blamed on women. And how especially true that was in the Ireland my mother had grown up in: sexual ignorance and shame, hand in hand. Now her daughter, who'd been brought up under the imperative to be perfect, her daughter had got herself into the same dirty stupid mess as her sister. But if it was impossible for my mother to speak, it would have been just as impossible for me to hear.

This taboo on openness between mothers and daughters, the secrecy which saps female self-worth, may seem to have been broken. The boundaries between what can and can't be said have certainly shifted. But girls quickly work out where the silences still fall and their mothers, poor dears, are not only women but *old* women. Sexism and ageism, that toxic combination, still alive and well.

At that time, I was myself a young woman fast-forwarding away from the past, away from my mother, just as she had done from hers. My mother was the only one of the Kavanaghs who left Ireland without her rosary or her prayer book. Part of her care of me had been to open her hand and let me swim free, unburdened. A priceless gift.

But of course the past was still powerfully at work in her, and it was this that had now reached out and grabbed me by the scruff of the neck. The past, the dead – as I understand now – never quite lose their power, neither in nations nor in individuals, never mind all the willed forgetting.

With time self-creation becomes – perhaps surprisingly – not second nature but an increasingly demanding and exhausting project. The forward-pointing arrow of time slows, and age brings an inclination to sink back into the earth, into one's roots. My mother's roots were in Catholic Ireland. As she occasionally said, 'It must be a wonderful thing to believe.' But the consolations of Catholicism were lost to her the moment she opened that letter from the Cúnamh Rescue Society in Dublin informing her that her sister Nancy's soul, and that of her newborn baby, were at risk of damnation. Agnes was the only one of the Kavanaghs who left Ireland without her rosary or her prayer book and although a sense of the sacred never left her, my mother's new life was lived out in what Seamus Heaney has called 'the weightless, profane spaces of the secular world'. And for the greater part she was content in that space which, as a young woman, she'd actively sought out. But in old age she might have been happier had she been able to reconcile her two selves:

her rooted Irish self, and the assimilated immigrant self who came into her glory in her middle years. Once Nancy died, however, the last meaningful link to her youth was gone. Often in this story I've remarked, 'she never said,' 'my mother never mentioned it,' or 'this was something my mother never spoke about,' a refrain which doesn't so much offer some kind of criticism as underline her loneliness, her never-to-be-lost status as an emigrant, which may have contributed to an inherited vulnerability to depression.

On what was to be our last Monday evening together my mother was tired. We were talking in a desultory way about her brothers and sisters when she remarked, 'Mother never used our names except to tick us off.'

'You don't use mine much.'

'Well there's only one of you, isn't there?' Then, 'I christened you Margaret. It was you who named yourself Maggie.'

Ah, yes. Existentialism! Self-invention. Child pitted against parent: 'I won't be what you made me. I'll be my own person.' Uncharacteristically, I pushed her a little.

'Don't you like it?' I asked.

She looked at me with surprisingly bright eyes.

'Oh I like it well enough,' she said.

So you see, those Monday evenings were important to us both. Although this was the period when I gave my mother many of the books she read with such quiet, reflective attention, and although we had a long-standing and easy modus vivendi – not least because of our love for my daughter – my mother and I still, in effect, stood either side of that black Dublin canal, in silence, unable to recognise one another. Now we were perhaps poised to speak, to see, to listen? Or maybe not. My mother, as

I have since discovered, had her own reasons for silence, which neither I nor my father knew anything of. Another reason was that we'd never entirely recovered from that explosive scene which had taken place between us nearly forty years earlier.

The only thing that would assuage my mother's pain was marriage – this in spite of the fact that she believed the marriage to be entirely unsuitable. Two months later, my father flew home from Belize (he was there on a short assignment which had, of necessity, been solo), I hired a fur cape from the Ladies' Department of Moss Bros. and, shaking in my winkle-picker shoes, John and I married at Kingston Register Office one snowy day in January 1963. Ironic, really. A shotgun wedding after the event. There was, after all, no baby, John by that time had rather gone off the idea of marriage, and I'd never been on it, seeing myself as a lover rather than a wife. My beautiful volatile young man's life had only just begun: he had left Trinity, Dublin, to become a student on a scholarship at RADA, and the world – some of it in the shape of very pretty young women – really was at his feet. I persuaded myself that marriage was a mere formality. Instead of church bells, we married with the dire predictions of family and friends ringing in our ears.

We were in love, but we were also young. Very young. I was twenty (just three months younger than my father when he married), and John reached twenty-three only five days before our wedding. In September that year I took up my hard-won place in the philosophy department at University College London, a married woman with no time for extracurricular life. Five years later I had my MPhil, John had begun a successful career as an actor, and we had our baby daughter. Still, there'd been grounds enough for the skeptics' fears.

John's godmother, Biddy, a worldly and sophisticated woman, had seen traits in me that would prove especially trying to her adored godson: I was 'too cold, too clever, too independent'. And, as my mother had seen, my husband possessed just those characteristics that would prove in due course especially tormenting to me. But then, in love, isn't torment what we look for as much as pleasure, instinctively seeking out the education of both our souls *and* our senses in the deep, secret battles and consiliences of marriage? My husband had reserves of loyalty and generosity my mother came greatly to love and appreciate and the fact is, nearly fifty years later, John and I are still together.

When I feel her, I feel her in my blood, in the set of my shoulders, in my DNA, in the dark. When I see her, I see her in the middle distance, walking away from me down an alleyway in Venice, picking an apple in a garden in France, always somewhat adream, and if our eyes meet, hers are a touch unfocused. When she looks at me I can't tell what she sees.

When I was thirty-two I had published a novel. A few nice reviews, pathetic sales. At the time I managed not to think about the issues in the book that my mother would have difficulty with, including the central character's abortion. It must have made painful reading, and though I honestly don't recall how much thought I'd given to her reaction, no doubt it wasn't enough; my book and my mother existed in different rooms in my mind. Now I acknowledge that I caused her real pain, bringing mess and stink like the foxes to her own front doorstep.

But she had loved the foxes, too.

At the time, mixed pride and embarrassment, a hint

of distress, were the only reactions to my novel that she shared with me. Until, that is, many years later on one of our Monday evenings together, when she told me she'd just reread my book and that she'd 'really enjoyed it', even that she 'admired' it. I was surprised and moved. There was a pause. We looked at one another and vast questions began to balloon on the air between us, but we let the moment pass. We didn't ask. Didn't speak. *I* didn't speak. It's only now I see it was my place to have done so, then, that evening.

I am left talking to myself.

So do I only have the courage to speak out now she's dead? Well of course the answer has to be 'yes', though perhaps 'courage' – with its suggestion of cowardice in not writing about her whilst she was alive – isn't the right word. 'Don't you answer back!' my mother used to say to me through gritted teeth when I was a lippy child.

The last time I saw my her well and at home was on the occasion of my husband's and my thirty-sixth wedding anniversary when my mother took us all, including our daughter, out to dinner. When I say she took us out, I mean she paid for it. My father was always good at recognizing and valuing the work my mother did in the house. He paid money directly into her bank account which it was her responsibility to manage, and she managed it very well. That money was hers, and they both saw it that way. So it was sometimes she who took us out, and doing so gave her huge pleasure, especially that night. Somehow we were all on especially good form and Shelley, who was thirty-two on that day, was spirited and beautiful. As we chose and shared dishes my mother's refrain was, 'Have plenty, have plenty!'

We were all very relaxed and my mother allowed her

feelings to show. Shiny-eyed, she kept looking from face to face and then around the pretty Italian restaurant with its elaborate sweets trolley and candlelit tables as if she'd found herself in fairyland. She was happy. She noticed things were good between my husband and me again and, with a raffish look in her eye, she raised her glass and said, 'Well, I don't know what it is he's doing, but it's obviously good for you!'

My mother wasn't much of a drinker and that evening she ended up tiddly. She was light-hearted and charmingly, a little awkwardly affectionate, holding on to her granddaughter's hand, linking her arm through both of ours and kicking up her heels as we walked back to the car. When we got home, she went upstairs, and after a few minutes I followed, to check that she was okay. I found her in their bedroom doorway, standing on one leg and helpless with laughter. The zip on her dress had caught on her petticoat and she'd got into an impossible tangle. I helped her out of her dilemma and then, leaning against the bannister, I laughed with her. The next time I saw her was in the hospital bed the day before she died.

Agnes outlived her own mother by twenty years. I go upstairs to the bedroom where my father has still left many of her things just as she used them: her talcum powder by the bed, her slippers, her silver-backed hairbrush on the dressing table. That photograph of her on the arm of a young man in the uniform of a British soldier. There's not just silence here but peace. Stillness. My mother's public persona – her manner, her voice, her touch – was notably gentle and sensitive. Yet in private, in times of intense emotion, what she revealed was a volcanic power which, as a young person, I took for her true inner nature. Knowing her more intimately, though at a distance, I see that gentleness and sensitivity were very much there at her core, too – as a girl, as my father's shy lover, as a young mother.

I go to stand at the window looking out. In the last years of her life, my mother slept badly. Sometimes, when she felt like the only human being awake on the entire planet, she used to get out of bed to make tea and from the darkened window she might see the fox – one of 'her' foxes fleeting away down the road. At the corner he'd look back over one shoulder, holding his brush horizontal, stiff as a shop bouquet in the hand of an iffy suitor. Then swiftly he was gone from sight, like a puff of smoke from a silent shot.

In later life, my parents seemed to be pulling in opposite directions. My father would very much like to have played bridge more often. Many of his activities took him away from the house, leaving my mother on her own. Recently, he said of himself, 'No one could live with me now.' Adding, 'I don't expect they ever could.' My mother, meanwhile, still had dreams of elsewhere. Her favourite dream was a cottage in Shere, the village not far from London where she'd enjoyed paddling with her granddaughter. Along the path that leads back to the village is a flint wall enclosing a vegetable garden where dahlias grow in amongst the runner beans. A line of cottages overlooks the garden, within sound of the river. This last dream of my mother's – not really within their grasp financially – was a modest version of the dreams my father had responded to when they were young, dreams which had propelled them up, up and away. But in later life, in this matter at least, my father's law prevailed and, having moved to their home in New Malden, that's where they stayed. Besides, my mother was tired. Only her ashes made it to the shallow river at Shere.

How was that night, that long last Sunday of their lives together? I'll never know, could never really know, even with every detail spelt out to me. 'Pity she didn't come to us sooner' the doctors had said. But my mother had fiercely resisted all suggestion of being rushed into hospital. Having talked it over in calmer times I understand that my father had repeatedly begged her to allow him to call the ambulance. That she had repeatedly said no. Heart attack or not, she was at her imperious best. Not until six in the morning, not until it was 'too late', had she given in. Did she perhaps understand more of what had happened than she let on, wanting above all else to avoid life as an invalid? The fact is that, with my father's support, she achieved that most lucky thing: a quick and relatively painless death. Had he acted differently it would have been a longer and much unhappier story.

A perfect early summer morning, presented like an expensive hotel breakfast, under a polished dome of silvery sky. The trees that stand along the driveway are composed all of light, gouts of bright light, green and yellow, verdigris gobbets flung down by the rain and sunshine, sparkling and shaking as if about to disperse, to vanish on the bright air. Through a gateway into the walled garden I can see a mass of wet, open, sun-warmed flowers. I am a step or two behind my mother who is walking slowly, putting her feet down softly like someone listening. The air is filled with the pulsing drone of wood pigeons. A young man with rolled-up sleeves and a shovel crusted with dark earth goes along the path. Otherwise the garden is empty. My mother's smile is dazed.

'How lovely,' she says, looking towards the sunlit trees. 'How peaceful it is here.'

The young man stops. His eyes follow hers.

'Yes,' he agrees, 'it is peaceful, isn't it.'

If the weather gets better then next week we'll go down to Shere, my father and I. Like Russian Orthodox Christians sitting on the family grave knocking back vodka and blinis, we too have a place to go to, to sit and remember. We'll pack sandwiches and a flask of tea, and we'll picnic – with neither vodka nor faith – on the grassy bank of the river where we scattered her ashes. 'If' – she will whisper in my ear as we pass through the kissing gate – 'if they really *are* my ashes.' And the following year, though I don't know this yet, my father and I will go to Shere again, on the tenth anniversary of her death, February 23rd, 2009, my father now aged ninety. A bright, cold day with brief flurries of snow falling on early daffodils.

As we stand on the little footbridge over the river, facing into the wind, my father will say, 'Your mother was the only person ever really to have any influence on me.' I am surprised and moved beyond replying. 'I always thought she was very brave to come over here like that, alone.' I, just as there are many occasions when I haven't spoken out, so there are lots of things my father hasn't said either. Different things from me, totally different. Different thoughts, different feelings. We both look down at the water rushing away beneath us. 'When my time comes,' he says, 'I hope you'll bring my ashes here, too.'

Over the years since my mother's death my father and I have grown closer. Sometimes in his company I get my childhood self back. He and I become part of the same chattering straightforward tribe, cheerful, busy, collecting

370

things, cracking corny jokes and whistling, happy as sandboys. Then, like a current in the air, a change in temperature, something halts me. I stand, struck silent maybe by the light, or a sound and I'm taken away, as at the call of my mother's voice, possessed by different gods, just as it was once believed that Pan would take you if you stood too long in the midday sun. It was our own story she wanted to tell. I picked up the thread, I took it and ran, terrified I might drop it and be lost. I've recorded as well as I'm able what I found, including forgotten names and things that were hidden. *Was that what she intended?*

By the time we get back to the house, a chill winter dusk has fallen. My father puts out scraps for the foxes. But later, when I go outside to look at the night sky, I sense they've gone, that where they had been, hungry and inquisitive, there's only darkness and a sense of tension. Above the trees the mineral stars don't even blink. There's a tug on the thread. I feel it slip through my fingers. Like all good storytellers my mother has led me here, and told me to continue alone. I let her go.

ACKNOWLEDGMENTS

My thanks to, firstly, my guide into this story, the historian Danny Grace, from whose books I have extensively quoted; to all those who generously shared their memories and stories with me; to my friend Francis Bennett for the kind of support and advice which enabled me to complete the project; to Penny Hoare, whose encouragement and incisive editing helped me to a final draft and, of course, to my publishers, Robert Davidson and Moira Forsyth, for believing in what I'd done; to my father, who gracefully withstood one of the worst things that can happen to anyone: a writer in the family. And, as always, to my husband, whose unfailing humour and stamina got me through the dark days.

Some names have been changed to protect identities.

BIBLIOGRAPHY

Books

–Gerry Adams, *Before the Dawn: An Autobiography* (Heinemann, 1996)
–Elizabeth Bowen, *Afterthought: Pieces about Writing* (Longmans, 1962)
–Gustave de Beaumont, *Ireland: Social, Political, and Religious* (first published by Michel Levy Frere, 1839)
–Clare Barrington, *Irish Women in England: An Annotated Bibliography* (Women's Education, Research and Resource Centre, UC Dublin, 1997)
–Diarmaid Ferriter, *The Transformation of Ireland 1900-2000* (Profile Books, 2004)
–Charles Foley, *Legacy of Strife: Cyprus from Rebellion to Civil War* (Penguin, 1964)
–R. F. Foster, *Modern Ireland: 1600-1972* (Allen Lane, 1988)
–R. F. Foster, *Vivid Faces* (Allen Lane, 2014)
–Tom Garvin, *Preventing the Future: Why Was Ireland So Poor for So Long?* (Gill & Macmillan Ltd, 2004)
–Daniel Grace, *The Great Famine in Nenagh Poor Law Union Co. Tipperary* (Relay Books, 2000)
–*Portrait of a Parish: Monsea and Killodiernan* (Relay Books, 1996)
–Lady Gregory, *Gods and Fighting Men* (Dublin, 1904)
–Alan Hayes and Diane Urquhart (eds.) *Irish Women's*

History (Irish Academic Press, 2004)

–Seamus Heaney, *Finders Keepers*: Selected Prose 1971-2001 (Faber & Faber, 2002)

–Brendan Kenelly (trans.), from 'The Penguin Book of Irish Verse' (Penguin, 1970)

–Finola Kennedy, *Cottage to Creche: Family Change in Ireland* (Dublin: Institute of Public Administration, 2001)

–F. S. L. Lyons, *Ireland Since the Famine* (Fontana, 1963)

–Jonathan Rosen, *The Talmud and the Internet: A Journey Between Worlds* (Continuum, 2000)

–Tim Robinson, *The Last Pool of Darkness, Connemara Trilogy* (Penguin Ireland, 2008)

–Patrick Shea, *Voices and the Sound of Drums: An Irish Autobiography* (Belfast, 2000)

–Eamon Slevin, *A Parish History of Borrisokane* (Nenagh Guardian, 1994)

–W. M. Thackeray, *The Irish Sketch Book* (1843)

–Gore Vidal, *Palimpsest: A Memoir* (Random House, 1995)

–Cecil Woodham-Smith, *The Great Hunger: Ireland, 1845-1849* (Hamish Hamilton, 1962)

Magazines and published papers

–Joe Hogan, *Irish Post* From 'The Irish Homestead' articles including: 'Household Hints' in March 1899; Elice Pilkington writing in April 1910; 'United Irishwomen' in November 1911; and 'Are Mothers the Ruin of Ireland' by Granis on February 1913 Carrigan Committee Report (1930)

–Niall Meehan 'Church and State and The Bethany Home'

(supp. to "History Ireland" Sep-Oct. 2010)

–Oliver St John Gogarty (quoted in the Irish Times in 1995)

–Susannah Riordan 'VD in the army: Moral Panic in the Irish Free State', a paper delivered to the St Patrick's College History Society in 2001 Magill Magazine, 1985